Information Modelling

BCS Practitioner Series

Series editor: Ray Welland

Information Modelling

Practical Guidance

Richard Veryard

MA MSc MBCS CEng

Prentice Hall

New York London Toronto Sydney Tokyo Singapore

First published 1992 by
Prentice Hall International (UK) Ltd
Campus 400, Maylands Avenue
Hemel Hempstead
Hertfordshire, HP2 7EZ
A division of
Simon & Schuster International Group

Typeset in 10pt Times
by Pentacor PLC

Printed and bound in Great Britain by
Redwood Books Limited, Trowbridge, Wiltshire

Library of Congress Cataloging-in-Publication Data

Veryard, R. (Richard)
    Information modelling : practical guidance / Richard Veryard.
    p. cm.—(British Computer Society practitioner series)
    Includes bibliographical references and indexes.
    ISBN 0–13–454182–0
    1. System design. 2. Management information systems. I. Title
  II. Series.
  QA76.9.S88V47 1992   92–2915
  004.2'1–dc20   CIP

British Library Cataloguing in Publication Data

A catalogue record for this book is available
from the British Library

ISBN 0–13–454182–0 (pbk)

3 4 5 96 95 94 93

Contents

Editorial preface

The aim of the BCS Practitioner Series is to produce books which are relevant for practising computer professionals across the whole spectrum of Information Technology activities. We want to encourage practitioners to share their practical experience of methods and applications with fellow professionals. We also seek to disseminate information in a form which is suitable for the practitioner who often has only limited time to read widely within a new subject area or to assimilate research findings.

The role of the BCS is to provide advice on the suitability of books for the Series, via the Editorial Panel, and to provide a pool of potential authors upon which we can draw. Our objective is that this Series will reinforce the drive within the BCS to increase professional standards in IT. The other partners in this venture, Prentice Hall, provide the publishing expertise and international marketing capabilities of a leading publisher in the computing field.

The response when we set up the Series was extremely encouraging. However, the success of the Series depends on there being practitioners who want to learn as well as those who feel they have something to offer! The Series is under continual development and we are always looking for ideas for new topics and feedback on how to further improve the usefulness of the Series. If you are interested in writing for the Series then please contact us.

Information is now recognized as a critical resource within commercial companies and information modelling is a key activity in making full use of this resource. This book goes well beyond the basics of information modelling and provides a wealth of practical examples to assist the information analyst in building complex information models.

Ray Welland
Computing Science Department, University of Glasgow

Editorial Panel Members
Frank Bott (UCW, Aberystwyth), John Harrison (BAe Sema), Nic Holt (ICL), Trevor King (Praxis Systems Plc), Tom Lake (GLOSSA), Kathy Spurr (Analysis and Design Consultants), Mario Wolczko (University of Manchester)

Preface

This book is intended for practitioners (but also students and teachers) of systems analysis and design, data administration and database management, and indeed all those who are (or want to be) either directly or indirectly involved in the structuring of information for a business or other organization.

Information modelling is a way of structuring the total information needs of a business or other organization. It is an important part of many formal methodologies, including information engineering and SSADM (Structured Systems Analysis and Design Methodology). This book goes beyond the simple, often trivial examples found in most introductory training courses and texts (including my own *Pragmatic Data Analysis*),[1] and shows how difficult yet common situations can be handled. It is therefore intended to equip the reader, both student and professional, to tackle real-life modelling problems.

Pragmatic is a good word, and I hope it will be seen to apply to this book, for four reasons:

1. It is aimed at practitioners rather than theorists. Although academics are welcome to read it, and to use it for teaching students, they should not expect to find such words as infological littering the text, nor will the mathematical foundations of data normalization be explained.
2. It arises out of practice rather than theory. The solutions I proffer in this book are largely based on the real problems of banks, oil companies, manufacturers, media organizations and all the other companies where I (and colleagues who have shared their thoughts with me for this book) have worked as consultant.
3. I have aimed to be short and stick to the point, rather than ramble on in the manner of a syllabus-filling textbook. The point is to produce models of business for business. (Here, I include non-profit organizations as businesses, since their management and information needs are broadly similar to those of commercial firms.)
4. The reader must also be pragmatic. The book aims to impart skill and understanding rather than abstract or generalized knowledge. The book offers guidelines and suggestions rather than strict rules. What you

I wanted to call the book Information Modelling Made Difficult. I only meant to make the subject less simplistic, and had no intention of making the book itself needlessly obscure. I thought this title would intrigue the potential reader, encourage browsers to look inside. But my colleagues thought the publishers wouldn't get the joke, the publishers thought the librarians wouldn't get the joke, and the British thought that Americans wouldn't get the joke. And vice versa. So I yielded. This demonstrates I do sometimes listen to advice.

do depencs on the situation you are trying to model, the particular purpose you have for building a model, and any formal methodological constraints chosen by your organization. Notations and structures should be guided by your own standards, or by the automated tools available to you.

For this reason, management and coordination is only described very briefly in this book. I hope to write another book to explore these subjects more fully.

When I started writing the book, I hoped to include material on managing and coordinating the modelling activity, as well as carrying it out. But it became apparent that this would make the book too long. The book you now hold concentrates on the concepts and techniques of information modelling, culminating in a wide-ranging survey of the things that are difficult to model. Here it is impossible to include a complete case study, but several real examples are included in the text.

How to read this book

Chapter 1

This chapter introduces the subject of information modelling, describes the background and rationale (usually within the context of a systems development project) and sets up the basic principles. Although some readers may wish to skim the background material, they should read and understand the principles (even if they do not agree with them).

Chapter 2

This chapter introduces, defines and illustrates the basic concepts of information modelling, including the diagramming conventions and recommended documentation. Readers new to the subject should read the whole chapter. Those familiar with the subject may prefer to skim or omit the chapter, and refer back to it (via the concept index) if explanation of specific concepts is needed.

Chapter 3

This chapter provides a set of techniques for producing information models, and shows how these techniques can be embedded into a formal systems development methodology (such as information engineering). I hope that even experienced readers will discover some new techniques in this chapter.

Chapter 4

This chapter provides a set of self-study exercises (with solution guidelines) for the new reader to test understanding of the concepts and techniques of Chapters 2 and 3.

Chapter 5

This chapter demonstrates the use of information models to support management information needs. The approach described in this chapter is the author's own, and is significantly different from the standard approach.

Chapter 6

This chapter introduces some of the main complexities and generic difficulties of information modelling. This is where readers new to the subject will discover what it is that makes information modelling difficult. Experienced readers will probably already know what the difficulties are, but should be interested in the way I tackle these difficulties.

Chapter 7

This chapter offers four partial case studies, which the reader may use as long examples to reflect on, or as further self-study exercises to practise on.

Chapter 8

This is the longest chapter in the book, and contains a series of situations and patterns that arise when modelling specific areas of business. Although it is possible to read this chapter sequentially, many readers may prefer to skim through the chapter initially, and then use it as a source of reference when tackling real-life modelling problems. The object index may be used to locate the relevant section(s).

Concept index

To assist the reader, when concepts are introduced they are printed in **bold type**. All references to these concepts are included in the concept index.

Object index

The names of all entity types and other objects used in examples or templates are printed in SMALL CAPITALS. The object index includes page references to these objects.

Acknowledgements

Many friends and colleagues have helped with the book. Since they are all so persuasive, I hold them jointly and severally responsible for any errors. (They can also claim credit for any new ideas this book contains.)

Every time I practise the subject, or try to explain it to others, I learn something new. So I have had hundreds of teachers. Where I have been able to trace the origin of an idea through the unreliable reaches of my memory, I have provided a footnote in gratitude. The rest must accept my thanks collectively.

Many people read various draft versions of the manuscript; my thanks not only to Richard Gilyead, Keith Short and Ian Macdonald for their feedback, but also to the publisher's readers (whose identities have been concealed from me – the topic of anonymity is discussed in Chapter 2). Thanks also to Ray Welland, the series editor, and to Prentice Hall staff, past and present.

For the case studies I was helped by Trevor Jones, Michael Roche, Terence Ronson, Trish Semmens and Jameela Siddiqi.

I am also grateful to my employer, JMA Information Engineering Ltd (now part of Texas Instruments), for encouraging the writing of this book.

1 Introduction to information modelling

This chapter provides a context for the book. What is a model, and what is it for? Why do we produce models at all? Why do we produce information models?

The rest of the book will explain how to produce information models. Here, we consider the why, what, who, where and when of modelling in general, and of information modelling in particular. We also mention the use of automated software tools to support information modelling.

1.1 Why model?

Information models are produced for a purpose, and should be sufficient for that purpose. The most common purpose is the design and construction of a computerized information (or data processing) system. Thus before building an information system to support a business activity (such as the purchasing of raw materials), an abstract model is produced that shows the structure of the business activity, and of the information needed to make the activity successful.

Information systems (IS) have not always been built this way. In general, there are two ways of building things. One is an amateur, unselfconscious way, based on tradition and common sense. The other is a professional, selfconscious way, based on scientific and technical knowledge. To illustrate this, let us compare an igloo with a geodesic dome. The Eskimo builds an igloo the way his people have always built igloos. The form has evolved over many generations, and it is now a very good solution to the original design problem: how to make a tent out of snow. In contrast, the inventor of the geodesic dome, Buckminster Fuller, was an architect and engineer, who calculated the form and construction of his dome using formulae of applied mathematics. Although bearing a superficial resemblance to previous domes, Fuller's structure was wholly new.

The Eskimo cannot afford the risk of radically deviating from tradition, or he may be buried under a mound of snow. It is impossible to be confident that a wholly new structure will be stable, without using the engineering knowledge that distinguishes the amateur from the professional. But it is impossible to rapidly develop wholly new structures by just following tradition. Evolution is a slow learning process, consisting of many cautiously accumulated changes.

1

The pioneers of computing had little knowledge about software and the nature of information systems. Application systems were built using an 'amateur' approach that rapidly became accepted tradition. There was no notion of analysing requirements formally. Programmers simply turned the existing paperwork system into a software replica. Gradually, as our knowledge has increased over the last few decades, more 'professional' approaches have evolved. Nowadays we have 'engineering' methodologies for the design and construction of software and information systems. These methodologies usually include some form of information modelling, the aim of which is to produce a coherent and self-contained model of the business, from which one or more systems can be designed and built but this is not the only possible use of an information model.

1.1.1 Uses of an information model

There are several uses to which an information model may be put, including:

- Strategic planning (information architecture) and system scoping.
- Information system design and implementation.
- Information system coordination and interfacing.
- Database design and implementation.
- International standardization.
- Data conversion and bridging.
- Evaluation and selection of packaged application software.
- Evaluation and selection of system software (including database management systems).
- Systems testing and impact analysis.
- Training in use of specific application system or database.
- As a framework for general training, identifying what information a person needs to perform a given job.
- As a training vehicle itself, i.e. to present the relevant information to the trainee in a clearly structured form.

As we shall see, the modelling approach depends crucially on the purpose for which the model is intended. As a preliminary illustration of this, let us compare the use of information modelling for systems development with the use of information modelling for strategic management.

1.1.2 Strategic modelling

Computerized information systems have the power to change the way the members of the organization think about their work. The more the organization relies on computers, the more power the systems have. This is one of the reasons why the conceptual structure of the systems deserves serious attention from the management of the organization.

One of the possible purposes of building an information model is to develop a strategy for the business. Long-term plans for information systems development are increasingly based on some kind of high-level model of the business entities and functions (often referred to as a **strategic model** or **information architecture**. The information architecture may include reference to the principal activities or functions of the enterprise (structured hierarchically, or as a value chain) as well as its important entity types. A model of the whole enterprise can be clustered into sub-models or business areas, each of which is then the subject of detailed analysis and IS development projects.

But the purpose of such strategic models need not be restricted to IS development plans. Strategic models can express the changing intentions and conceptual structures of the business, which may need to be reflected by new information systems, but which may also be communicated via information systems.

Thus an information architecture may have several purposes:

1. To provide a framework for formulating opportunities to obtain direct competitive advantage from information and systems.
2. To establish and maintain the link between the strategic business objectives and the systems development projects.
3. To define the scope of business areas and of information modelling projects.
4. To provide a framework for coordinating analysis and design projects.
5. To provide a framework for planning and implementing the necessary technical and organizational infrastructures.

To achieve these purposes, far more breadth is needed, and far less detail, than for designing a single application system.

1.1.3 Systems development

The benefits and advantages of information modelling for systems development include:

*   Providing a framework for development and repair projects,[1] discovering the detailed business requirements by a detailed analysis of business data, which enables a formal link between business objectives and information requirements, providing information plans to support business plans.
*   Increasing business understanding, since the business is described in simple diagrams and definitions instead of unreadable specifications; this enables rationalization of business processes, based on management of information. It also enables the expression of some strategic aim of the business (e.g. to extend the concept of CUSTOMER to include other business partners).
*   Reducing risk, since assumptions and structures are made visible and explicit, and can therefore be discussed and verified.
*   Supporting negotiations of computer system requirements between analysts and the target users of a planned computer system, or between different groups of users or managers.

- Providing a framework for identifying and evaluating opportunities to enhance the business, which may sometimes have nothing to do with information systems development; identifying opportunities to use information for competitive advantage, often extending or simplifying the boundaries of the organization; allowing traditional business processes to be rationally challenged.
- Supporting database/system design and development – structural decisions are made once only and carried visibly through the rest of a development project.
- Recognizing commonly recurring situations, so that appropriate existing solutions can be adapted and applied more easily.
- Supporting the integration of information, since a common model opens up possibilities for sharing both of data and processes. This in turn improves communications between parts of the enterprise, encourages decisions to be made on a common basis, and may help remove the inefficiencies of bridging and duplication.
- Establishing a common framework of concepts and terminology, to support and encourage consistent communication, especially across departmental boundaries.
- Establishing the central focus of a methodology for information management (which usually includes information modelling and other techniques), which should increase the quality of systems and the effectiveness of systems development.
- Enables the use of integrated computer-aided software engineering (I-CASE) tools. CASE is the term for software that is used to design and construct software application systems.

Sometimes these benefits are not foreseen but emerge as positive side-effects after the event.

1.2 Why automate modelling?

A fully integrated CASE (computer-aided software engineering) tool allows integration of information modelling in three dimensions (Figure 1.1).

Figure 1.1 CASE and information modelling

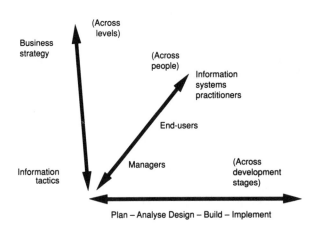

One aspect of integration is to allow the various people working on information systems to coordinate their work. This improves consistency and compatibility, both within and between project teams.

But this coordination does not only involve IS professionals; communications between systems developers and the end-users are also improved. The techniques of information engineering lead to a better understanding by the users of what they are going to end up with. This means that there is a much better chance of getting systems that fit the practicalities of the business. User participation has further benefits, including such intangible effects as spreading awareness and positive attitudes throughout the organization.

Another aspect of integration is to enable the different stages of a project to be coordinated. Until recently, you could expect a system development project to produce a succession of weighty documents. This succession was referred to metaphorically as a waterfall, since each document cascaded into the next, like a succession of rockpools. Much of the development work consists of translation and even transcription from one level of documentation to the next. A simple change to the system requirements would be a complex editing job, to ensure all the documentation remained up to date. (Often this would be skimped, resulting in documentation becoming worthless. The rockpool, as it were, became stagnant.) A methodology based on information models, together with appropriate tools (CASE) can rationalize away all this burden.

The most important aspect of integration is that the analysis can start at the very top of the enterprise, from the overall business strategy. An information model can be built at the strategic level, establishing a visible link between the business strategy and the provision of information. (This strategic model is sometimes known as the **information architecture**.) This is often a mutually rewarding process; a business can gain competitive advantage from using information creatively. Perhaps the most interesting are the symbiotic links between enterprises in different industry sectors, such as some recent joint ventures between retail organizations and banks, to debit your account automatically when you buy your week's groceries.

1.3 Historical background

Structured methodologies represent the fourth stage of the evolving relationship between users and information engineers. (By 'user', we denote a person for whom a computerized information system is a means to an end, rather than an end in itself; by 'information engineer' we denote such computer 'experts' as analysts, designers, programmers, engineers and operators, who work in the area known variously as computing, data processing and information systems.)

Stage 1: no division between users and information engineers

In the early days of computing, hardware and software were designed by the mathematicians that were going to use them. The code-breakers at Bletchley

Park during the Second World War, led by Alan Turing, provide the best known example.[2] Of course, there were differing specialities, but there were not yet clear boundaries between computer scientists and data-processing professionals on the one hand, and the 'users' on the other hand. The computer was used as a tool in a mathematical project.

Stage 2: back of envelope

When it became clear that computers would have commercial and administrative applications, as well as acting as giant pocket calculators, businessmen and generals started to commission specially programmed application systems, using general-purpose computer hardware. These systems were often designed from the bottom up, by self-appointed computer experts, with the businessmen and generals (and their subordinates, who would have to work with the new system) pretty much excluded from the whole process.

So the communication between the users and the information engineers would often be just an initial brief. Usually very brief – hence its characterization as fitting on the back of an envelope. The user's requirements were stated roughly on the back of an envelope, and these were translated somehow (each programmer working out his own procedure) into low-level machine code or assembly language. (Figure 1.2).

Figure 1.2 Back of an envelope brief

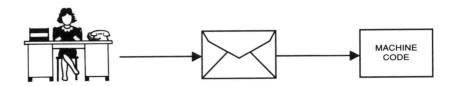

This process perhaps looks very efficient, but it was only capable of achieving fairly low levels of sophistication in the delivered system. Very few people were able to perform the direct translation at all. When the system was delivered, it was usually nothing like the users had expected, was sometimes quite unsuitable for the purpose for which it was intended, and had to be expensively maintained if any value was to be obtained from it at all.

Stage 3: voluminous specification documents

In response to this, during the 1960s and 1970s, many organizations introduced standards and procedures to make sure that the information engineers and the users remained in contact during the development cycle. The development process was divided into phases; at the end of each phase, a report would be produced by the information engineers, which would specify in great detail what the system would do when complete. (Fig 1.3).

Figure 1.3 Phased
specification

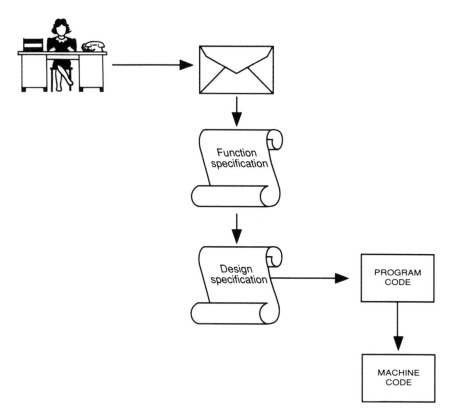

The effect of this approach was to subdivide the translation process into separate translation steps. (Figure 1.3 shows one version of this, although there were often more steps than are shown here.) This subdivision brought several benefits:

1. The first step (the functional specification) was often accessible to a subset of the user population. In other words, they could read it and get a rough idea of the intentions of the developers. (They might have wanted to get more than a rough idea, they might have needed a precise idea of relevant aspects of the developers' intentions, but usually they did not get it.)
2. Increased project control, since the development was broken down into separate project tasks which were standardized and made visible to the project manager.
3. Division of labour, as each step could be assigned to staff with specialized skills in that step (e.g. system design, program specification, program code).
4. As a result of (2) and (3), it became possible to build more sophisticated systems.
5. Opportunity to automate an individual step. The final step, from high-level programming language (such as COBOL) to machine code, could be carried out by an automatic compiler.

6. As a result of (5), the difference between the user's requirements and the form in which the requirements could be input to the computer itself (which we could call the translation 'distance') is reduced.

Thus both productivity (by the introduction of compilers) and quality were improved.

The documents produced at the end of each phase were known as 'deliverables' (presumably because you needed a delivery truck to carry them!); they allowed the users to be presented with several hundred pages of closely jargoned description. Good intentions, but these 'three-volume novels' were worse than back of envelope specifications in many ways: the good designer was inhibited by the bureaucratic, almost legalistic tedium of formulating the design in the correct style; the bad designer was excused from responsibility, provided he or she had obeyed the rules of procedure and layout, and obtained a formal sign-off from the users. Meanwhile the users, knowing that it would be impossible for them to understand the full implications of what was contained in the documents without spending months of study, were forced to sign them off unread, on blind trust, as correct statements of their requirements.

1.4 Structured methods

To address these problems, among others, many organizations have turned to such information management methods or methodologies as information engineering methodology, JSD (Jackson System Development) or SSADM.[3] These are structured in the sense that the structure of the computer system(s) is derived from the structure of the business, expressed as a series of business models. The database or file structure is derived from an information model, most commonly expressed as entities, attributes and relationships; the program logic is derived from a series of process models.

Prototyping is sometimes seen as an alternative to these structured methodologies, bypassing the need for business models. This is a false view: the technique of prototyping still requires an understanding of requirements and structure, which is best made explicit by a model – it is therefore not alternative but complementary.[4]

The tasks and procedures for information modelling will be laid down by such a method, or can be obtained from a standard text on systems analysis. It is not our intention to specify this task structure in this book. Some of the issues that will be addressed by such a method or task structure are as follows:

- Use of formal method or methodology, usually prescribing a fixed or semi-fixed sequence of tasks.
- Relationship between experts and 'locals'.
- Negotiations between interested parties.
- Coordination between models.
- Use of automated tools (e.g. workbench or CASE tools).

Information modelling can fit in many ways into a method or task structure, carried out at different stages of a project, to different levels of detail. Some methodologies specify a particular division of responsibility between analysts and users, or between data analysts and systems analysts. The techniques, patterns and attitudes described in this book are largely independent of these differences, although the modeller must of course be aware of such factors when building a particular model. Furthermore, the same techniques can be applied whatever the intended use of the model, but the resulting model should naturally be suitable for the purpose for which it was built.

There is a confusion of terminology here. There is no agreement in the literature of information science about the exact boundary between a method and a methodology. Some writers argue that 'ology' means study; it is used to name such theoretically based disciplines as geology, biology, astrology and sociology. Thus, just as 'technology' should denote the study of technical matters (techniques or technics) – and, for that matter, 'terminology' should denote the study of terms – so 'methodology' should be used to denote the study of method. But just as technology and terminology tend to be used in practice to denote collections of technics or terms, so methodology tends to be used to denote systematic collections of individual methods or techniques.

An I-CASE tool will generate applications and databases from a model, which contains a description of the business (a business model, produced by analysis) and a specification of an information system to support the business (a system model, containing design decisions linked to the business model). Only one translation step is now required: between the statement of requirements and the information model.

If the business strategy has been analysed, and if from this analysis a strategic plan for information management has been produced, there will now be the opportunity to build and maintain a strong link between the requirements of each

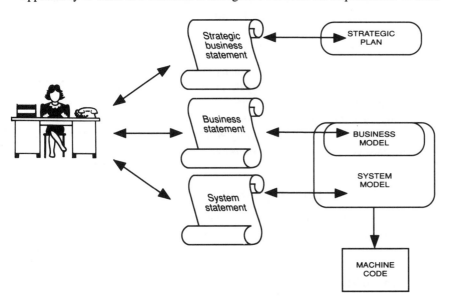

Figure 1.4 Initial use of methodology

Figure 1.5 Ultimate
use of methodology

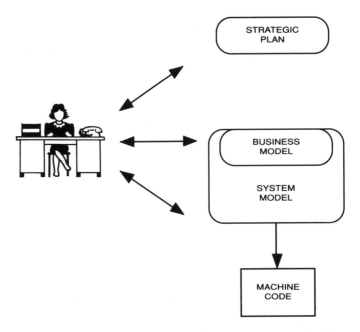

system and the overall business strategy (See Figure 1.4). Previously, any link with the business strategy was fortuitous, and was included into the statement of requirements only through the knowledge and understanding of the user(s), if at all.

The culmination of this progress is when the users can understand the information models directly (See Figure 1.5). The business models and associated documentation provide a complete representation of the business requirements of one or more computer systems, which is accessible to all interested parties. There is no need for redundant documentation or translation to any other form. In particular, there is no need for separate requirements documents.

This has already been achieved in many cases: *if* the business areas are small and well scoped, *if* the users participate in the actual model building, *and if* the information management staff are prevented from polluting the models with complexity, *then* the models do make sense to the business. (The factors leading to artificial and unnecessary complexity will be considered in Chapters 2 and 3, including systems design considerations and metadata.)

1.5 User participation

One of the concepts underlying most of the methodologies referred to above is that of 'user participation'. This participation is effected in one of three ways: (1) user input, (2) user review; and/or (3) user cooption. Thus some users may be interviewed before the models are built, some users may be shown the completed models for confirming their validity, while some users may directly join in the modelling activity. Thus the users and the information engineers together build easy to understand models of the users' business, on which the design is based. In all three types of participation, instead of making the users think in computing terms, the information engineers are supposed to think in business terms.

The aim of this user participation is to achieve the following:

1. *Design based on business models* – a business model is two things. First, it is a description of the business structure and operations. (This should reflect the 'deep' structure, not the 'surface' structure.) Second, it is a statement of intentions, both about the business and about the system design.[5] The idea is that if the models correctly reflect the business, then the ensuing computer systems will be suitable for the information processing requirements of the business.

2. *Business models based on user input* – the business models are based on interviews and discussions with users, as well as facts drawn from other sources (e.g. observation, experimentation, document and file search . . .).

3. *Business models reviewed by users* – the business models will be in the form of simple diagrams, which the users can appreciate and verify.

4. *Systems design controlled by users* – the information systems will be understood by the users while still in the planning and design stage, thus enabling the users to get what they really want from a systems development project.

As this participation is dependent upon good communications between user and engineer, some communication techniques are described in Chapter 3.

1.6 What is an information model?

In this book, the types of model we are particularly interested in are those that describe information in terms of entities and entity types. The basic model structure to be described in this book is the entity–relationship–attribute model. We shall augment this model with some discussion of entity subtypes, roles and lifecycles. Much of the book's contents can be easily translated into other equivalent analysis models, including object-oriented and knowledge-based analyses.

What kind of model is an information model? If we consider the characteristics of a scientific model, we shall see that an information model shares some of these characteristics, but does not entirely conform to the requirements of science. A complete systems development methodology may involve the production and management of several types of models, each describing different aspects of a business area, or of the system requirements and design:

- Information model, showing the business area in terms of its entity types, relationships, attributes, etc.

- Activity model, showing the business area in terms of its processes, process dependencies, events, etc.
- Interaction model, showing how the information in the information model supports the activities in the activity model.
- Distribution model, showing where the information and activities are located geographically or organizationally.
- Human computer interface (HCI) model, showing the external appearance and behaviour of a computer system.
- Data storage model, showing the internal design of databases and other computer files.

In this book, we shall be concentrating on the information model. However, it should be understood that for many purposes, an information model alone is not enough, but needs to be supplemented or complemented by other kinds of models. Thus an analysis project often produces information models and process models in parallel.

1.7 What is a model?

What is a model, anyway? In general usage, the word **model** is capable of various uses:

- Scientific theory or hypothesis.
- Abstraction (based on classification, aggregation and/or generalization).
- Objective description of a business situation.
- Plan/map/orientation.
- Architecture, pattern language, blueprint or template.
- Statement of business intentions and/or perspective.

Lowry divides models into four types, according to the general purposes of their application.[6] The four types are: (1) *descriptive models;* (2) *predictive models;* (3) *explorative models;* and (4) *planning models.* These senses of the word 'model' overlap, but cannot all hold true simultaneously. For example, sometimes the word is used to refer to the scientific link between the designed object and its desired properties. For example: 'A model, in the scientific sense, is a representation of a system which is used to predict the effect of changes in certain aspects of the system on the performance of the system.'[7] Thus a civil engineer uses formulae from applied physics to assure herself that her bridge will not fall down. But the same engineer may use a balsa wood mock-up of the bridge. It may seem confusing to refer to both the formulae and the mock-up as models. Each has a completely different status. The *scientific model* is based on testable theory, is about a reality out there, and is completely descriptive. The engineering model is part description, part prescription, and can be a proposal or blueprint. I have elsewhere referred to such engineering models, which communicate people's intentions as well as recording them, as *pragmatic models.*[8]

A toy plane in a wind tunnel is a hybrid model; it both communicates an intended wing shape, and tests its aerodynamic properties. Business models, including information models, are often hybrids in the same sense.

1.7.1 Scientific aspects of modelling

To the extent that a model is a factual description of an organization, or a business or business area, it is a **hypothesis** that can and should be tested, as well as an **explanation** or source of understanding. Four main principles of science are relevant here:

1. Lawfulness.
2. Shift of scale.
3. Experiment and test (trial and error).
4. 'The map is not the territory.'

First, let us consider lawfulness. In order to behave rationally and communicate intelligibly, individuals and organizations need a coherent framework of assumptions and values. Without such a framework it would be impossible to share ideas, or coordinate activities. Even a non-bureaucratic organization must have some structure, some regularity in its internal and external relations, some 'laws' of behaviour.

Even those who stand for constant change and uncertainty need to rely on some laws and principles. Within any situation of apparent instability, there will be points of stability.[9] (Otto Neurath has illustrated this with the metaphor of a ship, which was being rebuilt while in mid-ocean, but which needed to retain some structure, so that the crew and cargo remained afloat.[10]) Thus a marketing executive, who refuses to place *any* constraints on the types of products or services the future organization might trade in, is simply being unrealistic. Without at least *some* assumptions, it is impossible to think intelligibly about marketing (or market information systems) at all.

An information model shares this characteristic, as it captures some of the fixed, predictable aspects of an organization, the rules of the business. Management can be regarded as the legislators, who define the unbreakable laws within which the business operates; it is these laws (and their implications in terms of information structure) that are expressed in the information model. But there is a clear difference between the laws of Nature (which are outside human control) and the laws of a given organization (which can sometimes be altered – permanently or temporarily – by a simple memo from the Chief Executive).

Second, science often works by a shift of perspective. Certain phenomena are explained by looking through a microscope or telescope, so that events and objects visible to the naked eye are explained in terms of events and objects much smaller (or larger or slower or faster). Biology is decomposed into genes and cells, chemistry is decomposed into molecules, physics is decomposed into subatomic particles. This allows many apparently diverse events and objects to be explained in a common way: diverse everyday objects may often turn out to have the same inner materials and mechanisms.[11]

Some parts of a business fall easily into this type of analysis. Accounting information can be broken down into atomic transactions of income and expenditure; marketing information can (perhaps) be broken down into data about individual customers; geographical areas can be defined as collections of postcodes or zipcodes. But this type of decomposition has its limits, as we shall see later in the book.

Third, science depends on a combination of speculation and experiment. The creativity of a scientist often appears as a bold guess or intuitive insight, which is then verified by painstaking collection and analysis of experimental data.

Some people have complained that information modelling is not scientific, because it doesn't always produce the right answer first time, but sometimes requires some trial and error, some conceptual experimentation, before coming up with a good answer. This complaint betrays a misunderstanding of science, which is fundamentally experimental. Trial and error in science may result in small adjustments to theory, or radically new theory (so-called paradigm shifts). Trial and error in business modelling results in a good description of the actual business situation, rather than falling back on a standardized stereotype of business in general.

Done properly, information modelling follows a scientific approach. This means that a version of the model is produced as a hypothesis, and as a framework for further fact-finding and analysis. The model can be read as a series of assertions and assumptions about the business and its information structure. These assertions are then tested against the understanding of the business experts, and against any other available sources of business knowledge.

Therefore this book cannot be used as a substitute for proper fact-finding and analysis, although it can help you find a good answer more quickly, by suggesting possible hypotheses that you can build into your models in order to test, and by giving techniques for building and testing models more effectively and efficiently.

Finally, the good scientist always remembers that a theory is only a theory. Light may be represented as waves or particles. Motion may be represented by Newtonian or Lorenzian mechanics. But there is always a temptation to confuse symbol with reality, to confuse measurements with the things they measure. The founder of general semantics, Alfred Korzybski, called this tendency 'the illusion of mistaking the map for the territory'.[12] Or one might use the Sanskrit word for illusion: *maya*, which can be defined as the creation of form, relating to the endless play of forms and the void from which it springs.[13]

1.7.2 Pragmatic aspects of modelling

There is a myth that an information model is simply an objective description of an organization, such as could have been produced by an intelligent Martian. This is a fallacy. Each organization creates its own reality, containing concepts and frameworks which differ from those of its competitors, sometimes in small and subtle ways, sometimes in large and obvious ways. A Japanese car manufacturer, for example, is an entirely different organization from an American car manufacturer, not merely in structure, but in the concepts and terminology that are used to manage the business. It is this reality that must be captured in an information model.

Furthermore, a model is never built just for the sake of it, but always with a particular purpose, and this purpose implies some local values and intentions in addition to the general values and intentions of the organization. Thus a model is not just an objective description of a business situation, but expresses the intentions and perceptions of the key actors in the situation. For example, when analysing the requirements of a new computer system, these requirements result from a combination of facts about the business as it is, and intentions about the business as it should ideally be. Description may come from observation and documentation, as well as interviews. Often it is fairly junior members of staff that have the best knowledge of current operations.

But more important than merely knowing what the business does is knowing what the business would like to do. This comes from more senior personnel, and from future business plans and strategies. Thus the general approach is to analyse the facts and intentions in parallel, and put these together into a model that expresses a set of business requirements; this is illustrated in Figure 1.6.

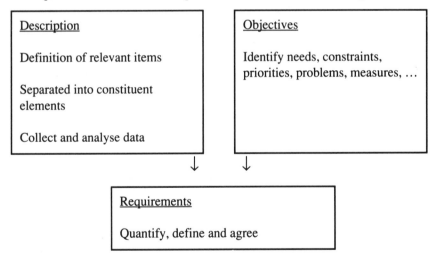

Figure 1.6 Sources of a business requirements model

1.7.3 Administrative aspects of modelling

Building any type of model involves adhering to some definitions of the constructs, and some constraints as to how the constructs are used. This is not to make the task of information modelling more difficult, but to make the task of interpreting and using the resulting information model easier. We do not want to have any ambiguity in the model.

In information modelling, we need carefully to distinguish the **model** itself, which is a system of concepts, from a **notation** which may be used to represent the model. Different notations may draw diagrams with boxes of different shapes; thus the same model may be represented in several different notations.

An information model is a structured collection of business concepts and rules. A model is expressed using a **notation**, which defines what kinds of constructs can be used, and how. A notation is just a system of symbols, which may have a **syntax**, defining formally how the symbols may be combined and manipulated. A notation also has a **semantics**, which defines how the symbols are to be interpreted and used.

In this book, our notation consists of entity types, relationships and atttributes (or, more accurately, symbols representing these objects). This notation will be introduced and explained in Chapter 2. A formal syntax for this notation (which can be found in many theoretical texts, but is not presented in this book, since it is not required for practical purposes) would specify how entity types can be combined, and so on.[14] A semantics for this notation would specify what an entity type meant, and so on.

This is not the same as the semantics of a given model, which defines the meaning of the business concepts themselves. Thus in a business model for raw material purchasing, there may be a symbol PURCHASE ORDER. This symbol has a meaning, i.e. 'an agreement with a specified supplier for delivery of specified quantities of specified materials within a specified time period'.

The notation may in turn be maintained with the help of a computer-aided software engineering (CASE) tool which displays the notation as a diagram on a computer screen, and allows an information engineer to perform manipulations consistent with the syntax. Today's tools are unable to support the semantics of the model, except by allowing free text description to be associated with some of the symbols. Thus a computer can check that your model is syntactically correct, but not that it means anything, let alone check whether it correctly represents anything.

1.8 Scope, perspective and purpose

A model requires three things: scope, perspective and purpose. Scope means what is included and what is excluded from the model, in other words where the boundaries of the model are. Perspective means whose views are incorporated into the model.[15] The model will be affected by the objectives of the people whose perspectives are captured by the model, and also by the objectives of the person(s) building the model. Thus the purpose of the model is also important; what is the model intended for?

The three are interconnected. Scope affects perspective; whom you ask and what you ask them about, and therefore the perspective you obtain, is determined by scope. Perspective implies an individual role. A model of a company's distribution may be partially based on the perspective of the warehouse manager, but ignores the fact that the manager is also a supporter of the sports team or orchestra sponsored by the company, or the fact that the manager is also a consumer of the company's products, because these facts are not relevant to the role of warehouse manager. Perspective affects purpose because the modellers should be sensitive to the business and other objectives of all the people involved, and these objectives depend on the context. Purpose affects scope; whether something is relevant and worth including depends mainly on the modelling purpose. A methodology should have some strategy for dealing with this circularity, so that the modelling team achieves something useful and avoids getting stuck in a perpetual loop.

1.8.1 Scope and context

A model of an organization does not usually have the same scope as the organization itself. For example, we would expect a sales model to include CUSTOMER (or its equivalent), but the customers are not actually part of the organization. (Or are they? Do not take such things for granted.) A methodology should provide rules and guidelines for deciding the scope of an information model. This may be done partly in advance, and/or partly during the modelling exercise itself. For example, information engineering contains formal techniques for dividing a business into business areas, each of which will be analysed and modelled semi-independently.

You cannot define the scope precisely at the start. The scope is only finally defined when the model itself is finished. The scope is just everything that the model includes. But you can indicate broadly the area that you intend to investigate, perhaps in terms of the major business functions that will be included or excluded.

A common way of defining scope is to list several areas, and specify that the model must cover at least these. If a broad model of the whole enterprise has been produced, the intended scope of a more detailed model can be specified by delineating part of the broad model. In any case, the scope remains provisional until the model is completed. The analyst reserves the right to request an extension of scope, in order better to achieve the purpose of the modelling exercise, or to request a contraction of scope, in order to focus the exercise better and produce something useful within the available time and resources.

The scope also defines the context. Every model is part of a larger system, which affects its meaning.

1.8.2 Perspective

Some methodologies make explicit statements about the perspective from which an information model is to be produced. This is usually stated as a contrast: for example, a methodology will commonly demand that the information model should express the user perspective rather than the IT (Information Technology) perspective, or that it should express a business perspective rather than a technical perspective.

Although these general statements offer useful guidelines about perspective, further thought and negotiation is usually required to determine, for a particular project, exactly which user, or which business. In some cases (especially if data sharing is a major objective) it may be necessary to consolidate several different perspectives into one model. This is one of the things that makes information modelling difficult, and should not be brushed aside on the assumption that the user, whose perspective is to be modelled, is a single and coherent body.

As a result of a good modelling exercise, a consensus may emerge. The skilled modeller may sometimes create a single and coherent perspective, by persuasion and group work. But even the most skilled modeller cannot always achieve such results.

1.8.3 Purpose

If you are not convinced that the purpose of a model affects (and should affect) its appearance, consider the map of the London Underground. The style (now copied by many other cities) was created by Harry Beck in the 1920s, and was a brilliant innovation in map making. This map, for distribution and display to passengers, shows only the stations, the lines and the intersections. It does not show the sidings or repair yards, which are of no interest to passengers. This exclusion does not invalidate the map as a model; on the contrary, it makes it easier to read. A model is a description of *relevant* aspects of reality, and since relevance depends on the purpose of the model, the contents of the model should also depend on the purpose. In the same way, the usefulness of a geographical map depends on getting an appropriate scale and including the right detail.

Purpose means what you do with the model when you have finished. How do you make use of it? So how much is it worth to the organization? So how much time was it worth spending getting it right? How much is the detail worth?

There are several possible uses of an information model. They include:

- Strategic planning (information architecture).
- Information system design.
- International standardization.
- Database design.
- Software package selection.

The level of detail needed, and the types of knowledge that must be captured in the model, vary enormously, according to which of these purposes is more important.

A model often serves as a statement of requirements, which may have several purposes in parallel. The user communicates requirements to a systems designer, and the designer communicates his/her solution back to the user. The cost–benefit justification of a project needs to be calculated and confirmed. The project manager needs a breakdown of the content and scope of the work in order to estimate the size of the development, to allocate tasks to members of the project team, and to prevent any escalation of scope after resource budgets have been fixed. These various things have to be communicated to/from various parties at various stages of a development project.

1.8.4 Complexity

Since each model has its own scope, perspective and purpose, there is potential even within a small organization for a multiplicity of models whose contents are not only different but in some ways contradictory, since there will be a multiplicity of purposes and scopes. Before analysis starts, there may be as many perspectives as there are people within the organization.

One of the greatest difficulties of information modelling is the management of multiple models, and of the overlaps, interfaces and conflicts between them. This management function is known by several names, including data administration, architecture administration and development coordination. This provides a framework in which information modelling can be carried out for the whole of a large enterprise.

There are three problems of coordination to discuss here. First, how to coordinate several models in the same style (i.e. entity–attribute–relationship), which have overlapping scope but different purpose or perspective. Second, how to coordinate these models with models and documents in some other style (process models, HCI models and system specifications). Third, these models change over time, in complex ways. A change may affect more than one model, and it may not be possible to carry out the same change to all affected models at the same time. Both for this reason, and for historical reasons (maintaining an audit or archive, so that past decisions may be reconstructed), it is usually necessary to have several versions of a model, representing the understanding at different times. (There are other reasons for needing multiple versions of a model as well.)

Some readers will be surprised by this assertion, since there is a widespread opinion that the goal of information modelling is to produce a single consistent and total model for an entire organization. But when this has been attempted, it either fails completely or results in a model with several hundred, perhaps even thousands of entity types, too large and complicated for anyone to understand. If it were easy to combine all the business areas into one model, then the value of such a global model would nonetheless be small. But it proves immensely difficult, often impossible to combine everything into one model.

Some information modellers believe this to be necessary, therefore always possible. The evidence points the other way: there are many information management organizations that have tried and failed to produce such a total model. And in any case, a total model is neither necessary nor sufficient to achieve the hoped for benefits, and so does not justify the effort even in situations where it may be shown to be possible.

In many large information management organizations, there is a group or department responsible for the integration of data and systems. Just as the name of the information management organization itself has undergone many changes of name, as fashions have changed (e.g. computer group → data processing department → MIS (Management Information Systems) Division → IT division), so the integration group may have had a succession of different names, as its perceived scope and responsibility has increased (database administration → data administration → development coordination). The members of such groups have sometimes invested a great deal of personal credibility and political goodwill in standing up within their organizations for a particular approach to achieving integration. So I do not expect them to receive this section gladly.

But to abandon the fruitless attempt to build a single global model does not mean we have to abandon the goal of integration across several dimensions. Perfect integration may be an unreachable goal, but by attempting the impossible, you may reach a worthwhile position. Development coordination is possible, using CASE software, but needs new techniques to succeed. It will be a subject for a separate book to describe these techniques of coordinating and integrating information models resulting from the analysis of several business areas within the same organization.

As an organization grows older, larger and more complex, it tends to become more formal.

> Growth tends to generate a reduction in the frequency and comprehensiveness of personal contacts among the key members of the original core group and between the original and new people in the system. This condition tends to result from the physical distance and organizational subdivisions which usually accompany increases in size.[16]

The first sign of this is often a formalization of information systems.[17]

This is confirmed by Mintzberg,[18] who argues that an organization tends to require different coordinating mechanisms as the environment's demands on it change. These assertions seem also to apply to subsystems within an organization, both activity systems and departments. (In this case we can regard the enterprise itself as a major component of the environment in which such a subsystem operates.)

Information management (IM) may be viewed either functionally or by department; in an abstract functional view, information management includes all activities supporting the enterprise, which need not be carried out by full-time members of an IM department. (Thus the steering committee for an information systems development project is included or excluded, depending on which view we take.) Thus the Mintzberg model predicts increasing formalization within information management, as the use of computer systems spreads within an enterprise, and as the average age of the software in use increases. This increasing formalization is also predicted by a well-known and simple model of the evolution of information management within an organization. According to Nolan,[19] information management passes through six stages of growth; as an organization grows more mature, its information systems become more integrated and better managed.

The traditional approach to computer systems development is suboptimal, because each system is designed and implemented as an isolated application. This tends to result in large inconsistencies or overlaps between systems, and unworkable interfaces between systems. This is a collective failure, not an individual failure. An individual manager may well recognize the suboptimality of his or her own systems, yet not have the resources to overcome this.

Methodologies such as information engineering are intended to remove this suboptimality. Among other things, it offers a number of coordination mechanisms, including standardization of skills, work processes and outputs, as well as mutual adjustment processes. These coordination mechanisms (which are partially automated through the use of a good integrated CASE software tool) enable decentralization and professionalization of information management, thus helping an organization achieve integration of systems and technology without excessive centralization.[20]

1.8.5 Decision-making levels

Information is used to make decisions. So it is useful to analyse the decision-making processes within a business area, to enrich the model, and to discover the most important entities from the business perspective.

Management information systems are usually built upon a base of operational data. Thus a common image is that of a pyramid, showing how strategic and tactical information required by senior and middle management is produced by analysis, selection and aggregation from the day to day business operations. For such systems, the most stable element is the information model, which describes the objects managed within the day to day business. Many methodologies therefore adopt a so-called data-driven design approach, basing all management information systems upon the stable foundation of an information model representing operational data (see Figure 1.7).

Figure 1.7 Information pyramid

However, this pyramid is misleading. It suggests that senior management have comparatively small amounts of information to take in. This is far from true. The higher up one looks in the management hierarchy, the smaller is the proportion of information that relates directly to the operations of the business itself, which can be derived from the internal operational data, and the larger is the proportion that relates to the outside world. (Figure 1.8).

Figure 1.8 Double pyramid

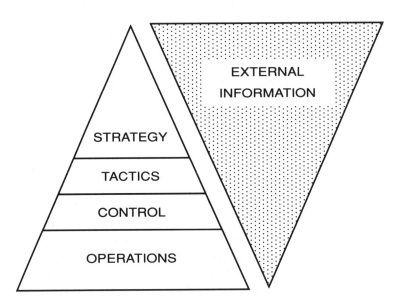

External information is particularly important within marketing functions. Because marketing takes a large amount of responsibility for managing the relationship between the organization and its environment, the information needs of marketing cannot be satisfied from internal sources, but require external data collection, including market research surveys. (Further discussion of marketing information can be found in the Martimark case study, in Chapter 7.)

1.9 Criteria for a modelling method

Information modelling generally consists of three interlinked stages: analysing a business situation, building a model of the situation, and then analysing the information model to gain further understanding of the situation. (The method described in Chapter 5, 'Modelling information needs', addresses the third of these stages.) Any information modelling method, addressing one or more of these stages, should have the following characteristics.

1. It should have a well-defined scope of applicability. In other words, there should be some advance indication of the kinds of situations it can handle, and the kinds of situation for which it would be inappropriate.

2. The results should be clear, simple and unambiguous. A model should serve as a communication tool. Therefore it should be easy for people from all backgrounds, with any level of experience, and with very little training, to read, understand and appreciate. It should also be fairly easy to learn how to produce a model, although we should not expect this to be quite as easy as reading a model. Similarly, the analysis based on the model should be widely understood.

3. The resulting model should be technologically stable. In other words, it should not be biased towards any particular technological implementation. Nor should any design decisions be hidden in the model. This includes the crucial design decisions concerning the positioning of the boundary between person and machine – in other words, which bits we are going to computerize and which bits we are going to leave unautomated. The point is that the model should be a statement of what person and machine together can do or should be doing, from which the actual design decisions can later be made. For example, a model of payments should not assume that all customers pay by writing cheques which are delivered by human postmen. Instead, the model should be generalized, to allow for future banking and mailing possibilities. In practice, this turns out to be an impossible demand. However, the attempt should still be made, to identify and eliminate as many technological specifics as possible. Furthermore, the modelling method should not be biased towards this or that technology. Information models may be used to design filing cabinets full of paper, hierarchical file structures, network or relational databases, or newer emerging technologies such as hyperbases (which may include text and image data, as well as traditional data records).

4. The method should encourage good analyst practice. The analyst should construct hypotheses, test the validity of his/her assumptions, and abandon those that cannot be supported. It is the ability and readiness to unbuild, rather than the ability to build, that distinguishes the good analyst from the mediocre one.[21] This is usually called 'iteration'. But the word often misleads: it is taken to mean doing the same thing repeatedly. The good analyst tries different things, is not satisfied with the first solution that occurs to him/her, tests the consequences of a particular solution, and is prepared to backtrack if the consequences are awkward. It is therefore essential that the tools and techniques used by the analyst help and encourage this search for quality. If even a minor change requires much tedious rework, even the most conscientious analyst may sometimes fail to correct minor errors.

5. The method should be robust, and self-testing. In other words, it does not depend on 100 per cent correctness at every stage, does not rely on the analyst always noticing something at the first chance, but is tolerant of errors and omissions, gives the analyst a second chance. (This is related to the previous point, which said that the analyst should be helped to *correct* errors and omissions. This point says that the analyst should also be helped to *notice* errors and omissions.)

1.10 Terminology

Finally in this chapter, a few words to clarify the terminology used in this book.

1.10.1 Data analysis

The activity of information modelling is often referred to as data analysis, and its result a data model. I used this terminology in my previous book.[22]

The trouble with the term 'data' is that it is too restrictive. There are various ways of defining the difference between 'data' and 'information', but most people agree that the term 'information' denotes a richer concept.

The trouble with the term 'data analysis' is that it is used by some people (such as statisticians) to describe the analysis of data *content*, whereas what we are here concerned with is the analysis of data *form*.

1.10.2 Object-oriented approach

There are several related approaches (including the object-oriented approach, and certain forms of knowledge engineering) which may have a different range of concepts, techniques and supporting software. I hope and believe that much of the underlying thinking of this book can be translated fairly readily into these other approaches. (My previous book has been widely referenced by object-orienteers.)

1.10.3 Who is the user?

By user, we denote a person for whom a computerized information system is a means to an end, rather than an end in itself; by information engineer we denote such computer 'experts' as analysts, designers, programmers, engineers and operators, who work in the area known variously as computing, data processing and information systems. (This term does not imply an adherence to, or understanding of, the information engineering methodology.) The term 'user' may therefore refer to any interested party or stakeholder outside the community of information systems and technology specialists. This may therefore include the actual users of existing systems, and also the potential users of planned systems (which may not be exactly the same group of people). In addition, we often need to include line management, auditors and controllers, as well as the target users (or their representatives). In some circumstances, people outside the organization may have a legitimate interest.

Other terms have been suggested as an alternative to user. Perhaps domain expert or application expert would be better? These terms, however, emphasize the user's knowledge, but ignore the user's status as an interested party. 'User' has wide currency, beyond information systems. 'Where the user understands nothing and cannot evaluate his tools, you can sell him anything. It is the user, said Plato, who ought to be the judge of the chariot.'[23]

1.11 Summary

In this chapter, we have outlined the context of information modelling – its historical emergence, its present-day context, and the purposes it may be used for. Some of the principles of information modelling have been mentioned, and these will be explored further in the rest of the book:

- An information model may describe both the present situation and the future intentions within a defined part of an organization.
- A model is produced for a purpose, which influences its content and structure. This is because the scope, perspective and required/relevant detail will vary according to the purpose.
- The meaning and possible use of a model therefore depends on its scope, perspective and purpose.
- Models (or pieces of models) can be brought in from elsewhere, but these should be tested for correctness before being used, since the structure and intentions of two organizations rarely coincide exactly.

Notes

1. System maintenance can be divided into three types: enhancement (which is really further development), conversion (e.g. from one technical environment to another) and repair.
2. A. Hodges, *Alan Turing: The enigma,* Burnett Books, London, 1983.
3. D. Avison and G. Fitzgerald, *Information Systems Development: Methodologies, techniques and tools ,* Blackwell Scientific Publications, 1988.
4. W. Morrison, 'Communicating with users during systems development', (*Information and Software Technology*, vol. 30, no. 5, June 1988, pp. 295–8.
5. R. Veryard, 'Computer systems analysis, models and prototypes: a reply to R. K. Miles' (*Journal of Applied Systems Analysis*, vol. 13, 1986. pp. 89–93.
6. I. S. Lowry, 'A short course in model design' *American Institute of Planners Journal*, May 1965, pp. 158–66. See also P. G. Rowe, *Design Thinking,* MIT Press, Cambridge, MA, 1987, pp. 166 ff.
7. D. Cleland and W. King, *Systems Analysis and Project Management* 3rd edn, McGraw-Hill, Tokyo, 1983, p. 33.
8. Veryard, *op. cit.*
9. A. Borgmann, *Technology and the Character of Contemporary Life,* University of Chicago Press, Chicago, IL, 1984, p. 19.
10. O. Neurath, 'Protokollsätze' *Erkenntnis,* Vol. 3, 1932, pp. 204–14.
11. A. Borgmann, *op. cit.*, p. 21.
12. A. Korzybski, *Science and Sanity ,* Science Press, New York, 1941.
13. H. Rheingold, *They Have a Word for It* Jeremy P. Tarcher, Los Angeles, 1988.
14. See for example P. Chen (ed.) *Entity Relationship Approach,* IEEE CS Press North-Holland, Amsterdam, 1985.
15. Perspective is sometimes referred to by the German word *Weltanschauung.* See P. Checkland, *Systems Thinking: Systems Practice*, Wiley, Chichester, 1981.

16. R. E. Quinn and D. F. Andersen, 'Formalization as crisis: transition planning for a young organization', in J. R. Kimberley and R. E. Quinn (eds), *New Futures: The challenge of managing corporate transitions*, Dow-Jones-Irwin, Homewood, IL, 1984.

17. D. Miller and P. Friesen, 'Archetypes of organizational transition', *Administrative Science Quarterly*, vol. 25, 1980, pp. 268–99.

18. H. Mintzberg, *The Structuring of Organizations*, Prentice Hall, Englewood Cliffs, NJ, 1979.

19. R. Nolan, 'Managing the crises in data processing', *Harvard Business Review*, March-April 1979.

20. C. Finkelstein, *An Introduction to Information Engineering*, Addison-Wesley, Sidney, 1989. See also J. S. Hares, *Information Engineering for the Advanced Practitioner*, Wiley, Chichester, 1992.

21. N. Vitalari and G. Dickson, 'Problem-solving for effective systems analysis: an experimental exploration' *Communications of the ACM*, 26 Nov 1983.

22. R. Veryard, *Pragmatic Data Analysis*, Blackwell Scientific Publications, Oxford, 1984.

23. P. and P. Goodman, *Communitas,* 2nd edn, Random House, New York, 1960, p. 14.

2 Concepts of information modelling

The aim of this chapter is to provide definitions and simple illustrations of the important terms in the 'language' of entity–relationship–attribute modelling. The concepts or constructs are introduced one at a time, and diagramming conventions are suggested. These diagramming conventions are probably the most widely used, but there is nothing sacred about them, and other equivalent diagrams would do as well. For example, we use a crowsfoot symbol to represent one of the properties of a relationship (its cardinality– see below), but the reader may encounter other symbols for the same property, perhaps single or double arrowheads, or trident symbols. It is of course, a good idea for a project or organization to choose a consistent set or symbols, either based on what the diagramming software offers, or (if the diagramming software offers a choice of conventions) based on existing documentation standards.

Some readers may already be familiar with some of these concepts. Reading this chapter will, I hope, give such readers the opportunity to deepen their own understanding of these concepts, by a process of cross-fertilization between their own ideas and mine. Even if you already understand these concepts better than I do, you may still learn something from my approach.

Figure 2.1 A picture is worth a thousand words

One of the reasons why diagrams are used to express complex structures, is that they allow much more efficient communication than is possible with words alone (See Figure 2.1). For this reason, all modern systems development methodologies are based on diagrams of one kind or another. This is, of course, greatly helped by the opportune availability of workstation graphics software, allowing such diagrams to be manipulated easily. However, the diagrams were being produced long before we had this kind of software, to automate them. (On the first data modelling project I worked on, back in 1980, there was a clerical assistant working full time on drawing, erasing and redrawing the models on large pieces of paper.)

Figure 2.2 A word explains a thousand pictures

However, a diagram alone is of limited value. 'A picture is worth a thousand words only with some person or caption to explain it – only when framed in words.'[1]

How many pictures of vehicles would we need to define completely the word VEHICLE? The word VEHICLE communicates less than the picture of a particular car, but it also communicates more, because it represents not one car but all cars.[2] Thus an information model is an abstract structure, that depends for its very power on words. Each box or line or other symbol on the diagram represents an object, and an object requires a name, and a clear definition.

We shall be constructing models from three main types of object: *entities, attributes* of entities, and *relationships* between entities. Further concepts and object types will emerge as we go along.

2.1 Entities

2.1.1 Entity types and occurrences

Figure 2.3 An entity and occurrences

Entity type: PERSON
Occurrences: Jack, Jill

Entity type: LIQUID
Occurrences: Water, Vinegar

An **entity** is any object of interest within the area being modelled, about which information may be collected, manipulated or stored. Entities can be people, material things, events, locations, or more abstract concepts and groupings. Entities are classified into types; an **entity type** is a class of similar entities. For example, in a payroll area, the relevant entity types could perhaps include EMPLOYEE, SALARY PAYMENT, TAX CATEGORY and EXPENSE CLAIM. A particular employee (Jacob Zlàddyr, for example) is said to be an **occurrence** of the entity type EMPLOYEE. Warning: sometimes, people use the term 'entity' when they mean 'entity type'. (I have done it myself, out of laziness, or the desire to spare my listeners the logical complexity which the word 'type' introduces.) However, it is important to keep the two concepts clear – they are at different logical levels.

There are certain conditions that a class of things must fulfil, to be allowed as an entity type within the model:

- First, there must be a clear boundary between the occurrences of the entity type, and the rest of the universe. In other words, if EMPLOYEE is to be an entity type, there must be no ambiguity as to who should count as an employee and who not.
- Second, the things that we are interested in about the entities must be reasonably alike, which then gives some structure to the entity type. (We shall define this structure below in terms of the attributes of the entity type, and the relationships between this entity type and other entity types.)
- Third, the entity occurrences must be identifiable in a standard way, and capable of being distinguished as individuals.
- Fourth, the entity occurrences must play similar roles in the business or organization. Using the concepts and terminology to be introduced in this chapter, we shall restate these conditions with more precision and detail in Chapter 3.

2.1.2 Entity definitions

There are two possible ways of defining an entity type. One way is to state a set of necessary and sufficient conditions for something to be a valid occurrence of the entity type being defined. The other way is to list some example occurrences, both normal and unusual. Often it is not enough to list unconnected examples, and it may be possible to describe them as members of a family, perhaps grouped around a central typical (or paradigm) case and linked with the latter by various direct or indirect links of logical connection and analogy.

Wittgenstein's attempt to define the entity type GAME is worth quoting here.[3]

> Consider for example the proceedings that we call 'games'. I mean board-games, card-games, ball-games, Olympic games, and so on. What is common to them all? – Don't say: 'There *must* be something common, or they would not be called 'games' – but *look and see* whether there is anything common to all. – For if you look at them, you will not see something that is common to *all*, but similarities, relationships, and a whole series of them at that. To repeat: don't think, but look! – Look for example at board-games, with their multifarious

relationships. Now pass to card-games; here you find many correspondences with the first group, but many common features drop out, and others appear. When we pass next to ball-games, much that is common is retained, but much is lost. – Are they all 'amusing'? Compare chess with noughts and crosses. Or is there always winning and losing, or competition between players? Think of patience. In ball games, there is winning and losing; but when a child throws his ball at the wall and catches it again, this feature has disappeared. Look at the parts played by skills and luck; and at the difference between skill in chess and skill in tennis. Think now of games like ring-a-ring-a-roses; here is the element of amusement, but how many other characteristic features have disappeared ! And we can go through the many, many other groups of games in the same way; can see how similarities crop up and disappear. And the result of this examination is: we see a complicated criss-crossing: sometimes overall similarities, sometimes similarities of detail.

For the purposes of communication and understanding, explanation by example may be better than a formal statement of the logical conditions of membership of the entity type. But such explanations, while good for the straightforward cases, may leave the status of unusual and exceptional cases unclear. So if the information model is to be used for developing formal systems, explanation by example will not be good enough, and a logical definition will be needed, covering the exceptions as well as the straightforward cases.

Why is careful definition important? Business rules are stated in terms of entity types, and we need to know when such business rules apply or not. And measures of business performance depend on knowing what is included or excluded.

My local library has a different procedure for borrowing books and borrowing tapes. Books are free, but tapes require a deposit. When a friend of mine was ill recently, I wanted to borrow a talking book – in other words, the content was book, but the medium was tape. Would I need to pay a deposit? The important point here is that I needed to ask the librarian – was this a book or a tape – since I could not determine this merely by examining the object in question. (If I had gone to a different library, I might have got a different answer, since two libraries may well choose to regard the same object in different ways, and apply different rules and procedures to it.)

To design a system for a library that will apply the correct procedures to books and tapes, you must know what counts as a book, and what does not count as a book. The definition of the entity type BOOK serves to communicate this knowledge to the designer of the library system. This knowledge is then built into the system, either through the training provided to the librarians, or through computer programs.

My library has another rule, which is that I can borrow up to eight books at a time. But this leaves me unsure whether a three-volume novel counts as one book, or three. This is another question that needs to be resolved by the definition of BOOK, so that the knowledge of how the particular library chooses to regard multi-volume works can be captured in any system.

Sometimes different parts of the organization may want to define an entity type differently. For example; the legal department do not regard a customer as a customer until the contract has been signed. But the marketing department regard him as a customer as soon as they get a verbal agreement. We could hit legal problems and/or annoy the customer if we fail to respect this subtle difference. This difference may also affect how the performance of the business is measured and reported. Top managers want to know, when comparing departments or divisions, that they are comparing like with like. So either all divisions should include pre-contract customers in their reported results, or none should.

These examples illustrate the importance of careful and precise definition of entity types, which should specify both a **membership rule** (when does something count as an occurrence of this entity type) and an **identity rule** (when does one occurrence count as the same as another occurrence). One of the skills that the analyst needs to develop, therefore, is that of spotting potential loopholes in an entity definition, and closing them. (This is akin to the skill of the lawyer, in drafting watertight contracts or legislation. However, unlike the lawyer, the analyst commonly assumes that false interpretations will be the result of misfortune, rather than the deliberate exploitation of ambiguity by interests contrary to his own.[4])

We shall return to these concepts in Chapter 3, where we consider some of the logical complexities of membership and identity rules, and show how to handle 'fuzzy' entity types such as Wittgenstein's GAME.

2.1.3 Entity type names

Each entity type must be given a name. In this book, as the reader may already have noticed, we show the names of entity types in small capitals. Often there is a difficulty in choosing an appropriate name for an entity type. This may be for several different reasons. One is that there may be an obvious name, but it normally carries an over-narrow meaning. The entity type may be a combination of several concepts, and although each concept has a name, there may be no commonly accepted name for the aggregate.

Some people argue that, unless an entity type already has an accepted name, then it cannot be important. According to this view, difficulty finding a name would be a symptom of bad analysis. However, this does not allow for the creation and emergence of new concepts. For example, the concept of employee may be commonly understood to exclude part-time or free-lance workers, but we may want to define an entity type that includes these workers as well. To use the entity type name EMPLOYEE, although it accurately describes most of the occurrences it is to include, does not exactly fit the entity type. Furthermore, the entity type may or may not include the employees of subcontractors.

The point here is not whether this concept already has a good name, but whether this concept is useful for the business. Continued failure to find an acceptable name may indicate that it is not useful, but it may also mean that there are several overlapping concepts that must be disentangled. For another example, the sales department may want to include within the CUSTOMER entity type not only the people they are currently doing business with, but also future prospects, potential rather than actual customers.

Another problem arises with synonyms and homonyms. A **synonym** is an alternative name for the same thing. Thus CUSTOMER and CLIENT may be synonyms, if they mean exactly the same thing. The trouble is that approximate synonyms are more common than exact synonyms. So SUPPLIER may not be an exact equivalent of CREDITOR if the latter includes the taxman and the former does not. Thus the occurrences of one do not completely overlap the other. But even if they do, even if the occurrences of A are all occurrences of B and vice versa, that is still not enough. What is required for A and B to be exact synonyms is that they *necessarily always* include the same occurrences, and that a future counter-example is therefore ruled out.

In practice, such perfectionism is excessive, and information models are usually built where the name of the entity type covers most, but not all of the occurrences, and the gap is filled by the definition. Or perhaps the name covers too much, and has to be qualified by the definition. Thus the entity type names EMPLOYEE and CUSTOMER may be used after all, provided that the definition is clear.

A **homonym** is a word that is used for two different things, depending on content. The most frequently cited example of a **homonym** is ORDER. If purchase orders, sales orders and works orders are modelled as separate entity types, then ORDER would indeed be a homonym. This can be resolved in two ways: either by introducing a qualifier to remove the ambiguity, or by merging all these different types of order into a single generalized entity type ORDER.

There are certain entity type names that trigger suspicion among experienced analysts: REPORT, LINE, ITEM, RECORD, CODE, RESULT. The suspicion is that these names refer to some existing way of representing entities, and should be replaced by a name that refers directly to the entity itself. Ask what a report or a line or a record contains or communicates, ask what a code represents. For example, on examining the putative entity type INSPECTION REPORT, it turns out to be nothing more than the INSPECTION itself, currently represented and communicated in the form of a report. An inspection has a result, but there is no need for an additional entity type INSPECTION RESULT, since this is nothing more than information belonging to the inspection itself. (If an inspection has many results, then they must be distinguishable in some way, they may perhaps be the results of different parts or aspects of the inspection, and that may point to the need for an entity type INSPECTION ASPECT or whatever.)

2.1.4 Two-faced entities

One difficulty with information modelling, is that of **two-faced** entity types that serve more than one purpose. This is found particularly with abstract entity types such as MARKET or ACCOUNT. The principle of data sharing seems to urge that each entity type serve as many purposes as possible, but there are situations where a single term hides a multiplicity of purposes, and must be pulled apart.

A more clear-cut example of a homonym is POLICY, *since there is little likelihood that* INSURANCE POLICY *and* ORGANIZATIONAL POLICY *can be lumped into a single, generalized entity type. More difficult to handle is where the homonymy is not so obvious to spot. For example, in a food manufacturer, some people may think that* PRODUCT *means a single can of beans, while others may think it means all cans of beans of a particular type. Or when one department of the company does some work for another department, there may be some confusion whether the department receiving the service counts as a customer. (For the sales department, it is not a customer, for the servicing department it may be. There may or may not be some notional 'payment' between the two departments, but this will be unlike a true financial transaction. We shall return to this example later.)*

Table 2.1 Intersecting entity types

	MARKET		
PRODUCT	Before sale	At sale	After sale
What the customer buys			
What the customer gets			

A good example of a two-faced entity type occurring in many models is PRODUCT. This has two aspects: what is bought by the customer, and what is delivered to the customer. Superficially these appear equivalent, but they often turn out not to be. Consider tinned peaches. The consumer selects a brand, and perhaps does not care where the peaches are grown. Indeed, the same brand of tinned peaches may contain Californian peaches at one time of year, and South African peaches at another time of year. Furthermore, peaches from the same source may be tinned under several different brand names (including supermarkets' own brand labels).

Thus we have many facts about a tin of peaches, including its brand name and retail price, as well as the source of the peaches inside. Confusion arises if we try to model all these facts in a single entity type called PRODUCT. Instead, it is usually a good idea to distinguish two entity types: PRODUCT and BRAND, with a many-to-many relationship between them.

The same physical object may be sold in a number of different contexts. A piece of foam rubber may be sold in sports shops as a mat, in specialized health care shops as a physiotherapy aid, in furnishing shops as a sofa lining, and in an art gallery (after some mutilation) as a sculpture. With software products, a similar situation seems to hold. The customer asks for Microsoft Word™, and gets Microsoft Word UK Version 4.0™. So the software title would be the BRAND, and the software version would be the PRODUCT. However, some customers may ask for a specific version, so the situation is more complex than with peaches, where the customer can only get what the manufacturer chooses.

One way to get yourself completely confused is to build an intersection between two two-faced entity types, for example PRODUCT and MARKET. Then the ambiguity is multiplied (see Table 2.1).

How do we recognize two-faced entity types? One sign is an apparent conflict of business objectives – for example to increase the flexibility of supply without proliferating brands, or to increase the segmentation of target markets without fragmenting the support infrastructure. Another sign is irreconcilable differences between rival descriptions of the entity type, such as in estimates of size.

2.1.5 Subject areas

Before we have identified specific entity types, we may want to refer to a broad field of information. We call this a **subject area**. This is useful during the early stages of planning and analysis. Some high-level information models consist entirely of subject areas rather than entity types. Before an analysis project starts, its scope may be defined in terms of the subject areas it is to decompose into entities (since the entity types themselves may not yet have been defined) and their relationships and attributes. And the concept of subject area also allows reference sideways, to aspects of data in other business areas, outside the scope of our own business area.

The usual convention for subject areas is to give them plural names, to distinguish them from entity types. Thus CUSTOMERS is a subject area, which may well include an entity type called CUSTOMER, but need not. (There could be several entity types, each modelling an aspect or class of customers, none of them called CUSTOMER.)

2.2 Relationships

2.2.1 Associations and pairings

A relationship is a pattern of association between two entities. Any two entities may be associated in a number of ways. For example, Sir Walter Scott is associated with the novel *Waverley*, in two ways:

1. The name Walter and the name *Waverley* both begin with the letter 'W'.
2. Scott was the author of the novel.

Scott is an occurrence of the entity type MAN, and *Waverley* is an occurrence of the entity type NOVEL. The two associations just listed can be generalized into two patterns of association between the two entity types. We therefore have two **relationships** between MAN and NOVEL, namely:

1. . . . begins with the same letter as . . .
2. . . . is author of . . .

A **relationship pairing** is, then, an association of one entity occurrence with another entity occurrence, according to a specific relationship. Thus <Francis Bacon, *Frankenstein*> is a pairing by the first relationship but not the second, while <James Joyce, *Ulysses*> is a pairing by the second relationship but not the first. One of these relationships is trivial, while the other is potentially interesting. I have deliberately included a trivial relationship in this example, in order to make the point that it is very easy to invent irrelevant relationships, and to clutter the information model with them. It is therefore very important to filter such rubbish relationships out.

Let us suppose that the second relationship *is author of* is relevant to the model. We shall need to depict, define and analyse the relationship. We start by considering two properties of the relationship: its **cardinality** and its **optionality**. We start by asking, for each occurrence of MAN, whether it can be associated with zero, one or many occurrences of NOVEL, and vice versa. We can show this as a table. (Table 2.2).

Table 2.2 Cardinality and optionality

	Zero	One	Many	
MAN	✓	✓	✓	NOVEL
NOVEL	✘	✓	✘	MAN

These tables are sometimes known as Rikkilae tables, after the Finnish eccentric Raimo Rikkilae.

We can read the first line of the table as follows. The first tick indicates that a man need not have written a novel at all, that there are some men not associated with any novel via this relationship. The second tick indicates that a man can be associated with exactly one novel, since some novelists stop after their first (e.g. Elias Canetti); the third tick that a man can be associated with more than one novel, since most novelists go on to write more. And we can read the second line of the table as follows. The first tick indicates that there cannot be a novel not associated with an author, or to put it another way, every novel has an author. The second tick indicates that there can be a novel with one author; the third tick indicates that there cannot be a novel with more than one author. In summary, the second line of the table asserts that every novel has exactly one author.

(Now this assertion may or may not be true. The advantage of drawing this table is that it makes this assertion clear, and raises the question: might there be anonymous or jointly written novels, and how do we cope with this?)

From Table 2.2, we can define the two properties of the relationship, mentioned earlier. Optionality is defined from the first column. If there is one tick in the first column, then the relationship is **partially optional**, while if there are two ticks in the first column, then it is **fully optional**. Thus the relationship is optional for MAN, but not optional (mandatory) for NOVEL, and is therefore partially optional.

Cardinality is defined from the third column. There are four possibilities for the cardinality of a relationship: **one-to-one** (if no ticks), **one-to-many** or **many-to-one** (if one tick) and **many-to-many** (if two ticks). In this particular example, the relationship is a one-to-many relationship: this means that one man may author one or many novels, but each novel is authored by one man.

What is the significance of cardinality? Why is the difference between one and two or more so important, while the difference between two and three or more is not. The answer lies with entity identification. We can identify Scott as the author of *Waverley*, because we know that *Waverley* can have only one author. But we cannot identify *Waverley* as the novel of Scott, because we know that Scott could have written more than one novel. (Of course, some writers do write only one novel. The phrase 'the novel written by Elias Canetti' does happen uniquely to identify a single novel, but the point is that such identification is not always reliable.)

The alert reader of this section will have noticed overlap between MAN, AUTHOR, WRITER, and so on. It is just this sort of confusion that the modeller must become sensitive to, and skilled in resolving.

For example, feminists will complain that many of the best novels are authored by women. I have used the male terminology here deliberately, in order to be able to address this point. This feminist complaint is legitimate, and the information modeller has three possible ways of answering it:

1. Define the entity type MAN to allow female as well as male occurrences. Thus not only George Orwell but also George Eliot would be included. We could also include child authors. This is a common strategy, but misleading. It is not always possible to find a name for the entity type that exactly matches the definition, but a name that ignores a good half of the occurrences would be too inaccurate.
2. Allow the relationship between MAN and NOVEL to be fully optional, so that novels written by women would not be associated (obviously) with a male author. (That solution would only work if we had a convincing reason for being uninterested in female authors.)
3. Change the name and scope of the entity type from MAN to PERSON.

In this particular example the third answer would probably the best. But the reason for explaining the other options is that they may be valid in other, more complex situations. What is the significance of optionality? If the relationship is optional then the business conditions governing the optionality must be analysed and described. Consider the difference between the following statements:

- All customers must have signed a contract. Only such customers can be serviced.
- Even customers that have not signed may be serviced.

If the relationship is mandatory, it makes servicing the customer easier, since we can assume there will always be a contract. (This ensures we know the customer address, credit rating, etc.) If the relationship is optional, we should ask which customers have not signed, and what difference it makes to the way they are serviced.

For a counter-example, read Cocktail Time *by P. G. Wodehouse.*

A third property of a relationship, of particular interest when the information model is implemented as a database, is whether it is **transferable**. A customer, having signed one contract, may cancel that one and sign a new contract. A contract may occasionally be transferred to a different customer (perhaps if the original customer is taken over). However, a novel cannot be transferred to a different novelist.

2.2.2 Entity–relationship diagram

The entity types and relationships are shown in Figure 2.4. The entity types are shown as boxes, and the relationships are shown as lines between the boxes. Optionality is shown by a circle on the line; a cardinality of 'many' is shown as a crowsfoot. Thus the relationship discussed above, between PERSON and NOVEL, can be shown.

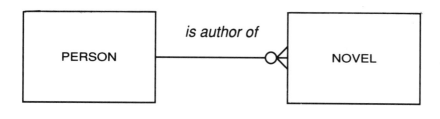

Figure 2.4
Entity–relationship
diagram with one-to-
many relationship

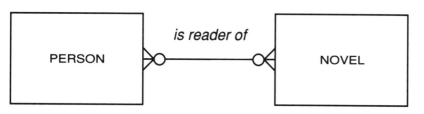

Figure 2.5
Many-to-many
relationship

This can be read as 'each person is author of zero, one or many novels; while each novel has exactly one author'. Different combinations of the same conventions are used to show relationships of other cardinality and optionality. Figure 2.5 shows a many-to-many relationship between PERSON and NOVEL. It also shows that possibly a novel could remain entirely unread. We might ask whether this is physically possible? Surely the author herself would have read the book? But does the author count as a reader? Does READER include employees of the publishing or printing firm? That depends what we *mean* by a reader. This example demonstrates the need to define the relationship, to remove any such ambiguities. Just as entity types have to be carefully defined, so do relationships, since their interpretation may affect business rules, or may influence systems design.

2.2.3 Relationship names

A relationship has no direction; it represents associations between two objects. (For this reason, we use the crowsfoot notation to indicate the cardinality of the relationship, rather than an arrow, which suggests a direction or flow.[4]) However, ordinary language is linear, so if we want to express a relationship in ordinary language, we must name one object before the other. There are therefore two names for the relationship, according to which object is named first. For example CUSTOMER *places* SALES ORDER and SALES ORDER *is placed by* CUSTOMER – these two names represent the same relationship. In this particular example, both names use different forms of the same verb: to place. In English, it is usually fairly easy to find two names r and r' for the relationship between two entity types A and B, so that ArB and Br'A are both normal English sentences. It is a good idea to use the same verb if possible, perhaps one active and one passive, but this symmetry is not essential, and should not be pursued if it makes the names sound awkward or unnatural.

The symmetry is a happy chance feature of the English language. This is because, in the English language, the name of an entity type is always the same, and its grammatical role (subject, predicate or object) is indicated by the position of the word in the sentence. (Interestingly, English is closer to Chinese than to other European languages in this respect.) In so-called inflected languages, the grammatical role is indicated by the form of the entity type name, and the sequence of words in the sentence may be irrelevant to the meaning. Thus whereas in English, the two names of a relationship both contain the names of the entity types in the same form, this is not true of all other languages.

- *Das Buch veredelt den Menschen.*
- *Der Mensch wird durch dem Buch veredelt.*

Therefore any such guideline about the naming of relationships cannot be an intrinsic component of entity logic, since it would vary from language to language. Use such language-specific guidelines if they help you keep a consistent style of naming, but do not get hung up over adhering to such rules, and do not sacrifice clarity or correctness for their sake.

Figure 2.6 Clockwise relationship names

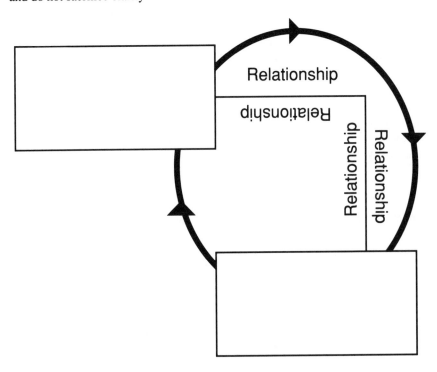

There is a simple convention about the placing of relationship names on the diagram: the names are read clockwise. (Figure 2.6). Thus a relationship name above a horizontal line is read from left to right, a name to the right of a vertical

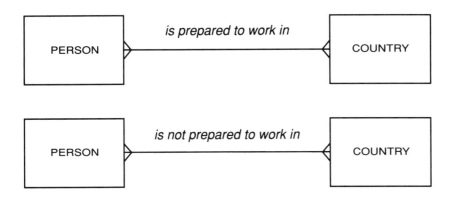

Figure 2.7 Positive and negative relationships

line is read from top to bottom, a name to the left of a vertical line is read from bottom to top, and a name below a horizontal line is read from right to left. (The names are not normally written upside down, however; this diagram is purely to demonstrate the clockwise rule.)

Relationships may be positive or negative. Consider the alternatives in Figure 2.7.

Clearly, if we know which people *are* prepared to work in, say, South Africa, then we also know (by elimination) which people are *not* prepared to work there, and vice versa. Therefore only one of the two relationships is required in the information model, and the other can be derived from it. But which of the two relationships do we include? The obvious answer would seem to be to always choose the positive one, and avoid the word 'not'. But this is not good enough, because it depends which verb we are using. In the above example, we could just as well have named the two alternatives *refuses to work in* and *does not refuse to work in*. A better way of deciding which of the two to include in the information model is to determine which of the two is the genuine information need, which is of more interest and importance to the business. Since information tends to be of greater value according to its unlikeliness (i.e. if you could have guessed it anyway, it was not worth very much), it follows that the less frequently occurring relationship is probably of more importance, thus we should choose whichever alternative will result in the fewer pairings. (This answer happens to be better for computer systems design as well, but this is a secondary consideration.)

Table 2.3 Pairings

	South Africa	Saudi Arabia	Sweden
John	✓	✓	✗
Deepak	✗	✓	✓
Winston	✗	✗	✓
Shelagh	✓	✗	✓

In Table 2.3 the tick indicates a pairing under the relationship *is prepared to work in* while the cross indicates a pairing under the relationship *refuses to work in*. In this particular example, there are more ticks than crosses, indicating that refusal is the exception rather than the rule. Therefore, following the guideline that we prefer to model the rarer of the alternative pairings, our model should include the relationship *refuses to work in*, and not the other, since it can be derived.

Drawing the relationship in this way, as a matrix with ticks and crosses, also allows us to see that there are some situations where a single relationship is not enough. Suppose we did not actually know whether Shelagh was prepared to work in South Africa or not. The matrix would then look like Table 2.4.

Table 2.4 Three-value matrix

	South Africa	Saudi Arabia	Sweden
John	✓	✓	✖
Deepak	✖	✓	✓
Winston	✖	✖	✓
Shelagh	?	✖	✓

Because the matrix contains three values instead of two, it is not possible to model it with a single relationship. In this case, the relationship *is prepared to work in* cannot be derived from the absence of the relationship *refuses to work in*, and we might need both, or some more complex structure.

Another situation where we might need a more complex structure is where we need to model the *reason* for the refusal, or alternatively the *conditions* for the acceptance. (For example, if Winston will only work abroad for a maximum of three months, or if John expects to take his wife and children on any long-term assignment.) Reasons and conditions will be discussed in Chapter 8.

2.2.4 *Singular versus plural*

One of the difficulties many people have when first faced with an information model is to distinguish between the singular and the plural. A box with a singular name in it (CUSTOMER, SUPPLIER, EMPLOYEE) is not an entity occurrence but an entity type, representing all possible occurrences. Reading a one-to-many or many-to-one relationship will be hard, until you have grasped this point.

Do not expect other people to grasp the point as quickly as you. Even intelligent people sometimes have mental blocks in this area, perhaps depending how well the modelling language was explained to them in the first place. It sometimes helps to draw rough diagrams of entity occurrences and relationship pairings, to show examples of the one-to-many and many-to-one relationships in action. Such diagrams can be used to convince people that a relationship is truly one-to-many or many-to-many.

In Figure 2.8, the names on the left denote some (but not all) occurrences of
PERSON, the names on the right denote some (but not all) occurrences of BOOK,
and the lines depict pairings according to the relationship *writes*. This shows
us that an author can write many novels, but a novel can have only one author.
Note that in such a diagram the pairings between entity occurrences do not
need arrows – a pairing has no direction. If 'a' is associated with 'b', then
'b' is necessarily associated with 'a'. Even if there was an entity where
we were unsure whether it was the name of a novel or the name of a novelist, the
ambiguity would be resolved by the layout of the diagram.

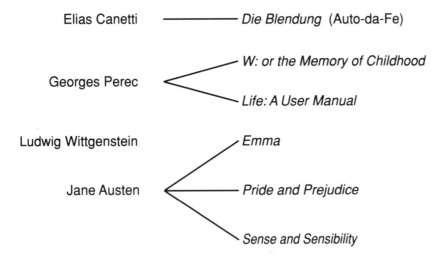

Figure 2.8 Different
types of pairing

Another symptom of this difficulty with singular and plural is the temptation
to show an entity occurrence as an entity type. But an entity type is expected
to have several occurrences. Thus, if all business is conducted in US dollars,
there is no interest in an entity type called CURRENCY. It is only if there is a
mix of several currencies that we need to associate each transaction with
a particular currency. Similarly, single-occurrence entity types called HEAD
OFFICE or PERSONNEL DEPARTMENT are almost certainly wrong. (These may,
however, be valid occurrences of such entity types as OFFICE LOCATION or
DEPARTMENT. I also know of one organization that for historical reasons has
seven head offices. They are in fact the regional offices of a decentralized
organization, but it is politically impossible to call them anything but head
offices.)

The only time it makes sense to have an entity type in the model with a single
occurrence is when there is only one occurrence *now* but the possibility of others
in the future. For example, while the company is operating only within one
country, it may deal with only one tax office. However, there might be a
business plan for overseas expansion, which would necessitate multiple
occurrences of TAX OFFICE. Such situations are rare. There are even rarer
situations where there are *zero* occurrences now, but there may be several in the

future. Therefore single-occurrence and zero-occurrence entity types always arouse suspicion and deserve a second look. An entity type that *necessarily* has only one occurrence is a sure anomaly, and should be removed from the model or generalized.

Also arousing suspicion is a **universal relationship**, a many-to-many relationship between entity types A and B where every occurrence of A is associated with every occurrence of B. Similarly, a **negatively universal relationship**, where no occurrence of A is associated with any occurrence of B. If a relationship is truly universal, or negatively universal, then it conveys no information at all: it is never worth asking whether a given occurrence of A is associated with a given occurrence of B, because you already know the answer. As with the single-occurrence entity type, the key question is whether the relationship is *necessarily* universal, in other words, whether it is possible that future occurrences of A and B might break the pattern. If a relationship is universal by chance, then it may be worth including, but if it is necessarily universal then it is certainly redundant.

An attribute that always takes the same value would be a similar error. Information requires difference (it is a 'difference that makes a difference', to quote Bateson), and so if something in the information model is devoid of difference, it is devoid of information, and therefore has no place in the model.[5]

2.2.5 *Relationship description*

One way we can extend our understanding of the cardinality and optionality of a relationship is by quantifying them. This can be done by replacing the ticks and crosses of the relationship table with the percentages of occurrences, as in Table 2.5.

Table 2.5 Occurrence percentages

	zero	one	many	
PERSON	95%	0.01%	4.99%	NOVEL
NOVEL	0%	100%	0%	PERSON

We already know (because the relationship is one to many and partially optional) that every novel is written by exactly one person. What we now see from the percentages is that most people do not write a novel at all, but that of those that do, most write several novels rather than just one. Furthermore, by extending the table, we may also document the average and maximum number of novels written by each novelist. This kind of knowledge adds richness to the model. Depending what your information model is going to be used for, such richness may be invaluable, or may be wasted effort.

2.2.6 Involuted relationships and implicit hierarchies

All relationships associate pairs of entities together. In the examples discussed so far, these entities belong to two different entity types. Some relationships, however, associate pairs of entities belonging to the same entity type: these are known as **involuted relationships:** for example, the relationship between employees shown in Figure 2.9.

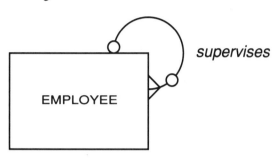

Figure 2.9 *Supervises* relationship

Note that such relationships often define a hierarchy – the supervisor is supervised in turn by another employee higher up in the organization. Such a relationship is almost always fully optional, since the employees at the bottom have no supervisory role, while at the top, executives are usually responsible to shareholders or members, institutions, civil servants or politicians rather than being supervised by other employees.

One of the characteristics of a hierarchy is that there can be no loops – in other words, an employee cannot be the supervisor of his supervisor, or the supervisor of the supervisor of the superviser of the same employee. Not all one-to-many involuted relationships define such hierarchies. Consider the relationship between the psychoanalyst and the patient. One of the rules of the profession is that each psychoanalyst must undergo analysis from a colleague. Thus the analyst of the analyst, or the analyst of the analyst of the analyst, may well be the same person: see Figure 2.10.

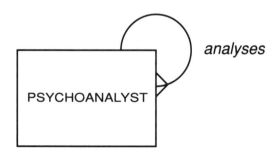

Figure 2.10 One-to-many involuted relationship

While a one-to-many involuted relationship can define a hierarchy, a many-to-many involuted relationship cannot. This is because a hierarchy must be a tree structure, with only one root, whereas a many-to-many relationship may have several roots.

In the example in Figure 2.11 there can be no loops – a part cannot usually contain itself, either directly or indirectly. (This is not always true – in manufacture with some materials, rejects may be melted down and reused, thus for example, a candle may be made from other candles.) Figure 2.12 shows an example where loops can be allowed.

Figure 2.11 Many-to-many relationship with several roots

Figure 2.12 Looped involuted relationship

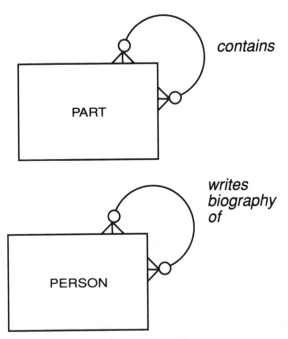

We asserted above that, when drawing diagrams of occurrences, it is not necessary to show any direction on the relationship pairings. But this changes when we come to look at involuted relationships, since if 'a' and 'b' are occurrences of the same entity type, it will not be clear from the occurrence diagram which way round to read it.

In the following diagram of the *contains* relationship, (Figure 2.13) the arrow shows that the bicycle contains wheels which contain axles which contain ball bearings. Bicycles and tricycles share some common components (e.g. the same saddle is used), which is why the relationship is many to many and not one to many. Figure 2.14 shows the *writes biography of* relationship. A biographer can write many biographies, and a person can be the subject of many biographies. Children writing biographies of their parents is common; parents writing biographies of their children is rare.

Whereas with the bill of materials structure, it may be appropriate to ban loops (since in many manufacturing situations it would be absurd for a component to contain itself), with the biographical structure there might easily be a loop: 'a' writes a book on 'b' who writes a book on 'c' who writes a book

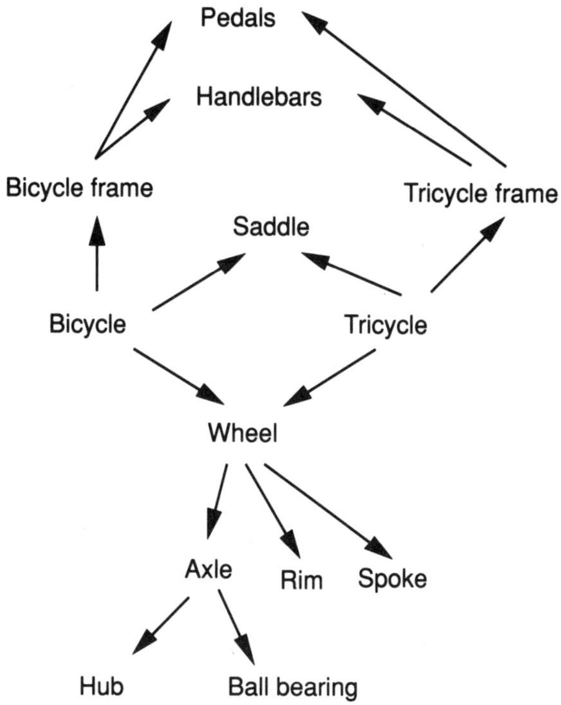

Pedals

Handlebars

Bicycle frame

Saddle

Tricycle frame

Bicycle

Tricycle

Wheel

Axle   Rim   Spoke

Hub   Ball bearing

Figure 2.13 *Contains*
relationship

Figure 2.13 *Contains*
relationship

on 'a'. However, I have not been able to find such a loop – any reader who
draws one to my attention will be suitably rewarded.

Later in this chapter, we shall return to these examples, to show how such
relationships can be analyzed further.

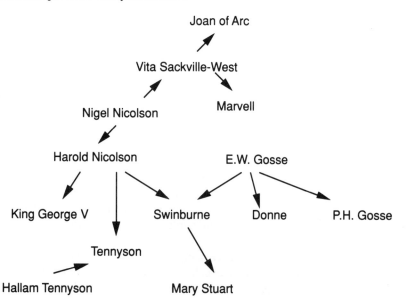

Joan of Arc

Vita Sackville-West

Nigel Nicolson

Marvell

Harold Nicolson   E.W. Gosse

King George V   Swinburne   Donne   P.H. Gosse

Tennyson

Hallam Tennyson   Mary Stuart

Figure 2.14 *Writes
biography of*
relationship

2.2.7 Explicit hierarchy versus involution

Sometimes the obvious way of modelling a situation is to represent it as a hierarchy. For example, accounting periods can be represented hierarchically, as days within months within years. Similarly, GEOGRAPHICAL AREA can be represented hierarchically, perhaps as towns within counties within countries. Alternatively, instead of having a separate entity type for each level of this hierarchy, it is possible to define a single generic entity type, lumping all the levels into one, via an involuted relationship.

Figure 2.15 A hierarchy

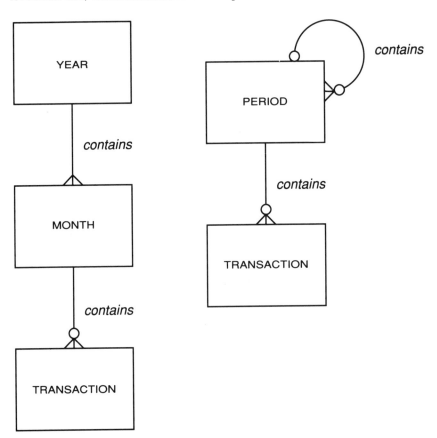

Thus consider the accounting example shown in Figure 2.15, where transactions are assigned to months within years. The solution on the left shows YEAR and MONTH explicitly, whereas the solution on the right has lumped both into a single entity type PERIOD, with an involuted relationship to associate each month with the year it belongs to.

We shall encounter this type of choice many times, not merely in modelling space and time, but also with such other hierarchies as ORGANIZATION UNIT (departments within divisions, etc). Some of the triggers that prompt the generalized solution are:

- Difficulty in knowing what level in the hierarchy you are at, since the levels may be relative rather than absolute.
- Difficulty in placing relationships at specific level.
- Difficulty in placing attributes (but do not be too concerned about derived attributes such as subtotals).
- Difficulty in identifying top or bottom level.
- Likelihood of additional levels being introduced.

Sometimes an explicit hierarchy is arbitrary. One project manager divides a project into phases, and the phases into stages. Another project manager divides a similar project into tasks, and the tasks into activities. Is there any reason for preferring one set of terms over another? Do the phases of the one correspond exactly to the tasks of the other, and does it matter? An explicit hierarchy can show different breakdowns between levels, while generalization can hide these differences. This brings both advantages and disadvantages.

The main advantage with involutions is the extra flexibility that they offer. For example, if the accountants decide to produce results quarterly as well as annually, this can already be supported by the generalized information model, since quarters can be introduced as additional occurrences of PERIOD. The non-generalized model would presumably have to be altered by the insertion of an additional entity type QUARTER.

One trouble with involutions is that, since the structure is hidden in the relationship, it is often necessary to define several complicated integrity conditions on the relationship. For example, that each month belongs to a year, but a month cannot belong to a month, a year cannot belong to a month, and a year cannot belong to a year. Perhaps all transactions are assigned to specific months, or perhaps some transactions cannot be assigned to specific months but have to be assigned to a whole year. In the model showing YEAR and MONTH explicitly, these integrity conditions follow automatically from the diagram, and do not need to be specified additionally.

2.3 Attributes

2.3.1 Attribute definitions and values

We have defined an entity as an object of interest to the business, or to the area being modelled. We can now define an **attribute** as an item of information that describes an entity. For example, the entity type PERSON may possess the attributes: NAME, ADDRESS, HOME PHONE NUMBER. An attribute is in fact a type of information, general to the occurrences of an entity type. Each occurrence of the entity type may have a **value** for the attribute. Thus for the entity type WAREHOUSE, three different occurrences may have attribute values as shown in the three columns in Table 2.6.

Each attribute may belong to only one entity type. An attribute may, however, be associated with other entity types via relationships. Thus for example, the warehouse has a location, and the manager of a warehouse also has a location; but the manager's location is not an attribute of the entity type MANAGER, since it is no different from the location of the warehouse that she manages. LOCATION is an attribute of WAREHOUSE, and is indirectly associated with MANAGER via the relationship between MANAGER and WAREHOUSE.

Table 2.6 Occurrences and attribute values

attribute	<<<<<<<<	values	>>>>>>>>
LOCATION	Newton	Milton	Crichton
CAPACITY (sq. metres)	20,000	5,000	12,000
FRIDGE CAPACITY?	Yes	No	Yes
TELEX NO.	457246	568358	578396

An attribute should represent a single fact. Composite attributes (where several independent facts are represented by a single attribute) should be decomposed into atomic attributes. An attribute should also be **single-valued**, which means that each occurrence of the entity type may have only one value for the attribute at a time (although this value may change over time). A **multi-valued attribute**, where an occurrence can have more than one value at the same time, is a sure sign of incomplete analysis.

Often, when an attribute turns out to be multi-valued, it may be necessary to add an extra entity type. So, for example, if one of the attributes of EMPLOYEE is JOB TITLE, and if it turns out that some employees have more than one job title concurrently, it will probably be necessary to add the entity type JOB to the model, with a relationship to the EMPLOYEE entity type. (JOB TITLE is then an attribute of JOB.)

However, there may be other modelling options. If a person has two home phone numbers (one for weekdays and another for weekends), then a single attribute HOME PHONE NUMBER would be multi-valued. In this situation, instead of adding an entity type, it will sometimes be good enough to divide the attribute into two: WEEKDAY PHONE NUMBER and WEEKEND PHONE NUMBER.

We discussed above the anomalies of the single-occurrence entity type and the universal relationship. Here there is the anomalous case of the **fixed-value attribute**, where every occurrence of the entity type takes the same value for the attribute. Again, we must ask whether the attribute just happens at present to have this property, but could in future have different values. If it is necessarily fixed value, then it conveys no information, and adds nothing to the model.

2.3.2 *Attribute properties*

It is sometimes useful to define a **domain** for an attribute, or for several attributes. This represents the set of possible values for the attribute(s). For example, the attribute WAREHOUSE CAPACITY may take numeric values within the range 0–1 million square metres. Some modelling tools allow standard domains to be defined, with fixed length and other properties; thus for example, all monetary values can be represented in a standard fashion. However, since some modelling tools only offer a limited range of domains, and do not allow additional domains to be defined, some organizations define procedural standards for the names and lengths of such domains, as well as standard operations on them.

Some modelling tools expect attribute lengths to be defined as part of the information model. However, it is not always appropriate to fix the length of an attribute during analysis. Often all that can be determined is the longest value known to date. And the designer may choose to provide a field that is longer or shorter than the longest known value.

This corresponds roughly to the distinction in the Spanish language between 'ser' and 'estar'.

An attribute may be **mandatory** (where every entity occurrence must have a value) or **optional**. An attribute may be **essential** (where once an entity occurrence has a value, this value cannot be changed) or **transitory**.

2.3.3 Data and information

In traditional computing systems, the only attribute values that could be stored were in the form of binary data. Even modern databases concentrate on storing data, such as numerical values, dates, codes and so on. However, there is increasing demand for computerization of other forms of information – textual, graphical, audio, video and so on. Any of these may be legitimate domains for an attribute. A personnel system may wish to store colour photographs of all employees. So, in analysing this requirement, we may define an attribute EMPLOYEE APPEARANCE, whose values are not verbal descriptions but pictures.

It is to emphasize that we are not restricted to traditional data values, that we now refer to our models as information models, rather than data models.

2.3.4 Fluctuation of values

On the smallest scale, change is sudden and discontinuous: electrons jump from one energy state to another without passing through states between. Similarly, even if attributes change their values continuously, our process models are based on discrete change. (One of the consequences of this is it enables us to represent the models on digital computers.)

For example, the attribute BLOOD PRESSURE of a person goes up and down all the time (well mine does, anyway) so does it make sense to have a single-valued attribute in this situation? We have to go to the purpose of the information – from what perspective are we interested in blood pressure? If we were building a medical support system, for people in intensive care, it might be appropriate to monitor their blood pressure continuously. Then we might have an entity type BLOOD PRESSURE MEASUREMENT, and there could be thousands of occurrences of this entity type per day for each PERSON.

For an employee health scheme, on the other hand, we might just be interested in the normal blood pressure as measured at the most recent check-up. Although

Figure 2.16 Attributes

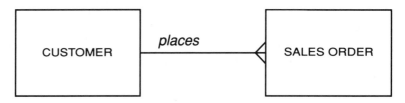

Figure 2.16 Attributes

an employee may have several check-ups over time, we are only interested in the most recent one – so we can safely define the attribute to refer to this one. Perhaps we need another attribute called MOST RECENT CHECKUP DATE.

2.3.5 Where do attributes belong?

We have already stressed that an attribute only belongs in one place. (For the reader with experience in relational databases, this means that there is no need for 'foreign keys' in the entity model, although there may be foreign keys in the subsequent database, to implement the relationships.) For example, where does the attribute CUSTOMER NUMBER belong?

In Figure 2.16 it is an attribute of CUSTOMER. It is associated with SALES ORDER via the relationship *places*. Therefore it is not a direct attribute of SALES ORDER. The same is true of other attributes of CUSTOMER, such as CUSTOMER ADDRESS, CUSTOMER CREDIT LIMIT, and so on.

So let us give some guidelines for deciding which entity type an attribute belongs to, given that each attribute can belong to only one entity type. If you want to associate an attribute with more than one entity type, there are two possible ways of dealing with this:

1. It is the same attribute. For example, if you have ADDRESS both of OFFICE and of WORKER, it may turn out that the address of the worker is the same as the address of the office in which the worker is located. The model should contain the attribute ADDRESS only once, as an attribute of OFFICE; the attribute is associated with the entity type WORKER via the relationship is located in between OFFICE and WORKER.
2. It is in fact two different attributes. For example, if you want to have PHONE NUMBER both of OFFICE and of WORKER, it may turn out that these are not the same, because the phone number of the individual includes an extension number, whereas the phone number of the office does not. In such a case, we need to have two attributes, with two different names, to avoid any confusion.

2.4 Subtypes and roles

2.4.1 Entity subtypes

If an identifiable subset of an entity type has special and relevant attributes and/or relationships, we can mark this in the model as an **entity subtype**. For example, in a sporting example, we may wish to highlight CAPTAIN as a subtype of PLAYER. There are two ways of showing this diagrammatically. The complex way is to draw a hierarchy of entity subtypes – we shall illustrate this below. The simple way is to draw a box within a box, as in Figure 2.17.

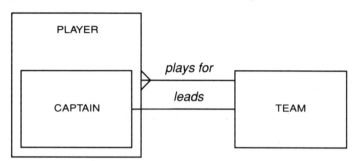

Figure 2.17 Entity subtypes

Sometimes several non-overlapping subtypes can be usefully identified. This is known as **partitioning**. For example, hospital staff can be divided (or partitioned) into DOCTORS, NURSES and OTHERS, as in Figure 2.18

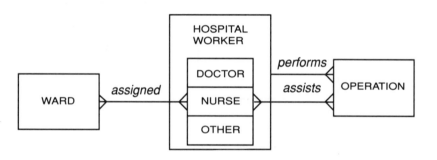

Figure 2.18 Partitioning

Subtypes may themselves be subdivided. For example, we may wish to distinguish SURGEONS from other DOCTOR: see Figure 2.19.

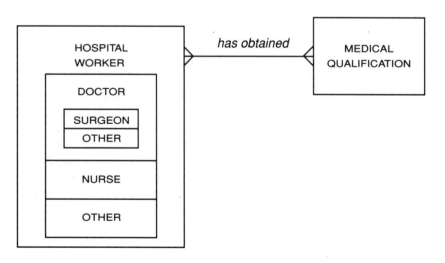

Figure 2.19 Partitioned subtypes

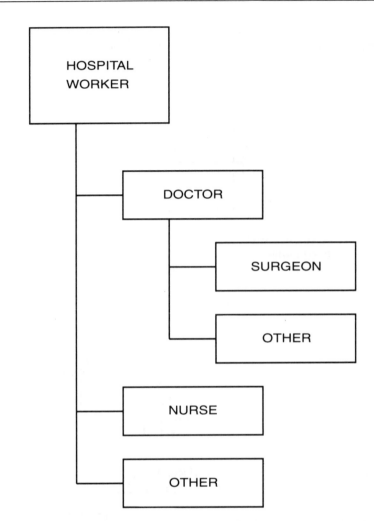

Figure 2.20 A hierarchy of subtypes

*OTHER is not a very good name for a subtype, since it defines an object in terms of what it is **not** rather than what it **is**, but it serves here to illustrate the concept.*

Another way of depicting this is to draw a hierarchy, separate from the entity–relationship diagram itself: see Figure 2.20. Two branches of the hierarchy may not overlap.

The same entity type may be partitioned in more than one way. Thus for some purposes we may wish to divide customers into two subtypes: HOME CUSTOMER and EXPORT CUSTOMER, while for other purposes we may wish to distinguish between actual and prospective customers, thus we would want two further subtypes: CURRENT CUSTOMER and PROSPECT CUSTOMER. Let us assume that all four combinations are possible: CURRENT HOME CUSTOMER, CURRENT EXPORT CUSTOMER, PROSPECT HOME CUSTOMER, PROSPECT EXPORT CUSTOMER. Therefore, as none of the four subtypes is a subset of another subtype, the two partitions are independent of one another. We show this as a double hierarchy, or by two separate nests of boxes. (See Figure 2.21.)

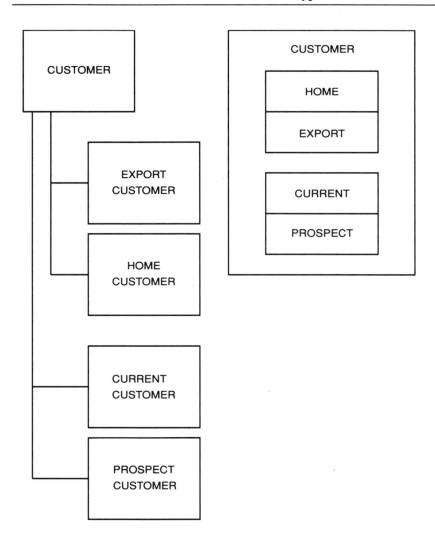

Figure 2.21 Double hierarchy – two alternative notations.

Here, although EXPORT CUSTOMER may not overlap with HOME CUSTOMER, and CURRENT CUSTOMER may not overlap with PROSPECT CUSTOMER, there may well be overlap between subtypes within different partitionings.

This can lead to very complex structures, with several independent multi-level hierarchies within a single entity type. Common sense must be applied, to ensure the model remains comprehensible.

2.4.2 Entity roles

A person can own a car. A company can also own a car. Therefore a car can be owned either by a person or by a company. Car ownership is therefore a **role** played by both entity types PERSON and COMPANY. We can sometimes model this

Figure 2.22 A mutually exclusive relationship

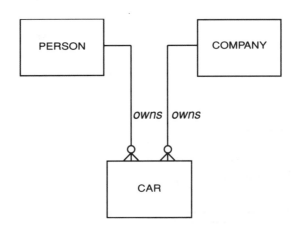

using a **mutually exclusive** relationship, which is to say that each occurrence of CAR must be either related to a PERSON, or to a COMPANY, but not both. This is illustrated in Figure 2.22.

But sometimes there may be some additional attributes associated with the role of car ownership, such as the insurance no-claims bonus. In this case we may require four entity types: PERSON, CAR, COMPANY and CAR-OWNER, with the last representing the role. The relationships between PERSON and CAR-OWNER, and between COMPANY and CAR-OWNER, are mutually exclusive one-to-one relationships of a special kind. They are usually given a standardized name, such as *takes role* or *same as*. (Figure 2.23 shows both, but consistency would be better.) A very common situation to which this applies is where payments are made to external parties other than suppliers (e.g. refunds to customers, parking fines to magistrate courts, etc.). We could have a role entity type called PAYEE, containing bank details and other relevant attributes, with the special role relationship to SUPPLIER and other entity types. An alternative to this would be to use subtyping, with SUPPLIER, CUSTOMER and COURT being subtypes of the general entity type EXTERNAL PARTY. This can become extremely cumbersome, with several complicated partitions and competing hierarchies, and role entities may be easier for the users to understand. There are no fixed guidelines when to use subtyping and when to use role entities; it is largely a matter of taste and style.

Figure 2.23 Role entity type

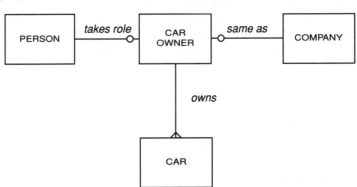

Sometimes similarity and difference does not follow a hierarchical structure. P may be similar to Q, and Q similar to R, but that does not imply that P is similar to R. Suppose it is not. What do we do?

1. Lump Q with P, and ignore the similarity with R.
2. Lump Q with R, and ignore the similarity with P.
3. Lump P, Q and R together, and ignore the lack of similarity between P and R.
4. Use non-hierarchical role constructs rather than hierarchical subtype ones. Look for the role shared by P and Q, and the role shared by Q and R. Thus Q plays two conflicting roles. (This non-hierarchical structure may be more difficult to manage than the hierarchical one. Often one of the other options is acceptable.)

A frequent example of an entity type with two conflicting roles is SUBCONTRACTOR. For the purposes of production planning, a subcontractor is equivalent to an internal department or organizational unit, and in this role it shares such matters as task responsibility, work scheduling, use of raw materials, etc. We can call this role WORK UNIT. Meanwhile, for the purposes of accounting, a subcontractor is equivalent to a supplier, and in this role it shares such matters as invoicing and payments, contracts, etc. We can call this role CONTRACT PARTNER. There are common attributes, relationships and integrity conditions associated with each role. It would be difficult to model this with a hierarchy of subtypes, without making everything a subtype of a very broad entity type that will probably be too generalized to be useful. So in this case we could model each role as a separate entity type, as in Figure 2.24.

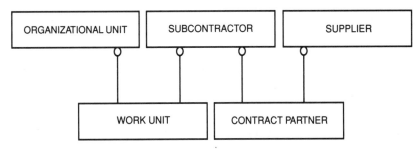

Figure 2.24 Modelling overlapping roles

Another situation in which entities may be included in the model to represent roles, is where several occurrences of the same entity types participate differently in the same event. For example, consider a wedding. (I shall use the Christian form of the ceremony, but this can be easily translated into other cultures.) There are four roles: bride, bridegroom, priest and witness. No person can perform more than one role in the same wedding, but a person may be able to perform different roles on different occasions (subject to sex and denomination).

These roles may involve preconditions and changes of state, which will be modelled in the entity state model. Three of the roles require the person to be suitably qualified: only a spinster can play bride, only a bachelor can play bridegroom, only an ordained person can play priest. Two of the roles involve a change of state. Thus being a bride involves a change of state from spinster to wife; being a bridegroom involves a change of state from bachelor to husband. The other two roles do not involve a change of state; there are therefore no restrictions on the frequency with which a person may act as priest or witness. (The entity state model will define whether, and under what circumstances, a married person can revert to the unmarried state, allowing them to be married for a second or subsequent time. This is, of course, a question of religious denomination.)

This structure is probably more elaborate than would be required in most business situations, but there is often a need to prevent an occurrence of an entity type playing more than one role at the same time, for example where craftsmen are required to inspect one another's work, but are not allowed to inspect their own work (for obvious reasons). Another business example is in the guaranteeing of financial transations, where a company or individual customer cannot be its own guarantor.

2.4.3 Pseudo entities and dummy entities

Discussion of roles allows us to define a related concept, that of a **quasi subject** or **pseudo entity**. This is something that, under certain conditions, acts as if it were an occurrence of a particular entity type. Often it may be a complex object masquerading as a simple object. In accounting, for example, it may be easier to regard a complex adjustment as if it were a straightforward transaction, rather than introduce additional entity types to cater for exceptional situations. (Accounting packages for general ledger usually adopt such simplifications, so that the package is usable without needing to represent the full complexity of the business.)

A **dummy entity** is similar to a pseudo entity, except that whereas a pseudo entity exists in a more complex form, a dummy entity does not exist at all. One reason for dummies is to seed the database with test occurrences – this may be required for business as well as technical reasons (for example, direct mailing lists are usually seeded with dummy names and addresses, so that abuse of the mailing list can be detected).

Another reason for introducing dummy occurrences of an entity type is to preserve the integrity conditions. If there are exceptional circumstances where the factory itself may generate production requirements of its own, it may be better to introduce a dummy occurrence of CUSTOMER to represent the factory itself, rather than to allow there to be an occurrence of CUSTOMER ORDER that is not associated with any CUSTOMER. By forcing the relationship between CUSTOMER ORDER and CUSTOMER to be mandatory rather than optional, the data processing may well be simpler. (There are many situations, such as this, where there is a trade off between the complexity of the information structure and the complexity of the information processing, between the information model and the process model.)

2.4.4 Partition definition

Each subtype or role should be separately defined. There should be a definite way of determining which subtype(s) a given entity occurrence belongs to, and which role(s) it plays. The most common way of distinguishing one subtype from another is through the use of a **partitioning attribute**. In the hospital staff example, the partitioning attribute may be JOB TITLE. We may be able to list the value(s) of the partitioning attribute that correspond to each subtype. Or there may be a formula that determines subtype, for example {if AGE > 18 then ADULT else CHILD} would be the partitioning formula for the following subtype hierarchy. This is illustrated in Figure 2.25.

Figure 2.25
Partitioning formula

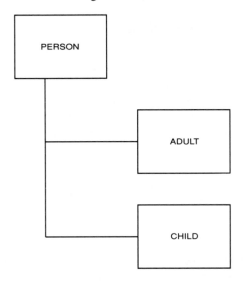

Instead of a partitioning attribute or formula, the partitioning may be determined through relationships to other entities. Thus in the hospital staff example, DOCTORs may be distinguished from NURSEs not via JOB TITLE but via MEDICAL QUALIFICATION TYPE which is an attribute of MEDICAL QUALIFICATION. (Figure 2.26).

Figure 2.26
Partitioning by relationship

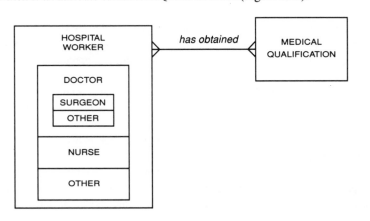

2.5 Resolution and intersection

Additional entity types are often uncovered during detailed analysis of an information structure. There are two main cases we must consider:

1. The introduction of a new entity type, when resolving a many-to-many relationship into two one-to-many relationships. This is called **binary intersection**.
2. The introduction of a new entity type to represent a non-binary relationship (i.e. an association between more than two entity types). This is called a **multiple** or **n-ary intersection**.

2.5.1 Binary intersections

A many-to-many relationship between two entity types often hides some information, since there may be attributes that cannot properly be assigned to either entity type. In detailed information modelling, therefore, it is customary to resolve many-to-many relationships by replacing them with extra entity types and several one-to-many relationships. For example, we may have a many-to-many relationship between SUPPLIER and PART (Figure 2.27).

Figure 2.27 Many-to-many relationship

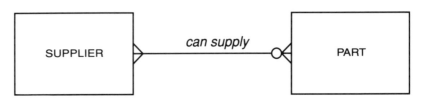

This hides the differences between the suppliers – for example, two suppliers may supply the same part at two different prices. It also hides the differences between parts – for example, the same supplier may have a standard delivery lead time of three weeks for some parts, and twelve weeks for other parts. These facts cannot be modelled either as attributes of SUPPLIER or of PART. Instead, we probably have to introduce an intermediate or **intersection** or **associative** entity type PART FROM SUPPLIER: see Figure 2.28.

The intersection entity type is almost always identified by its relationships to the entity types it sits between, and its name will often be a combination of the names of the entity types, perhaps linked with a preposition, as in this example.

As a special case of the resolution of many-to-many relationships, we can consider involuted ones. Recall the relationship *writes biography of* in Figure 2.12 (p.45).

We can resolve the relationship by adding another entity type BIOGRAPHY, with two one-to-many relationships. This allows us to capture the title and publication details of the biography itself, which was not modelled previously. This model also allows for a person to write more than one biography of the same subject; we now have Figure 2.29. This model appears not to be

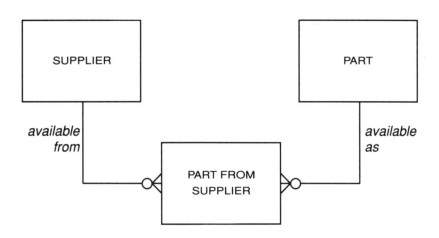

Figure 2.28
Intersection or
associative entity type

quite equivalent to the previous one, since it only allows each biography to have a single subject. The occurrence diagram (Figure 2.14) shows that Nigel Nicolson wrote about both his parents; but it does not show that this was a single book: *Portrait of a Marriage*. And Gosse's book *Father and Son* was about himself as well as his father. But although we may choose to define BIOGRAPHY as 'A book containing biographical material about one or more historical persons', we could alternatively define it as 'The biographical material about one historical person, contained in a specific book'. Both definitions are plausible interpretations of the common-sense usage of the word, but whereas the first definition results in the book *Portrait of Marriage* being a single occurrence of BIOGRAPHY, the second definition results in it being two occurrences.

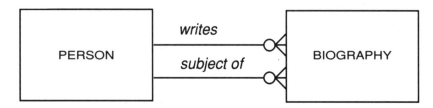

Figure 2.29
Biography–person
relationship

However, it may not always be meaningful or necessary to resolve *all* many-to-many relationships; a model that includes some many-to-many relationships is therefore not necessarily wrong. We have seen an example of this already, where we may just be interested in the acceptability of certain locations to certain employees. Whenever a many-to-many relationship can be fully depicted by ticks and crosses on a matrix (i.e. each cell of the matrix only needs to be either 'true' or 'false'), then there is no point in resolving it. Only resolve if this adds further information or properties (which, by the way, it usually, but not always, does).

And if the information model is not intended to give a detailed representation of the area, but is for broad planning purposes, then it may be inappropriate to resolve any of the many-to-many relationships, since it may obscure the essential structure if too much such detail is included.

2.5.2 Multiple intersections

We defined a relationship as a pattern of association between two entities. If we had wanted to be more precise, we could have called this a **binary relationship**. What about a pattern of association between three or more entities, which we might call a **multiple** or **n-ary relationship** (where n is the number of entities involved)? Some modelling languages allow such n-ary relationships to be defined and drawn, but the entity–relationship approach only allows binary relationships.

To see what we might be missing, let us look at an example of a tertiary (3-ary) relationship: it is between the three entity types COMPETITOR PRODUCT, OUR PRODUCT and MARKET AREA, and is called

> *... competes with ... in ...*

Thus, for the Coca-Cola Company, Diet Pepsi competes with Diet Coke in some countries, but not in others. This fact is clearly of no small interest to the marketing department.

As we go up to quaternary (4-ary) relationships, and beyond, it becomes progressively more difficult to think of plausible examples. It can be shown that any multiple relationship can be replaced with several binary relationships. This is what allows us to restrict ourselves to binary relationships, which are usually easier to understand. But often, in order to perform this replacement, we need to add an intersection entity type. Because of its origins, we can refer to this new entity type as a **multiple intersection**. In the above example, we might wish to add an entity type called MARKET COMPETITION, defined as any combination of COMPETITOR PRODUCT, OUR PRODUCT and MARKET AREA which possesses the association: see Figure 2.30.

Figure 2.30 Multiple intersection

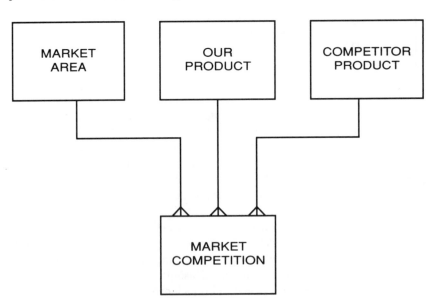

As with the binary intersections discussed in the previous section, we usually discover that the new entity type has attributes of interest to the business. We find, for example, that the relative market share (e.g. of Diet Coke versus Diet Pepsi in Germany) will be an attribute of MARKET COMPETITION.

2.5.3 Problems with intersections

There are two main problems with these intersection entity types. First, it is often hard to find meaningful names for them. A common solution is to include the names of all the intersected entity types in the name of the intersection, but this is cumbersome, and not always very informative. It is better to name the intersection after the relationship that it replaces.

The relationships between the intersected entity types and the intersection can also be difficult to name. It is often tempting to include the names of the other intersected entity types in the relationship name, as in Figure 2.31. Second, it is not always easy, in a complex structure, to determine how many intersection entity types are needed. There are no universal rules on how to address these difficulties but we should be able to offer a few tips as we go along.

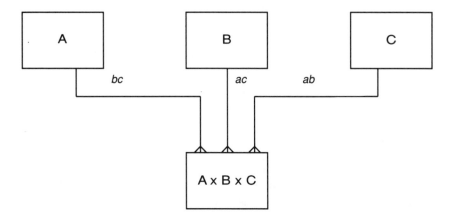

Figure 2.31 Naming intersection entity types

2.6 Redundancy

One of the aims of information modelling is to identify and (perhaps) remove redundant objects. We define redundancy to mean that a fact is represented in the model twice. Since facts are represented by objects, or combinations of objects, this is equivalent to saying that one object in the model can be derived from other objects in the model.[6] Some writers insist that all possible redundancy should be removed; here we take a more moderate approach, and insist that the redundancy should be analysed and controlled, but not necessarily removed.

There are two reasons for removing redundancy: to make the model simpler (and thus easier to understand and use), and to make the ensuing system more efficient. During analysis, we should only remove redundant objects for the first of these two reasons, since the second reason is a matter for systems design, but we need to establish all the facts of redundancy at this stage.

Storing a fact more than once opens the door to inconsistency, if the two versions of the same fact are incompatible. Thus non-redundancy makes it easier to ensure consistency. However, some situations demand a higher level of control, where consistency needs to be actively checked, rather than merely automatically ensured. Two or more versions of a fact are deliberately captured, so that they may be compared, and discrepancies highlighted. The classic example of this is double-entry book-keeping, which indicates its redundancy by its very name.

2.6.1 Types of redundancy

There are four types of redundancy:

1. **Redundancy by repetition** – two or more objects in the information model representing the same fact in the real world. For example, if the price on a customer invoice for an item is always the same as the price quoted in the catalogue, it would be redundant to represent this price twice, as an attribute both of PRODUCT ITEM and of CUSTOMER INVOICE ITEM.

2. **Redundancy by derivation** – an object in the model can be logically or arithmetically calculated from other objects in the model. For example, the price on a customer invoice for an item is always equal to the price quoted in the catalogue, minus the discount negotiated with that customer. Some further examples of derivation are listed below.

3. **Partial redundancy by repetition** – two or more objects in the information model sometimes or usually represent the same fact in the real world, but there are some exceptions. For example, the price on a customer invoice for an item is always the same as the price quoted in the catalogue, unless the sales manager has authorized a different price for this sales order.

4. **Partial redundancy by derivation** – an object in the model can sometimes, or usually, be logically or arithmetically calculated from other objects in the model but there are some exceptions. For example, the price on a customer invoice for an item is always equal to the price quoted in the catalogue, minus the discount negotiated with that customer, unless the sales manager has authorized a different price for this sales order.

2.6.2 Derived attributes

The most obvious form of redundancy is where attributes are repeated. More complex forms of redundancy arise where an attribute can be derived from one or more other attributes. We can identify the following common types of derivation:

1. To change units of measure (fixed) , e.g. to switch between feet and metres, multiply/divide by a constant.
2. To change units of measure (variable), e.g. to switch between dollars and pounds, multiply/divide by a currency exchange rate obtained by table look up.
3. To extract data (fixed), e.g. to derive a calendar month from a date.
4. To extract data (variable), e.g. to derive the age from the date of birth (depends on the current date).
5. To obtain a derived attribute by (arithmetical) manipulation of the other attributes of the same entity occurrence, e.g. GROSS AMOUNT equals NET AMOUNT plus TAX AMOUNT.
6. To obtain a single numeric value from a series of (input) numeric values. The simplest case is where the inputs are the values of a single attribute of a defined set of occurrences of some related entity type, and the derivation is based on a function such as COUNT, TOTAL, MINIMUM, MAXIMUM or AVERAGE. For example, ACCOUNT CLOSING BALANCE equals ACCOUNT OPENING BALANCE plus sum of (TRANSACTION AMOUNT)s.

In some of these examples, there is a loss of information in the derivation, in other words the derived attribute contains less information than the attribute(s) from which it is derived. In such examples, the derivation is necessarily one way. So although we can derive the age of a person (in years) from his/her date of birth, we cannot derive the date of birth from the age alone. (This loss of information, or one-way derivation is sometimes referred to as **information entropy**.) In such examples, there is no difficulty determining which attribute is derived and which is non-derived.

In other examples, however, the derivation could be two way. Thus we can either derive a measurement in feet from the measurement in metres, or the reverse. Thus it may be difficult to determine which of the two measurements is derived, and which is non-derived. The decision may finally be arbitrary, or based on majority convenience.

2.6.3 Derived attributes – design considerations

A derived attribute can be implemented in two ways: either stored and restored whenever the attribute values change, from which it is derived; or calculated and recalculated whenever its value is needed.

In the former approach, the derivation is performed at the earliest possible moment; in the latter approach, the derivation is performed as late as possible, on a just-in-time basis. (There may be other, more complex design solutions, where the derivation is performed neither at the earliest possible, nor at the latest possible moment, but at some intermediate point in time; for example, by a batch update program run overnight, when there maybe spare computing capacity. Such solutions, although common, are more complex because the status of any given data item may beunclear.)

The choice between these approaches is a design decision; it has nothing to do with the meaning and use of the attribute itself, and has only to do with the technical efficiency of the computer software. This decision, therefore, should be left to the latest possible point in the software development process. (However, some CASE tools blur this distinction between analysis and design, and encourage such design decisions to be made prematurely, in order to streamline the software development process.)

2.6.4 Inclusion of derived attributes

A derived attribute should be included in the information model:

1. When it represents a key performance measure (KPM) for the business or business area. Many managers measure performance of a business unit by a small number of ratios, and every such ratio is a derived attribute.
2. When it represents a shared information need of several users.
3. When it is required or referred to by several business processes.
4. When it is required as a status, partitioning or identifying attribute.
5. When its derivation is non-trivial.

During the early stages of analysis it may be difficult to be certain whether to include a particular derived attribute in the information model. If in doubt, it is usually better to include it anyway, and then review the situation when analysing the logic of the business processes, or towards the end of the whole analysis project. At this stage, the necessity of including a particular derived attribute should be clearer, and unnecessary attributes can be deleted from the model. (Note: this requires conforming to strict model management procedures.)

2.6.5 Specific derivations

In some circumstances, a derived attribute or relationship may turn out to be **specific**. This means that the derivation specifies a particular attribute value or entity occurrence. For example, if there is a basic attribute AGE, then the user may have information needs such as OLDER THAN SPOUSE, OLDER THAN 18, OLDEST IN AREA or OLDEST IN LONDON, all derived from AGE. These may be what is meaningful to the user. Such specific derivations must be treated with especial caution, because of the danger of their proliferation. (If OLDEST IN LONDON, then why not also OLDEST IN WEST LONDON, OLDEST IN EALING or OLDEST IN WEST EALING?)

The contrary should also be considered: a non-derived relationship or attribute may be specific, in the sense that it specifies some other object or value, but that object or value is not represented in the model. For example, there might be an attribute OLDEST IN LONDON, but no entity type of which London is an occurrence, and no attribute of which London is a permitted value. Such a relationship or attribute is, of course, not derivable from anything in the model. However, there may be a strong argument for considering adding the specified object(s) to the model, in order to define the specific derivation within the model.

2.6.6 External derivations

Any attribute which is outside the control of an enterprise can be considered basic for the enterprise. Thus the postcode or zip code is under the control of the Post Office, and could be derived from the address and other geographical information. However, it is usually not necessary to model such complex geographic derivations explicitly.

When attributes are outside the control of the business area being modelled, but within the scope of some other business area within the enterprise, then its derivation will be controlled as part of the coordination function.

2.6.7 Derived relationships

A relationship can also be derived if it duplicates information represented elsewhere in the model. The most common situation is where one relationship is the sum of two other relationships: see Figure 2.32.

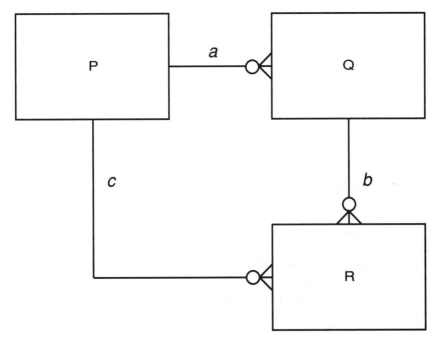

Figure 2.32 Derived relationship

Before you read further, think of at least one situation, fitting this structure, in which c is redundant, and at least one situation in which c is not redundant.

When I teach classes in information modelling, I display this structure and ask which is the redundant relationship. There is always someone who tells me that the relationship *c* can be derived from the other two, and is therefore redundant. But I have not yet explained what the letters stand for, so it is a trick question! Redundancy cannot be determined from structure alone, but depends on an equivalence of meaning.

If the relationship *c* between P and R is exactly equivalent to the relationship *a* between P and Q plus the relationship *b* between Q and R, then the relationship *c* can indeed be derived from the other two, and is therefore redundant.

Figure 2.33
Redundant and
derived relationship

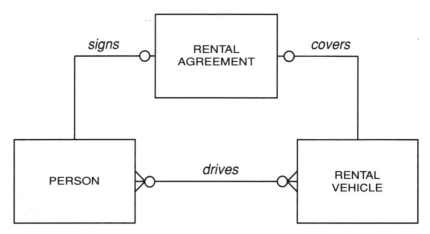

Suppose a business insists that the only person that can drive a rental vehicle is the person that signs the rental agreement. We can express this by saying that, for each occurrence of RENTAL VEHICLE, the occurrence of PERSON that you get by following the *covers* relationship followed by the *signs* relationship is the same as the occurrence of PERSON that you get by following the *drives* relationship (in short: *drives = signs + covers*.) Then the *drives* relationship is redundant, because it represents a fact that is already otherwise represented: see Figure 2.33. On the other hand, if the person that drives the vehicle need not be the same as the person that signs the agreement, then the *drives* relationship is not redundant, since it represents an independent fact. This notion becomes more difficult to apply, however, when we progress to more complex examples.

Figure 2.34 is an example modified from a real project. The two intersection entity types are PRODUCT OPTION VALIDITY, which indicates that a particular PRODUCT OPTION TYPE is available for a given PRODUCT, and PRODUCT OPTION CHOSEN, which indicates the options selected by a given CUSTOMER, within a given PRODUCT SALE. The entity type PRODUCT OPTION VALIDITY is basically a look-up table, indicating to the salesman what he or she can offer to a customer. The entity type PRODUCT OPTION CHOSEN is basically a sales order detail. The relationship *validates* between them has a bad name, and raises all sorts of problems about exceptions and changes. (What happens when

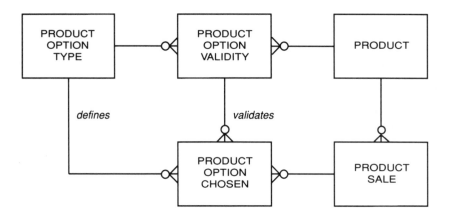

Figure 2.34 An example

a large customer is allowed a non-standard option? what happens when a product option is discontinued?) Whereas the relationship *defines* is much clearer, and allows changes and overrides to the look up table to be managed properly.

Thus we would want to remove the *validates* relationship, and retain the *defines* relationship. Or if only the *validates* relationship were included, and the *defines* relationship were missing, we would want to replace the *validates* relationship with the *defines* relationship. This is a special case of the structure shown in Figure 2.35. Suppose that $a + d = c$. In other words, for each occurrence of S, you get the same occurrence of P via the relationship c, as via the two relationships a followed by d. Suppose also that $b + d = e + f$. In other words, for each occurrence of S, you get the same occurrence of R via the two relationships b followed by d, as via the two relationships e followed by f.

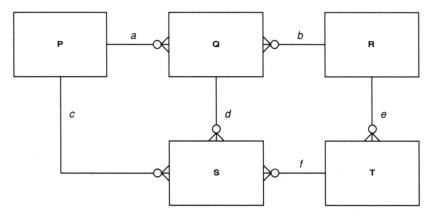

Figure 2.35 A special case

Clearly there is some redundancy. Which relationship is redundant? We could remove relationship c, without any loss of information, since it is equivalent to $a + d$. In the absence of R and T, this solution would probably be adopted. But in this example, removal of *c* only addresses one of the two redundancies. And once *c* is gone, all of the remaining relationships are required (i.e. none of them could be removed without loss of information from the model). However, if *c* is retained and *d* is removed, it does away with *both* redundancies. Navigation between Q and S requires the intersection of the two navigation paths *ac* and *bef*.[7]

If we have a model with *d* but without *c*, we have a situation we can call **partial redundancy**, since there is no relationship that is entirely redundant. There are many other possible structures with this property. Such situations often emerge when entity types have many-to-one relationships to entity types that are merely intersections. It is recommended, wherever this is found, to follow the following procedure:

1. Verify that the relationships concerned are mandatory.
2. Verify that the two (or more) navigation paths always yield the same result, in other words that the two (or more) 'foreign keys' truly have the same meaning. If they do not, make sure this is clear from the names of the relationships.
3. Seek to restructure the information model to remove the redundancy. If the model does not have the relationship *c*, it may need to be added, so that the relationship *d* can be eliminated.
4. Alternatively, build the necessary integrity conditions into the process logic to control the redundancy, if it is convenient to retain it. (This is not addressed here.)

Besides the redundancy argument, there is another advantage of replacing *d* with *c*. It is that a relationship to an intersection entity type is often hard to name and define, whereas a relationship to a non-intersection entity type is often more meaningful and stable. Thus the change not only improves the logical quality of the information model, it may also improve its clarity and relevance to the business.

In conclusion, we should note that there are very complex structures that can arise in an information model, and considerations of relationship redundancy are by no means always easy to resolve. The analyst must understand and confirm the business rules and integrity conditions that are being expressed. Weaknesses in an information model will show up as awkward or redundant structures in the database. A good modelling tool makes this visible, which should provide help to the analyst.

2.6.8 Derived entities

If all the attributes and relationships of an entity type are derived, then the entity type itself is derivable. Such an entity type may be useful, however, because it encapsulates some information that is required frequently, perhaps by several different business processes. For example, if a supermarket has electronic point of sale equipment, to record details of each item sold, the current stock levels could be derived from two entity types: DELIVERED ITEM and SOLD ITEM (perhaps together with a factor for breakage, spillage and shoplifting). However, it may be useful to define a derived entity type called STOCK ITEM. This enables the derivation algorithm to be defined in one place (against the derived object), rather than repeatedl for each business decision process that refers to the stock levels.

2.6.9 Benefits of derived objects

Defining an algorithm once, rather than repeatedly, has three benefits:

1. It reduces the amount of analysis work, since the algorithm only has to be defined once.
2. It reduces the amount of system development and maintenance work, since any code required to implement the algorithm only needs to be generated once. Subsequent changes in the algorithm can be carried out in one place.
3. It ensures consistency of decisions made using these derived data.

This is one of the ideas behind the object-oriented approach, but can equally be supported using the entity–relationship–attribute model, since entities, relationships and attributes can all be regarded as 'objects' (in a very abstract sense).

2.7 Identification

2.7.1 Purpose of identification

It does not make sense to have an entity type whose occurrences cannot be told apart. With every entity type in the model, therefore, there must be an identifier. An identifier serves a number of purposes:

1. When we discover a fact about an entity, we have to be able to state unambiguously which occurrence the fact relates to.
2. When we carry out some operation on an entity, we have to ensure that we do it to the right occurrence. It would be embarrassing if a credit organization sent bailiffs to collect money from the wrong customer. It could be dangerous if a prison released the wrong prisoner.[8] And it could be disastrous if a nation voted for the wrong politician.
3. When we want to know something about an entity, we have to be able to specify which occurrence we are interested in. Thus if you need a telephone number, you probably need to state the address (or at least the district) as well as the name.
4. When we encounter two entities under different circumstances, or playing different roles, we have to have some way of knowing whether the two entities are the same or different.

The identification of an entity is sometimes dismissed as a purely technical question, to do with the design of key structures on computer databases. This is a mistake, since the identification often raises important and strategic business issues. For example, the way a credit card company identifies its customer makes a significant difference to the way the customer is handled, and to the way business performance is measured. They even affect the way business strategies are to be interpreted.

Thus if a person holds a card in her own name, and also a card in the name of her employer, is she one customer or two? This depends how we identify credit-card holders.

- By card number?
- By name?
- By name and address?
- By name and date of birth?

2.7.2 Direct identification

The identifier may be complex or contingent. For example, if there is only one residence within a building, it can be identified by the postal address of the building. But if there are several flats within the same building, then the identifier will have to consist of the postal address of the building together with the flat number. For another example, in a schoolroom, most pupils can be identified by surname, but if there are two pupils with the same surname, then the teacher will have to use some other way of referring uniquely to each. (In old-fashioned schools, the Grimm brothers would be addressed as Grimm Major and Grimm Minor.)

Note that this does not prevent the teacher from continuing to use the surname to identify the remaining pupils. (This complexity may cause difficulty with computer implementation, however, as most present-day software will need to have uniform keys for each record type. But we should try to ignore such technical constraints when building information models.)

2.7.3 Indirect identification

Some identifications rely entirely on relationships. The house that Jack built. The assassin of Abe Lincoln. The assassin of the assassin of Jack Kennedy. (Does this rely on the disputed fact of Lee Harvey Oswald's role in Kennedy's death?) Identifications such as these rely on the existence of relationships between the entity types. (Or perhaps an involuted relationship on PERSON called *assassinates*.) As discussed above, if a single relationship is to be used to identify all occurrences of an entity type (as opposed to merely identifying some of them) then it must be a many-to-one relationship. However, there will be situations where several relationships combine to identify an entity type.

One paradox is in the identification of a so-called unidentified flying object. How can such things be identified? If twelve residents of the housing estate and a passing policeman saw a large glowing object at 11.45 p.m. on Friday night, then the identification is *the* object seen by these people on this occasion. But if another group of people a few miles away saw a similar object at 12.05, is it the same UFO? Thus it turns out that all we can identify is a UFO SIGHTING.

This is a fairly common situation – that the apparent concept must be replaced by something more definite, which we can identify clearly and uniquely, whereas the original concept was unable to be properly identified. We shall discuss the possible ambiguities of indirect identification and reference in Chapter 3. Although these problems can be avoided or ignored in simple models, they become increasingly relevant when intelligent activity is being modelled.

2.7.4 Identification in time

Suppose something exists in time, and is one of a series, distinguished from the other members of the series only by the time it occurs. What do we need to identify each occurrence of the series?

1. If each member of the series is an instantaneous event, then we merely need the date. And if two can occur on the same day, we also need the time of day.
2. If each member of the series exists until the exact moment its successor is created, then we need its creation date/time, but not the date/time of its being superseded, since this is necessarily the same as the creation date/time of its successor.
3. If the creation of the next occurrence is not necessarily synchronized with the disappearance of the previous occurrence, then we may need both start date/time and end date/time.
4. Examine the process that results in a new occurrence of the series. Is anything else created or altered at the same time? If so, it may be useful to model the synchronicity by representing the event as an entity type.

2.7.5 Limits to identification

We must be able to recognize when two occurrences are the same or different. Sometimes, this makes a simple or natural definition of the entity type impossible, since the information needed to equate two occurrences is not available. If I visit the same grocery store on two occasions, am I one customer or two? If the store has no way of recognizing me as the same customer, it will be forced to regard 'me on Monday' as a different customer to 'me on Wednesday'. When it adds up the number of customers it has had during the week, it will be forced to count me twice. This results in a rather weird and discontinuous notion of customer, but that is all they have to support the information. They do not have the information about me to support a more coherent definition of CUSTOMER.

A bank may be able to identify some of its customers, but not others. For example, if I buy travellers' cheques using a cheque drawn on my account, then the bank can identify me. But if I buy travellers' cheques from the same bank using cash, then I become anonymous.

If you cannot distinguish between two pencils, then PENCIL is not an entity type. But you can distinguish between pencils and typewriter ribbons, so STATIONERY ITEM may be an entity type.

If you are unable or unwilling to distinguish between two occurrences of an entity type, then you have defined the wrong entity type. However, an inability to identify such entities coherently may sometimes be overcome if the managers of the business think it important enough. It is often part of the business information strategy of a company, to move from an incoherent view of CUSTOMER to a coherent view. This requires new or enhanced collection or processing of data, but often creates business opportunities and advantages, since it enables the business to manage the relationship with the customer more effectively.

2.7.6 Multiple identification

We need to establish the identity through an identifier. In other words, we need to be able to say *this* entity, with no fear of ambiguity. In one oil company, there were over fifty different ways of identifying products. Each department had a different coding system for the different grades of petrol. There was clear business advantage to be gained in reducing this complexity. A project was launched to reduce the number of coding systems. Although it failed to achieve total consensus (i.e. there remained several rival coding systems), it was still worth doing.

2.7.7 Changing identification

There are two situations to be discussed in this section. One is that the means of identification changes. A person is identified by name, but the name may change on marriage or (in Britain) on elevation to the peerage. This may cause problems over the transition period, while the person continues to answer to the old name as well as to the new. Not just computer systems, not just formal systems, but people, too, have problems with such name changes.

Streets, towns, nuclear power stations, companies and even countries are wont to change their names on occasion. In the course of twenty years, Cambodia changed its name three times: first to Khmer Republic, then to Kampuchea, then back to Cambodia. When a company changes its name, it may remain the same CUSTOMER, but not be the same LEGAL ENTITY. But it would be difficult to argue that Cambodia had not remained (despite political turmoil) the same country. On the other hand, the Federal Republic of Germany retained the same name after merging with the former German Democratic Republic, although some would argue it was no longer the same country.

If an entity is identified by a combination of relationship pairings and attribute values, then this situation may arise both when a relationship is transferred and when an attribute value is altered. Some database software, and even some CASE tools, disallow any changes to identifying attributes or relationships, since record keys must be fixed. This is a local technical constraint, and has nothing to do with the conceptual information model. It merely forces artificial system measures (deleting and recreating records) to represent situations where names change in the real world (Such a CASE tool thereby abrogates its usual role of maintaining data integrity.)

The other problem arises with duplicate and partial identifiers. Is the John Doe cited as a hostile witness in this traffic accident the same as the John Doe whom we made redundant last year? This is a familiar problem to database administrators: how to handle duplicate names. There are two possible solutions:

1. Assume they are the same until proved different. Thus there will initially be one occurrence of PERSON. If it emerges later that it is not the same John Doe, then it will be necessary to undergo a process for separating out the attributes values and relationship pairings into the two occurrences.
2. Assume they are different until proved the same. Thus there will initially be two occurrences of PERSON. If it emerges later that both occurrences represent the same John Doe, then the attribute values and relationship pairings will have to be merged.

There are difficulties with both approaches. What counts as a valid proof, of identity or difference? What happens if you make a mistake? In the first approach, when you come to pull the two occurrences apart, how do you know which information is associated with which occurrence? In the second approach, when you come to put the two occurrences together, what do you do if there are minor incompatibilities between the information belonging to each occurrence?

On the whole, however, the second approach is usually regarded as safer than the first, because it is easier to merge than to separate.

2.7.8 Anonymous objects

Some companies know the names of all their customers, while others know few or none. For example, a sweetshop owner selling chocolate bars may recognize many of the regular customers, but not know their real names. (Some shopkeepers invent private names for their customers, like Grey Moustache or Shaggy Perm.) There are many situations where it is meaningful to refer to an entity type without identifying it properly. For example, to preserve the anonymity of examination candidates, the examiner may be prevented from knowing the identity of the candidate. Instead, the script is identified by an arbitrary number, assigned by some system. The examiner uses this number in discussions with other examiners, and with the examination administrators. If the candidate is personally unknown to the examiner, this mechanism is intended to prevent the examiner being able to guess the sex, race, religion, social class or age of the candidate from the name. And if the candidate is personally known to the examiner, the examiner may be less likely to recognize an exam script from the style of the answers than from the name.

However, the anonymity of exams can only be partial. Handwriting may reveal the sex and the age of the writer, even when the reader is not a trained graphologist. (Even I can usually tell whether someone went to school in the days when they taught copperplate handwriting with fountain pens, or whether they grew up with biros.) And of course the prose style reveals far more about the writer than his or her handwriting.

But in any case, the candidate's number is really only a surrogate identifier. The candidate must have a name, which will be known to the administrator, even if it is not known to the examiner. Reverse anomymity may also be required by the situation, so that the identity of the examiner is not known to the candidate, but again must be known to the administrator. A similar situation holds with referees reviewing papers for academic journals.

Considerations of data protection and privacy may produce further examples. These situations may be handled by having an artificial name or code number to identify each occurrence of the entity type. Military or strategic business operations often have false or cryptic names, so that the identity and location of the operation can be kept secret until the last minute.

Figure 2.36
Temporary anonymity

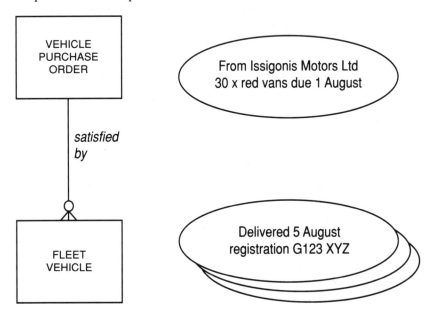

Sometimes anonymity may be temporary. For example, when I order a new car, I do not know its registration number plate until it is delivered. A company may order a fleet of identical vans, which only become separately identifiable when they are delivered: see Figure 2.36. This situation can be handled by having a separate entity type for the VEHICLE PURCHASE ORDER and for the FLEET VEHICLE when delivered. (This resembles one possible approach to modelling the links between PLAN and ACTUAL, which will be discussed in Chapter 8.) For another example, when scheduling a project, the project leader may not yet know the names of the people that will be available, so the schedule may contain a mix of real people and anonymous people (often temporarily named A.N. Other or TBA).

Intentions often refer to arbitrary or anonymous objects, but the resultant actions may have to refer to real objects. For example, a robber can only rob a specific man, but he can set out to rob a non-specific man.[9]

2.8 Integrity

The structure of the business or business area (or rather a particular aspect of this structure) is represented through the entity–relationship model. This structure can be regarded as a collection of rules. For example, that a given relationship is mandatory or many to one can be regarded as a rule – it rules out certain states of affairs. To put the same thing another way, each of the diagramming conventions defined in this chapter can be thought of as a pictorial representation of a rule. We have thereby already covered many of the most important and most useful aspects of the information structure. However, additional rules can be defined where necessary to add further structure to the model. These may include logic to describe:

1. Dependencies between attributes.
2. Mutually exclusive relationships.
3. Existence rules.

This logic can usually be expressed in declarative form. Simple CASE software may be able to deal with logic containing AND, OR and NOT, together with simple arithmetical calculation. Predicate calculus (ALL and SOME) and counting operations may require more sophisticated CASE software than is widely available at the time of writing.

It is one thing to express an integrity rule, another thing entirely to enforce it. Software developers may adopt different tactics for implementing the logic expressed in an integrity rule, but this is a design issue beyond the scope of this book.

2.9 Metadata

The prefix 'meta' is a warning that you are about to see an abstract concept. Metaphysics is a abstract way of talking about the physical world – so abstract, that some philosophers have dismissed it as total nonsense.[10] Even the word 'method' has this derivation; it contains the prefix *meta* as well as the Greek word *hodos*, which means 'path'. Thus the concept of method starts with the concept of a specific path, and then rises to a higher level of abstraction.

A **metamodel** is an information model at a higher level of abstraction, in which ENTITY may itself be an entity type! Metamodels are essential when designing tools for information management, including CASE tools and data dictionaries. However, problems arise when different logical levels are combined within the same information model: both data and metadata. **Metadata** can be defined as objects in a conceptual business model that refer to information, and not directly to the real world. It may sometimes be regarded as extreme generalization. Generalization relies on recognizing the same concept in many places, while extreme generalization has abandoned any pretence that a single concept is being modelled. The purpose of this section is to discuss when metadata are legitimate within information models.

Metadata complicate the model. They make an information model more remote from reality – it still may represent the business indirectly, but it no longer represents the business directly. This makes the model harder to understand, both for users and for information engineers.

So why do we get metadata in our models? There are several reasons:

1. During information strategy planning, information resource management is identified as a major business function. It therefore results in one or more business areas in its own right. These business areas produce information models from which the requirements for data dictionaries, CASE tools and other systems-related systems can be derived. These information models are likely to include such entity types as ENTITY, PROCESS, etc. Thus the models for these business areas inevitably include metadata. This is one good reason (there are others) for keeping the models for these business areas separate (although coordinated) with the models for other business areas. (This comment also applies to generalized decision-support functions.)

2. The product provided to the customer is (or includes) a flexible information service. For example, a financial service may include some *ad hoc* financial reporting. Then the content of the product might have to be defined as metadata, since it might be any combination of attributes.

3. The external source, accuracy and acquisition date of data must be captured. This leads each attribute to possess an indication of how up-to-date and reliable its value may be. Alternatively, we need to know which attributes (or rather which values of which attributes) have been revealed to the customer. (In the situation where the customer is given an embossed plastic or magnetized token of his relationship with us,

we need to know what attribute values are embossed or encoded on the current card.)

4. There are regional or operational variations. If the organization has many different products or locations or departments, each with different information requirements, it may be difficult to cater for these differences without extreme generalization. There may also be interface variations, for example tape formats.

5. When the analysts build the business model for a given business area, they are uncertain what the future business requirements will be. They may even be uncertain what the present requirements are. They respond to this challenge by extreme generalization. For example, instead of listing the known attributes of a given entity type, they introduce a new entity type called CHARACTERISTIC or VARIABLE, with a one-to-many relationship to the first entity type. Then (they argue) any attribute can be added at any time, simply by adding a new occurrence of CHARACTERISTIC.

   This approach arises from practices that were suitable for designing hierarchical databases, in which it was always easier to change or extend the use of an existing field than to add a new field. Since relational databases allow the addition of new fields more easily than hierarchical databases did, it makes less sense than it used to to complicate the data structure in order to anticipate every possible future requirement. There may well need to be a process to define a new attribute of a given entity type; but this process will belong to the information resource management function, and cannot be fully automated, since the computer cannot invent a definition of an attribute. (Note: it may still be possible for this process to be executed without involving information engineers – it is purely a matter of the information architecture, not one of organizational responsibilities.)

6. Some processes will be simplified if the information they have to manipulate is all in one place. This raises the question whether the processes are overgeneralized, or insufficiently sensitive to the business. There may also be other processes made more complex by having to handle metadata, so the overall complexity of the process model may be increased or decreased. However, the overall comprehensibility of the process model is almost certain to be decreased. So this seems another poor reason for complicating the information model.

Where metadata are mixed in with the normal data, it is more difficult to handle than where the metadata are kept in a separate model. Our recommendation is to avoid mixing metadata in the same models as other data. Instead, separate models should be created. This certainly applies to (1), and probably also to (2) and (3). We have already rejected (5) and (6) as reasons for having metadata. That leaves (4).

The crucial question with variations in requirements is how important the variation is to the business. If it is important, then perhaps we should not be trying to cram two or more radically different structures into the same model. If the Japanese operation is radically different from the French operation, then we should build two models, one for each perspective. If, however, the differences are trivial or undesired, then it should be a business question: to obtain a suitable consensus between the different perspectives, in order that they can be represented in one model. 'Agree to differ' effectively means two models (although we can still act to coordinate the models as much as possible, and not rule out sharing of systems, or even a future merger). There is also the question of how the models will be used: coordination of changes between models is a relevant consideration here.

A final warning against mixing logical levels: it bears a close formal resemblance to the family communication processes that cause schizophrenia, according to Gregory Bateson's theory of the 'double bind'.[11] Until the consequences of the double bind in organizations (and their supporting IT systems) have been analysed, it would be wise to treat metamodels with caution.

2.10 Summary

In this chapter, we have introduced a large number of the basic concepts of information modelling, thus indicating the form of a model, and particular aspects requiring analysis and documentation. The level of analysis and documentation depends, of course, on the purpose for which the model is built. Therefore you should not expect to deploy all the concepts on every project.

We have also laid down some rules, which apply to the use of these concepts, individually or in combination. For example, the rule that an entity type must have a satisfactory means of identifying its occurrences. We have also explored some of the implications of these rules.

2.10.1 Key rules

1. An entity type must have a membership rule defined – what things do or do not belong.
2. An entity type must have an identity rule defined, enabling us to distinguish individual occurrences. This entails an identifier that tells us for sure whether this occurrence is the same as that occurrence.
3. Information can be defined as 'a difference that makes a difference'. Therefore, an information model represents relevant differences between things. Each entity type must differ from other entity types, each entity occurrence must differ from all other entity occurrences, each attribute must be capable of taking different values, and so on.

4. It follows from (3) that each fact should only be represented once. Some purposes may require multiple representations of the same fact, but this redundancy should be clearly understood and strictly controlled.

2.10.2 Key recommendations

1. Use diagrams – but do not just use diagrams. Define the boxes and lines carefully.
2. Use a software tool to manage the diagrams and the definitions.
3. The occurrences of an entity type should have plenty of information in common, i.e. the same or similar set of attributes and relationships. This is likely to be the case when the occurrences play similar roles.
4. Look for loopholes in definitions of all objects.
5. Avoid using a single object to represent several overlapping concepts.
6. Do not model everything; model only what is relevant.
7. Document any logical constraints (integrity rules) applying to the objects in your model.
8. Avoid metadata – mixing form and content in the same model.

Notes

1. Paul Levinson, 'Impact of personal information technologies on American education, interpersonal relations and business, 1985–2010', in Paul T. Durbin (ed.), *Technology and Contemporary Life*, D. Reidel, Dordrecht, 1988, pp. 177–91.
2. Thanks to Krysten Nygaard for reminding me of this.
3. L. Wittgenstein, *Philosophical Investigations*, Basil Blackwell, Oxford, 1953, § 66.
4. The analyst tends to assume that everyone is on the same side. In some organizations, such an assumption would be naive, but that is beyond the scope of this book.
5. G. Bateson, 'Form Substance and Difference' *General Semanticcs Bulletin*, no. 37, 1970.
6. Devotees of the relational model often use a different definition of redundancy, tied to the specifics of *n*th normal form. Note that some intelligent translation of such concepts is required between the relational model and the entity–relationship model.
7. It will be seen that this solution assumes the intersection of *a* and *b* is unique. In other words, for each pair <p,r> of occurrences of **P** and **R**, there is exactly one occurrence of **Q**. But if this is not true, there will be another identifier of **Q** that can be 'normalized' out, and separately related to both **Q** and **S**.
8. Some religious implications of this are explored by the Monty Python film *Life of Brian*.
9. Kit Fine, *Reasoning with Arbitrary Objects*, Basil Blackwell, Oxford, 1985.

10. A. J. Ayer, *Language Truth and Logic*, Victor Gollancz, 1936.
11. G. Bateson, D. D. Jackson, J. Haley and J. H. Weakland, 'Towards a theory of schizophrenia', *Behavioural Science*, vol. 1, no. 4., 1956.

3 Techniques

This chapter describes some tasks and techniques relevant to information modelling. It does not aim to provide a complete methodology, but includes some advice to supplement the contents of any given methodology, such as information engineering.

We can define a project as a series of tasks or project steps, which may be scheduled and controlled. In order to complete these tasks, some techniques are required. A very experienced analyst may be able to perform these tasks without thinking too much about the techniques used, because she is so familar with them as to be almost unconscious of them. If an apprentice analyst works with an experienced analyst, there may be several places where questions arise: how did you arrive at this structure? How did you discover this counter-example? And so on. These questions are useful, because they force the experienced analyst to make her thinking explicit, and enable a transfer of skills to the apprentice. Each analyst develops some useful techniques (or heuristics) for developing models and for solving or resolving modelling problems. In this chapter, I describe some of mine.

Whereas the individual analyst within a large organization may be given little or no choice of the task structure, and may be required to document results in a particular style and format, it is seldom useful to make the use of particular techniques compulsory. The analyst should be free to use whichever techniques work for him or her in a given situation. If a particular technique does not solve a particular problem, then it is the responsibility of the analyst to obtain or invent a different technique. If what you are doing does not work, try something else.

Therefore, we start the chapter with an outline of the tasks (i.e. what needs to be done) of a typical requirements analysis project, and then continue the chapter with some useful techniques (i.e. how to achieve the tasks).

3.1 Task structure of analysis projects

At the highest level, a systems development methodology will usually divide the development activity into a requirements analysis phase and a series of design phases, culminating in construction, testing and implementation of one or more information systems. Information modelling plays a central role in the requirements analysis phase, and a lesser role in some of the other phases.

An analysis project will include several tasks. The following list of tasks is typical (the list concentrates on the tasks related specifically to the information modelling – a methodology such as information engineering may contain other tasks not described here)

1. Plan project

Define the purpose and scope of the modelling project. In information engineering, this would be based on a strategic plan for the whole enterprise, dividing a business into business areas. Alternatively, the scope may be equal to that of an existing computer system.

2. Interview users

Talk to the users, at various levels, individually or collectively, to discover the decision-making and control processes they are responsible for, the performance measures they use, and the needs they have for information. Collective interviews (often known as user workshops) can be much more productive than individual sessions, if properly managed. Good facilitation or moderation is required, to ensure the session achieves a useful result.

3. Document information needs

Record some of the information needs discovered in the interviews, relating each user to his/her needs. Document how business objectives and critical success factors are supported by this information. Circulate this documentation, and allow each user to register an interest in additional information needs. In a collective interview, where the discussion may be lively and non-sequential, it may be difficult to record which information need was stated by which user. However, if the session records a collective consensus, with important differences resolved, and with development priorities ranked, this documentation may not be necessary.

4. Develop information model

From the interviews and other sources, develop an entity–relationship–attribute model of the business or business area. Sometimes, it may be possible to create this model during the user workshops themselves, allowing for immediate resolution of issues and confirmation of models.

5. Analyse information needs

Select a representative sample of information needs for detailed analysis. Analyse each selected information need in terms of the information model. (This technique is described further in Chapter 5.)

6. Develop process model

From the interviews and other sources, develop a process model of the business or business area.

7. Analyse process information accesses

Analyse the information accesses required by each process in terms of the information model. (This technique is described further in Chapter 5.)

8. Revise scope and information model

Examine any information needs and processes not supported by the information model. Consider whether they are within the scope of the analysis project. Present the model, together with an explanation of its implications, to the users for confirmation. Conduct quality reviews of the model, and check its stability. Amend and extend the information model where necessary, to enable it to support all the information needs and processes that are within the scope.

9. Document distribution of information and process models

(This task will be useful for organizations spread across several locations, when the intention is to produce a distributed database system.) Produce a matrix that shows where each information need occurs. Produce a matrix that shows where the event occurs that triggers each process. From this matrix, produce a matrix that shows where access is required to each entity type.

10. Plan use and maintenance of information and process models

If the models are to be used for development of new information systems, or for the selection of packaged application software, or for any other purpose, the final stage in the analysis project is to determine the objectives, scope, cost–benefit justification and other planning considerations for their effective use. Furthermore, depending on the purpose of building the models in the first place, it may be necessary to keep them up to date. In this case, some on-going activity may need to be planned, to ensure that the models are reviewed regularly, or whenever changes occur.

3.2 Alternative starting points

There are several different approaches to starting work on an information model, and then pursuing it to completion. It is customary to draw a distinction between the top-down approach and the bottom-up approach, which are the two best known.

In the **top-down** approach, the analyst starts from the organization's goal and tactics, and goes on to identify the major information needs – in other words, the information that is required to make the major decisions – and to discover the structure of these information needs. In the **bottom-up** approach, the analyst starts from one or more existing systems (which may be wholly or partially computerized, or may consist entirely of paperwork), analyses the forms and layouts of these systems to determine the elements of data, and pieces these data elements together to construct an information model, using techniques such as normalization and canonical synthesis. This model is then refined, to remove specific shortcomings in these systems.

Some methodologies, such as information engineering, are chararacterized as top down, while others, such as SSADM, are characterized as bottom up. However, this is merely a difference of emphasis. A model produced top down will usually need to be compared to the existing systems, both as a check for completeness, and as a necessary preparation for replacing the existing systems with systems designed from the top-down model. A model produced bottom up will usually need to be compared to the business goals and objectives, to ensure the relevance and value of any subsequent development work.

Where there are several existing systems performing overlapping functions, each may have a somewhat different data structure. In the bottom-up approach, these structures need to be consolidated into a single generalized structure. This consolidation forces the analyst to make choices, which should be based on the business goals and objectives. Table 3.1 shows some of the main differences between the two approaches.

Table 3.1 Top-down and bottom-up approaches

Top-down approach	Bottom-up approach
Enables radically new solutions to business problems	Likely to stay fairly close to existing solutions, although allowing elimination of specific shortcomings
Requires some analytical flair and experience	Can be performed semi-mechanically by inexperienced analysts
Quantity of analysis not easily predictable in advance	Quantity of analysis roughly predictable in advance
Danger of lengthy analysis projects, unless strictly controlled	Project management can follow predictable lines
Project scope determined by architectural arguments	Project scope determined by scopes of existing systems
Details fit into rational framework	A rational framework may not emerge, and the analyst is left with a mass of detail

3.2.1 Referring to existing systems

How much should existing systems be allowed or encouraged to influence the models? Should the analyst seek to represent the existing models exactly, or ignore them completely? There is no general answer to this question. It depends on a number of considerations and, most importantly, on the objectives of the information modelling exercise.

Let us suppose that your objective is to develop a new system to replace an existing system. If you slavishly follow the existing system, then you can scarcely expect to make any significant improvements over it (except purely technical ones), but if you ignore the existing system, you may fail to improve over it.

Although bottom-up methods demand that you identify problems with the existing system, relate these problems to their effect on business objectives, and try to address these problems in the new system, they do not encourage you to challenge the assumptions embedded in the existing systems. This may result in your merely altering the symptoms, and not resolving the real problems.

The psychologist Kirton divides mankind into the adapters and the innovators.[1] A high adapter always seeks to work within a system, whereas a high innovator prefers to break free from the existing system. We should therefore expect adapters to take more notice of the existing system than innovators.

Use of codes from existing systems

Particular care needs to be taken when data are going to have to be converted automatically from existing files into a new database designed from your information model. Often the existing system will include codes that have no direct business meaning, and which serve only to identify records uniquely. Without these codes, there may be no way to construct bridges from the old systems to the newly developed systems. It is usually necessary, when the modelling is part of a systems replacement project, to include the old codes as attributes within the model. However, it may be wise to avoid using them as genuine identifiers, unless you are satisfied with the quality and data integrity of the old system. Normally, a strategy is required to migrate away from the old codes (which may include weaning the users away from them, if they have become accustomed to using these codes).

Another common feature of old systems is the presence of Miscellaneous Information or Comment fields, which, on perusal, turn out to contain a wide variety of different attributes. Any attribute that you can positively identify (and which is of genuine business value) should be modelled explicitly. It may be necessary to provide fields in the new database into which the miscellaneous data values can be stored. However, the designer will probably want to place traps on any user trying to update or enter values into these fields, to ensure the integrity of the database and the quality of its interfaces to other systems. When a user wants to put data into such a field, he or she will be invited instead to define a new attribute. After a decent interval, perhaps depending on the elimination of interfaces to old systems, these miscellaneous fields can be removed completely.

Perversion of system by users

Users of inflexible systems often find ingenious ways of getting around the controls built into the system by its original designers, or of getting the system to do things that it was never designed to do. One accounts receivable system failed to handle direct debits. This was solved as follows. The customers who wanted to pay by direct debits were set up as subsidiaries of a fictional corporation headed by a clerk in the accounts department. As pseudo holding company for these customers, this clerk received all their invoices, and then followed the following procedure:

1. Manually enter the invoice details onto a direct debit request sheet.
2. Place a stamp on the invoice to inform the customer that payment would be extracted automatically from its bank account in ten days time.
3. Mail the invoice to the customer.

It follows that, if you are going to copy the existing system, you have to analyse carefully how the system is being used, and what data are actually stored in the files, rather than merely examining the specification and other documentation.

Model business, not paper

Paperwork is itself a model of the business and often not a very efficient or effective one. Many business entities appear to be structured with a header and several lines. INVOICE and SALES ORDER are two common examples of this structure. The structure occurs frequently because of its convenience, especially in paperwork systems, for representing a one-to-many relationship. On-line computer systems are often given the same structure, with the layout of screens similar or identical to the layout of the paper forms. There is a potential ambiguity with this structure, when you have an XYZ (header) and XYZ lines. The term XYZ is ambiguous, referring either to the header or to the header together with the lines.

Another way of putting this is that one of the entity types at one level of detail has the same name as a broader concept at a higher level of detail. This can be managed by having two separate models, at the two levels of detail. Perhaps one model is 'normalized', and the other not. Then two objects in two models have the same names. This is no problem, as long as you know which model you are in.

But there is a deeper question, whether the ORDER and ORDER LINE structure is an accurate way of representing a business at all. The focus of the model should be to represent the underlying business concept, rather than merely a piece of paper (which is, of course, merely a component of the existing system). This is discussed further in Chapter 8.

3.2.2 Using templates

A **template** is a model of a business area that has been obtained from an outside source. It may be a model that has been developed for a specific organization (presumably with similar requirements to our own), or it may be a model that has been constructed as a hypothetical exercise. Some of the information requirements of a business organization will be standard. (This is what makes it possible to develop computer packages for such applications as accounting and payroll.) So why go to all the trouble of analysing the data structures from scratch, when another company has already done this work? (One of the principles of engineering is to reuse rather than reinvent.) The difference between using a template and using an application package is that the template is much easier to modify. If CASE tools are used, which enable a system to be generated very rapidly from a correct model, then tailoring of a template can be a powerful way of implementing something rapidly.

A template (as any data model) has two parts – its **structure** (syntax) and its **meaning** (semantics). Thus when we use a template as a starting point, we need to examine and modify both the structural elements (is this relationship really only one-to-many, or do we need a many-to-many relationship here?) and the definitions (is the scope of this entity type appropriate for our business?)

3.2.3 Brainstorming

One way of completing a model is to forget the practical constraints of computing, or the costs of information processing, and enter the realms of logical possibility. Ask: what could possibly be known or discovered about this entity or type. This may be very useful in breaking free of the assumptions and limitations of an existing computer system. This is neither top-down, nor bottom-up, but lateral thinking. This may be a useful way of encouraging people to be creative about the potential future uses of information, possibly even identifying opportunities to use information and systems for competitive advantage.

However, do not just brainstorm attributes for the hell of it. It will be necessary to establish some business interest in the information. Thus, like any brainstorming activity, it must be followed by an evaluation and selection activity, to discard anything that there is no good reason to retain.

3.2.4 Conclusion

Whereas the book generally describes information modelling starting from the requirements (i.e. top-down), in this section we have looked at alternative starting points, including existing systems and templates. The main message is that the choice of approach (or the mixture of approaches) depends on the purpose for which the model is being built. It may also depend on the skill level and quantity of resources available for the project.

3.3 Developing the model

3.3.1 Asking questions

Many people have a somewhat irrational response to the process of asking and answering simple logical questions. They are uncomfortable with the implications of their not knowing the answer, or with the expectation of a follow-up question.

Part of the popular image of the High Court judge is his remoteness from the real world. (At the time of writing this, there are very few female judges in the UK, and none in senior positions, so I shall use the male pronoun.) The popular press is always amused when a judge asks clarifying questions, such as the possibly apocryphal question 'What is a Beatle?' A recent example at the time of writing concerned a litigant who was described as a leading footballer. The judge asked whether he played rugby or association football. Scornful headlines filled the next day's tabloid newspapers, because the judge seemed not to have heard of the sports hero they nickname 'Gazza'.

Let us consider such clarifying questions from the judge's perspective. He is not completely ignorant, he probably had a fairly good idea who 'Gazza' was. But in order to make judicial decisions, a fairly good idea is not good enough. He has to be absolutely sure he knows exactly what the lawyers and witnesses are talking about. When there is a jury in the case, the judge also has to be sure that all the members of the jury understand such references. And there is a third reason for clarification: the case may become a precedent to be cited many years in the future, long after we have all forgotten who 'Gazza' was. To support arguments in some hypothetical future, the court record must be a self-contained document. (This reference to 'Gazza' will probably appear out of date or obscure to many readers. This is the very reason for including it as an example: to make the point that similar ephemeral references should not be left unexplored or unexplained, simply because one is embarrassed to examine the obvious.)

Some of these considerations apply to the analysis and modelling of a business area. No analyst should hesitate to ask a clarifying or confirming question, for fear of appearing ignorant or irrelevant. (However, the analyst is not under as much pressure as the judge, to ask even irrelevant questions because they might become relevant later. It is usually possible for the analyst to postpone questions of dubious relevance. For the judge, this is unsafe, because the witness may not be available again.)

There is another difficulty about asking questions, especially when they include the word 'Why'. People are accustomed to 'Why' questions leading towards a challenge. 'Why' questions, especially about decisions within the area of responsibility of the interviewee, often trigger quite inappropriate responses – from apologies and promises of future change, to aggressive self-defence – that do not actually reveal any reasons for the behaviour or decision. Thus sometimes the interviewee's reply is an answer not to the actual question, but to the presumed follow-up question.

Experienced analysts therefore separate 'what' they want to discover from 'how' they want to elicit this information from the interviewee. They are sensitive to the culture of the organization and style of the individual, and know how to pose questions tactfully and effectively.

Genie Laborde, in another context, describes the use of five questions for clarifying another person's meaning[2]:

1. Explore vague nouns (such as 'quality' or 'productivity') by asking 'what'.'What kind of ...? ''What do you mean by ...?' 'What ... specifically?'

2. Explore vague verbs (such as 'decide') by asking 'how'. 'How, specifically?'
3. Challenge modal operators (should, shouldn't, can, cannot) by asking 'what if'. 'What would happen if it did?' 'What could happen if it didn't?'
4. Explore comparisons (better, best, easier, easiest) by asking 'than what' 'Better than what, for what, when?'
5. Challenge generalizations (all, always, never, everyone, nobody) by raising your eyebrows quizzically.

She goes on to warn the student not to use these questions aggressively[3]:

> These questions are pointed, like lances or the verbal jousts of a cross-examination. People do not take kindly to having the limitations in their thinking exposed. ... Add softening phrases such as:
>
> • 'I'm wondering what, specifically, you mean by . . . '
> • 'I'm curious about . . .'
> • 'Would you be willing to tell me how, specifically, to . . . '

3.3.2 Discovering entity types

One of the requirements of an information model is to discover and define entity types. Here is a technique for doing this, broken down into several steps. In practice, these steps may overlap, but for the moment we shall pretend that they can be taken one at a time.

1. List candidate entity types (nouns, objects)

The first step is to make a list of the possible or **candidate** entity types. A useful starting point is to obtain a description of the business area, and to pick out the key nouns:

1. Look for a description of what the business is doing, and ask what are the people or things that are subject to these activities. For example, if we sell products to customers in shops, this suggests PRODUCT, CUSTOMER and SHOP as three candidate entity types.
2. A number or quantity or date may be an attribute of some entity. What kind of entity may have a similar number or quantity? For example, if a bag of flour has a sell-by date, what other things have such sell-by dates? This question may lead us to a candidate entity type called GROCERY ITEM.
3. A proper name (of a person, or place, or whatever) could be the identifier of an entity occurrence. For example, if we have a shop in Basingstoke, the name 'Basingstoke' identifies the shop's LOCATION.

Here are some questions to ask about these candidate entity types:
1. How does it enter the world of interest? How long may it have existed before we became interested in it? Are we then interested in its history before that point (i.e. backdated interest)?

2. How does it leave the world of interest? Does it continue to exist in some sense outside the world of interest? Can it then re-enter the world of interest, and do we care to connect it to its previous manifestation?

3. How does it change? How much does it have to change before it becomes something else?

4. Can it merge with another entity? Can it exchange aspects of itself with another entity? Can it divide into two or more entities?

5   How do we count several occurrences of the same entity type? How do we tell that we only have one occurrence, rather than several, or several rather than one? What does this mean, for this entity type?

6. What roles does it play? Do the answers to the above questions differ according to the role we are focused upon?

7. How do we discover that two entities we have met playing two different roles are in fact the same? What does this mean? How does it change our perception (if at all) to assert identity between two previously separate entities?

Having considered each of the candidate entity types from a number of angles, as suggested by these questions, we then see if we can make the model more powerful and broad by distancing it a little from the specific business situation we started with. This is known as **abstraction**, and there are three methods of doing this.

Abstraction clears away some of the specifics, and allows us to see the structure. If abstraction is taken to the extreme, no specifics are left at all. Except for skilled mathematicians, who are trained to understand highly abstract structures with no direct relationship to the real world, most people find such a model incomprehensible. Thus abstraction should be practised in moderation, leaving a sufficient amount of specifics for the model to remain meaningful.

> The relationship between the ease with which a model can be understood and its abstraction level does not appear to be a simple one. As one attempts to be more all-embracing on a given abstraction level, the ease of understanding ... will surely deteriorate.
>
> As the abstraction level increases from the lowest possible level, the comprehensibility will initially increase because of the reduction in the number of concepts ... to assimilate. As the abstraction level is raised further and further, the sheer abstractness counterbalances the gains achievable by abstracting.[4]

2. Introduce abstraction by classification

One of the ways we simplify and make sense of the world is by dividing people and things into classes. This reduces the amount of information we have to collect, maintain and consider. If a teacher assumes that all 8-year-old boys are the same, if a recruitment officer assumes that all black women engineering graduates are the same, or if an advertising draftsman assumes that all consumers of chocolate are the same, this saves the trouble of considering each individual separately.

Classification of some sort is a necessary fact of life. We want to be able to discriminate between capable and incapable, safe and dangerous, polite and rude, even perhaps good and evil. But sometimes classification is arbitrary; and there may be as many classifications as there are interested parties. The very word 'discrimination' is often used to denote unjust or unfavourable treatment of an identifiable group of people. But it is a fallacy to think that classification itself, or discrimination are themselves inherently undesirable. After all, unfair discrimination can only be recognized (let alone corrected) by a similar (but not necessarily equally unfair) discrimination: if a black woman engineer wishes to prove that she has been unfairly discriminated against because of her colour or sex, she must herself classify herself in this way.

Classification of people is not just a necessary evil, but is (most of the time) a useful and acceptable procedure. Consider schools, for example, where at first sight the word 'class' appears to have a rather different meaning. However, schoolchildren are divided into classes by some classification, based on age (usually), sex (often), ability (possibly), mother tongue (perhaps), or some other characteristics. (For the rich, for the physically disabled or musically talented, and for religious minorities, there may even be separate schools.) Too great a diversity of children within a class makes it impossible for the teacher to communicate effectively with the whole class. Educationalists may argue at great length exactly which characteristics should be used, and exactly how much diversity or uniformity is desirable, but few of them would expect a 16-year-old bookworm, who spoke three languages but whose English was rudimentary, to be forced to learn alongside a 9-year-old who could not yet read, and only spoke English.

Classification of physical objects causes much less concern. British Rail may classify its buildings into stations, offices, workshops and so on. This could result in a classifying entity type BUILDING TYPE, related to the entity type BUILDING. This would for example enable policy decisions (such as frequency of repainting) to be made once for each type of building, instead of once for each building, thus reducing the number of decisions that have to be made.

A good way to discover such classifying entity types is to examine the attributes of an entity type, and ask why a given occurrence of the entity type has a particular value. For example, in a building supplies wholesaler, the entity type PRODUCT has an attribute UNITS OF MEASURE, as shown in Table 3.2.

Table 3.2. Products and units of measure

Product Name	Units of Measure	Product Type?
Wallpaper pattern 4711	Metres	Wallpaper
Wallpaper paste (domestic)	Litres	Paste
Wallpaper paste (industrial)	Litres	Paste
Wallpaper pattern 4712	Metres	Wallpaper
Crimson gloss paint	Litres	Paint
Paintbrush 6 inches	Each	Tool
Wallpaper brush (9 inches)	Each	Tool

If all patterns and textures of wallpaper have the same units of measure (i.e. metres), and all colours and consistencies of paint have the same units of measure (i.e. litres), then it may be worth introducing a second entity type (as implied by the third column in the table), and making UNITS OF MEASURE an attribute of PRODUCT TYPE instead of PRODUCT.

Modelling purists may argue that this type of classification should always be done, even if it has no immediately obvious benefit. They believe that this kind of classification is needed to give the maximum flexibility and the minimum redundancy to a model. If you have read thus far, you will not expect me to preach any such dogmatic principles. Nonetheless, this kind of classification is often useful, and always worth considering.

3. Introduce abstraction by aggregation

Aggregation is the putting together of different things, to form a coherent whole. Thus, instead of talking about BUILDING and STREET and TOWN and COUNTY and POSTCODE, these may all be lumped together as ADDRESS. Or instead of talking about a CPU and a keyboard and a disk drive and a monitor, these may be bundled together into COMPUTER. People may be aggregated into teams or departments; products and services may be aggregated into compound products (thus, for example, when you buy a hifi, a one-year guarantee and repair service may be bundled in as part of the product price).

This form of abstraction is useful when decisions are made at the level of the aggregate or compound. However, sometimes what is required is the opposite of aggregation: the analysis of information down to **data atoms**. A data atom is the smallest unit of information, free of interpretation or ambiguity, that cannot be derived from any other information. Information needs are usually compound rather than atomic. In Chapter 5, we will show how complex information can be built up from data atoms, and conversely how compound information can be decomposed into data atoms.

It is often asserted that a computerized information system should capture information at the atomic level, and then provide various levels of summary and aggregation, depending on the level of interested management, or on the purpose for which the information is required. This is indeed an attractive approach, because the structure of the atomic data is likely to be more stable than the structure of the day to day information needs compounded from it, but it is not always practicable. Sometimes the information does not exist in atomic form, and it would be a burden to the business to create or collect it.

Consider the Post Office. The atomic entity is a single letter being posted. It is almost certainly impractical to capture data on each individual letter. However, information is required about the throughput and bottlenecks of letter handling. There are various ways of providing this information. Perhaps the letters are batched into bundles, and data are captured for each bundle. Or perhaps instead of tracking every single letter, a random sample of letters is selected and tracked in detail. Thus the simple and atomic entity type LETTER (with millions of occurrences per day) is not modelled; instead the model includes complex entity types such as LETTER BUNDLE or LETTER TRACKING SAMPLE (with far fewer occurrences per day, allowing monitoring and control processes to be carried out effectively).

The trouble with such aggregated or sampled entity types is that they are arbitrary. Whereas the entity type LETTER would provide stability to the information model, because it is fundamental to the business of the Post Office, the compound entity types are not stable. The Post Office could want to change its bundling mechanism, or its sampling mechanism, and thereby invalidate the definition of the entity type in question. Therefore a system designed on the basis of LETTER BUNDLE or LETTER TRACKING SAMPLE is less flexible, more vulnerable to changes in the business procedures, than a system designed on the basis of LETTER.

An alternative is to design a computerized information system to break the data down into data atoms. This is already done with some marketing systems, where you start with the total sales figures, and then use statistics from market research to break these figures down. Clearly such a breakdown will be an approximation, but perhaps other situations could be conceived that would be wholly accurate.

4. Introduce abstraction by generalization

Generalization is the putting together of similar things, by selectively ignoring their differences. For example, photocopiers are not the same as computers, but a model might usefully lump them together as OFFICE EQUIPMENT ITEM.

Generalization is a useful way of reducing the number of entity types in a model. Generalization is unavoidable in building an information model, since without any generalization at all, each entity type would have only one occurrence. Thus, as with the other forms of abstraction discussed in this section, the key question is not whether to generalize at all, but how much to generalize, and where to stop generalizing.

3.3.3 Analysing relationships

In Chapter 2, we defined certain properties of relationships: cardinality, optionality and transferability. The weakest form of relationship is a transferable fully optional many-to-many relationship, since this imposes fewest restrictions on the entity types. A mandatory one-to-many relationship is much stronger, since it rules out many possible combinations.

Some modellers prefer to start with relationships in their strongest form, and then look for counter-examples. They will therefore assert, for example, that every CUSTOMER always does business in a single CURRENCY, until they can find evidence to the contrary. Other modellers prefer to start with relationships in their weakest form, and then add properties to the relationships only when these can be demonstrated. They will therefore assume that at least one CUSTOMER does business in more than one CURRENCY, unless they can find a good reason to restrict this.

The advantage of the former strategy is that the models will be simpler and easier to understand. Complexity is added only when required, and it is added progressively, thus enabling participants to follow the process. The disadvantage is that many people become attached to their models, and find it difficult to motivate themselves to find contrary evidence. Thus the model remains simple, and fails to reflect the true complexity of the area being modelled.

The advantage of the latter strategy is that it is safer. The model will be more powerful, and the modellers will be motivated to find as many valid simplifying restrictions as possible. The disadvantage is that the initial version of the model may be extremely complicated, and thus exclude some participants from the process.

3.3.4 Relationships versus attributes

There are often situations where we are not sure whether to model a particular property of an object as an attribute of the entity type, or as a relationship to some other entity type. The tendency to describe a property as an attribute of a single entity, when it should properly be described as a relationship between two entities, is known as **fetishism**. (Marx identified economic forms of fetishism; Freud identified psychological forms; both follow the same logical structure.) A good example of this is where an attribute represents a subjective assessment of the entity type. For example, in the EMPLOYEE entity type, there might be an attribute called PROMOTION PROSPECTS. This is potentially misleading, because it hides the source of the assessment. Or in the PROJECT PROPOSAL entity type, there might be an attribute called ESTIMATED BENEFIT. This is also potentially misleading, because it hides the source of the estimate.

On the other hand, the opposite tendency, which creates an overabundance of classifying entity types, making the model difficult to use, must be resisted.

Let us consider the kinds of things or properties that an object can have (those facts about it that we might want to model).

1. A state or condition or other quality

For example, a person can have a particular state of health, or knowledge, or virtue. The best way to model such properties depends on how complex the state or condition is (and how complex our *use* of this information is). For example, if we want to roughly classify workers as skilled, semi-skilled or unskilled, then all we need is an attribute SKILL LEVEL of the entity type WORKER. If we want to capture the particular specialist skill of each worker, then an attribute such as SPECIALIST SKILL may be appropriate. But if we want to allow for the fact that some workers have *many* skills, then it may be better to have a relationship from WORKER to a separate entity type SKILL. And if there are other properties of each skill that are to be modelled, then the entity type SKILL becomes necessary.

2. A quantity

For example, a person can have a given height or weight. Such quantities are usually simple numbers (with or without decimal places); although sometimes a unit of measure (e.g. feet, metres, pounds, kilograms ...) must be included. This would be necessary if there was no consensus across the organization as to the units of measure to be used, so that some people in Germany would be measured in metres, and people in America would be measured in feet. (The organization may agree to convert all measurements to common units, but often does not.) Thus we may either have the attribute HEIGHT-IN-METRES or the two attributes HEIGHT and HEIGHT-UNITS.

However, if the model must include several different measurements of height or weight for the same person (e.g. over time), then a separate entity type MEASUREMENT (with an attribute of DATE-MEASURED as well as QUANTITY) may be required. This would allow the growth of a child, or the success of a slimmer, to be monitored. There is then a possibility of generalization: if we are measuring both the weight and the height of a child, (or both the petrol consumption and the top speed of a car), then we may either have a single entity type MEASUREMENT, differentiated by the attribute MEASUREMENT TYPE, or a different entity type for each type of measurement.

3. A sign

For example, a particular rank in the army has three stripes on the arm. Or a particular brand of the product has a green label. Often the relevance of such properties is that they assist in the identification or classification of the entities having the properties. The property is therefore a *sign*, and the sign has a *meaning*. It is then often argued that the sign must be an entity type, and the meaning is then an attribute of the sign. This is usually represented in computer or other systems by a code/description table, where the code represents the sign and the description contains the meaning. For example, the code 'GS' could stand for gasoline station, and be used to classify suppliers.

But in the real world, signs and symbols do not have to be composed of letters and numbers. Gasoline stations could be depicted on a map with a gold oval. For this we would need a symbol/description table, where a visual or other symbol is used rather than an alphabetic or numeric code.

4. A constituent part

For example, a warehouse has three loading bays. What we have to discover here is how this fact is to be used by the business. Are we interested in the loading bays as separate entities, or is the number of loading bays only relevant so that we know the throughput capacity of the warehouse itself?

5. A contents

For example, a lorry has three grand pianos loaded. How to model this depends on whether we are interested in the container, or the contents, or both. Usually the type of contents (in our example, grand pianos) will be a separate entity type. (This is discussed further in Chapter 8, when we talk about how to model SUBSTANCE.)

6. A possession

For example, a peasant has a house and a field. Do we want to know anything about the possessions as separate entities? We may just want to group people into three classes: tenant, rentier or owner-occupier. Or to classify them in some more complex way, perhaps according to the value of the property. (This might be appropriate for classifying potential customers, or when selecting targets to receive a mailshot.) This could be modelled in the same way as (3) above, attributing a sign to the consumer to indicate his/her purchasing potential. But in some cases, we want to include more in the model.

It is of little value just to know that an employee has a telephone at home; what is of value is to know what the telephone number is. So HOME TELEPHONE NUMBER becomes an attribute of EMPLOYEE. But because we probably do not want to know anything further about the employee's home telephone, it is unlikely to be needed in the model as a separate entity in its own right. However, the employee's car might be more important. It might be necessary to know whether it is an estate car, or even what make/model it is. In this case, the possession could be modelled as a separate entity type.

7. A relative

For example, a husband has a wife, and the wife has a husband. (In some societies, this is an asymmetric relationship of possession. In other words, the husband owns the wife, having bought her (with dowry payment) from her father. In other societies, a dowry is paid by the *bride's* family, implying that the bride has negative value.)

Summary

The essential question is whether the attribute values are needed in their own right and can be identified with their own properties.

3.3.5 Feature analysis

Some users will be able to provide immediate and precise definitions of the objects in the model. Some users, however, will find this difficult. The technique of **feature**

analysis is designed to draw out useful answers from relatively inarticulate users, or those who find systematic analysis difficult.[5] It is played like a card game. (Use of such games for creative management purposes has been popularized by Edward deBono, so there is no need for the user to feel he or she is being made fun of.) This technique can be used either with individual users or in group sessions.

The names of candidate entity types and/or occurrences are written on cards. Three cards are selected at random, and the user is asked to select the odd one out. In doing this, and explaining why, he or she will implicitly identify a similarity between two of them, not shared by the third.

> To demonstrate this, I have just drawn three cards from a DeBono pack: fish, scissors, octopus. Which is the odd one out? Scissors, because it is not edible. This implies a common feature (viz. edibility) of fish and octopus.[6]

Sometimes the user will be able to point out several features that the cards have in common. All features identified by the users are potentially important, whereas features identified only by the analyst are potentially unimportant. This is repeated with new cards, until a long list of features has been produced. Then a matrix is constructed, showing all the objects against all of the features. (This matrix is sometimes known as a **repertory grid.**) The user is taken systematically through each combination of object and feature, and asked whether the object possesses the feature. (There are three possible answers: yes, no, depends.) Finally, the matrix is clustered, to bring objects with similar features together. These features will be important points in the documentation and description of the objects within the model.

3.4 Defining entity types and identifiers

In this section, we take a more abstract look at the way entity types are defined and identified.

Two logicians dominate the nineteenth century: George Boole, the father of syntax, and Gottlob Frege, the father of semantics. Boole is honoured wherever binary logic hardware is designed; Frege should be equally honoured wherever information modelling takes place. In this section, we use his ideas to help us define and refine **membership rules** and **identity rules.**[7] Using these concepts, we shall see how information modelling can be extended beyond the areas in which is commonly applied, into areas of artificial intelligence, where similar techniques can be applied to far more difficult problems.

The **membership rule** (also known as **criterion of application**) tells us when an entity belongs to a particular entity type. For example, the membership rule for the entity type PRODUCT tells us how to distinguish products from things that are not products. The **identity rule** (also known as **criterion of identity**) tells us when an entity is distinct from another entity of the same type. In Frege's phrase: 'how to recognize the object as the same again'. For example, the identity rule for the entity type PRODUCT tells us how to distinguish one product from another product.

There are important pragmatic reasons why we want to get these rules right. Membership of the entity type PRODUCT probably implies many rules and procedures, to do with the administration and control of products. For example, company X manufactures and sells not only equipment but also training courses, which teach people the correct use of the equipment. If it regards both the equipment and the courses as products, then the same techniques of marketing or quality control will be applied to courses as well as equipment. But if it regards the equipment as the only product, and the courses as mere support activities, then it may fail to manage the courses properly. And when an information system is developed to assist product management, the information engineer must know what kinds of products the information system will have to handle, i.e. the membership of PRODUCT.

The identity rule of the entity type PRODUCT is also important. To continue the previous example, we have to know whether a given change in the equipment specification creates a new product, and whether it requires a new training course, whether it is the same again.

Thus, at least for most purposes of information modelling, all entity types must have both a membership rule and an identity rule. The way to test whether the membership and identity rules are adequate is to try to count the actual members of an entity type; if this proves impossible, then there must be something wrong with one or other of these rules. Or perhaps one should say that there is something wrong with the entity type. For example, if two people disagree as to the number of occurrences of PRODUCT that exist, they may sometimes be in possession of different facts. But it usually turns out that they are working on a different understanding of what PRODUCT actually is, with different membership and/or identity rules.

A useful way of using these concepts is to start with the desired membership and/or identity rules, and work backwards to obtain the underlying entity type. This may sometimes be the only way to produce a coherent information model.

3.4.1 Membership

Finite observation

In some cases, it may not be possible to be sure of classifying an entity correctly, because observation is inconclusive. (Philosophers refer to this as the problem of induction.) Consider the entity type VEGETARIAN. One observation of a person eating a steak is enough to deny membership of the entity type, but any number of observations of a person eating a salad is not enough to confirm membership. Such words as 'always' or 'never', 'necessarily' or 'possibly', 'can' or 'cannot', tend to cause difficulties when they appear in entity type definitions because membership thereby becomes non-verifiable.

Many marketing operations have difficulties defining PROSPECTIVE CUSTOMER. Who is more likely to buy a lawn-mower: someone who has previously bought a lawn-mower, or someone who has never bought a lawn-mower? Information modelling in these areas can often highlight logical errors in marketing tactics. Computer systems for generating junk mail should be able to select likely members of the entity type PROSPECTIVE CUSTOMER, based on previous buying behaviour or other known characteristics.

Another common example of this kind of difficulty is the entity type SCENARIO. Intuitively, one wants to define SCENARIO as 'anything that might happen', but this is so vague as to be almost useless. Instead, it may be necessary to define SCENARIO as the outcome of a specific scenario-building process, thus enabling us to place sensible limits on what counts as a scenario and what does not.

Characteristic and specific features

Some useful thoughts on membership rules can be obtained from Wittgenstein, whose followers distinguish between **characteristic features**, which are likely to belong to an object of a given class, and **specific features**, which are common to all members of a given class. Some more jargon has been introduced by anthropologists, which can borrowed here. **Monothetic classification** defines a class in terms of specific features. **Polythetic classification** defines a class in terms of characteristic features. Information scientists have usually assumed class membership can be defined monothetically, despite Wittgenstein's famous counter-example, based on his definition of the class GAME, quoted in Chapter 2.

Whereas operational entity types (such as EMPLOYEE) can usually be defined monothetically, strategic entity types (such as COMPETITIVE THREAT) often cannot. The natural definitions of such entity types may include words like 'typically'. To avoid this, the model may fall back on definitions that make the *ad hoc* judgement explicit, by specifying a judge, or a judging process. ('A competitive threat is anything identified by the strategic planning director as a competitive threat.') However, it is still useful to document the characteristic features.

The behaviour of an entity is usually a characteristic feature, rather than a specific feature. Thus it is usually inadequate to define an entity type merely in terms of what it does (or what its occurrences do). This can be like defining a dog as something that eats dog food. A good definition of an entity type specifies what it is (or what its occurrences are).

A definition of an entity type in terms of what the occurrence *might* do (as with COMPETITOR or DANGEROUS DOG) is even more difficult to treat objectively. What the marketing department (or the dog-catcher) needs is a way of recognizing members of the entity type *before* they display the potential behaviour. Thus DANGEROUS DOG may have to be defined by specific characteristics, such as breed or size. COMPETITOR may have to be defined in terms of those characteristics that make an organization capable of mounting a competitive threat, rather than in terms of competing products already on the market.

Fuzzy logic

Japanese manufacturers have started to produce consumer goods that incorporate techniques of artificial intelligence (AI). Popular journalism characterizes these techniques under the heading of 'fuzzy logic'. In fact, some of these consumer goods appear merely to perform a few calculations – such as a washing machine that senses the weight of clothes and reduces the usage of water accordingly, or a video camera that senses and compensates for the wobbling of the cameraman's arm.

True fuzzy logic is an alternative to Boolean logic. The best-known application of non-Boolean logic is in military intelligence and police detection work. In order to produce a fairly short list of likely suspects, the detective defines some characteristic features of the criminal (e.g. sudden wealth following crime, previous record of this kind of crime, lack of alibi, right blood group, etc.). Probably thousands of people satisfy at least one of these criteria, and possibly none satisfies all of them. The computer searches through the files to find people that are suspicious enough to warrant further investigation. We can express this as a derived entity type called SUSPECT, with a polythetic membership rule.

This kind of approximate deduction or selection is what logicians call fuzzy logic. Fuzzy logic can be translated, accurately enough for most practical purposes, into Boolean logic, in order to be executed by a digital computer whose internal structure is Boolean, but the Boolean equivalent would be long-winded and clumsy, and it would be very difficult for the policeman to state his requirements in this form.

Another way in which polythetic classification is attempted by artificial intelligence systems is in visual pattern matching. Programming a robot to recognize a chair, or a spy satellite to distinguish a tank from a lorry, is an extremely complex task.

Although not all artificial intelligence and robotics can be understood in these terms, it is worth acknowledging the practical strides that have been made by the AI community in formalizing these fuzzy logics. Although commercial data processing is less glamorous, there are many applications for these techniques, especially in marketing and planning, where expert systems and other AI-based technologies can be combined with information modelling and CASE technologies.

Re-cognition

Much of the effort of artificial intelligence goes into cognition, or re-cognition. There is, of course, a bias in our language, where nothing is supposed to be new. Research implies re-discovering forgotten facts from the lucky dip bag of the collective unconscious. And re-cognition implies an object's returning into the visual (or other sensory) field. Thus the researcher teaches the machine to see/discriminate/classify as the researcher herself would. The advantage of the machine is that, once taught, it can carry out the task millions of time without falling asleep. Thus the machine is an extension of the researcher-as-teacher. Even when the task enters non-human sensory fields (such as infrared scanning), the same teaching process works by analogy. So arguably, it is still the researcher (or research team) whose cognition is repeated by the machine.

We are here not interested in the physiological limitations of the human sensory apparatus. We assume that the human observer can deploy any available instrument to enhance his/her ability to discriminate. In a small business, a human expert can recognize patterns. But a business may grow faster than the expertise. So the expert needs to teach a computer to recognize these patterns. What patterns of late payment, for example, indicate the possibility that a customer may be in financial difficulties? What patterns of repair indicate that a machine is obsolete and needs replacement?

Definition by pictures

Identification by pointing is inherently ambiguous, as has been explained by many modern philosophers (including Wittgenstein and Quine). This is because there is usually no 'meta' language to explain exactly what it is that you are pointing at. Quine illustrates this by imagining a linguist in the bush, trying to learn a native language.[8] A rabbit scurries by, the native says *Gavagai*, and the linguist notes down the word 'rabbit'. But perhaps the word *Gavagai* means 'scurrying', or 'white', or 'bushy tail', or 'let's have one of those for dinner'.

If I point at a man, am I pointing at the whole man, or his chest? How do I point at him to make it clear I mean his chest, rather than the whole of him? How do I point at a dent in my car, differently to how I point at the car itself? Pictures and pointing at things only make sense within some context, provided by words. And it does not matter how many pictures you produce. Two pictures, together with the instruction to find what the two pictures have in common, may eliminate some of the possible misunderstandings, but by no means all. (There is a paradox here. It is by pictures (and other examples) that we learn language in the first place. Some concepts are defined through words, but many, perhaps most, concepts are learned by abstraction from experience. It is precisely the unreliability of experience as a grounding for conceptual thinking that concerns many philosophers.)

To find an equivalent situation in business modelling, let us imagine that the user produces a piece of paper, and says the word 'requisition'. The analyst may think he or she knows what the word requisition usually means, but cannot be sure whether the user attaches a special meaning to the word. Nor can the analyst be certain exactly what aspect of the piece of paper to look at:

- The piece of paper is a green copy from a rainbow set. Is it only the green copy that is called a requisition, while the pink copy is called something entirely different? Or is there one requisition, represented by a green copy and a pink copy?
- The piece of paper consists of a pre-printed form that has been filled in and counter-signed. Would a blank form be called a requisition? What about a form that has been filled in, but not yet authorized? What about a form that has been filled in and signed, but then cancelled? What about a form signed by a manager who has been fired? Does it make a difference whether he or she signed it before or after being fired?
- Does the form have to be correctly filled in, before it counts as a requisition? If the form referred to non-existent products, or specified an impossible delivery date, would it be a valid requisition?

Some of these questions could be answered by producing further examples of pieces of paper, which either are or are not requisitions. But since some of the questions refer to non-existence or impossibility, and since these concepts cannot be illustrated but must be explained in words, it follows that these questions cannot be answered without using words. (And even with words, some ambiguity may remain.[9])

3.4.2 Identity

Poetical example

In his essay on Keats's 'Ode to a nightingale', Jorge Luis Borges points out that an individual nightingale is unidentifiable. Keats regards the bird he heard as immortal; this is because the same bird was heard (and extolled) by Chaucer and Shakespeare, Milton and Swinburne. Borges goes on to quote Schopenhauer, who wrote:

> Let us ask ourselves sincerely whether the swallow of this summer is a different one than the swallow of the first summer, and whether the miracle of bringing something forth from nothingness has really occurred millions of times between the two, to be mocked by an equal number of times by absolute annihilation. Whoever hears me say that this cat playing here now is the same one that frolicked and romped in this place three hundred years ago may think of me what he will, but it is a stranger madness to imagine that he is fundamentally different.[10]

What is it here, that is the same again? Not the (mortal) bird, but the (immortal) species. Thus it is the assertion of identity between two birds that demonstrates to us which entity type is being spoken of.

The practical relevance of this concept is that, instead of starting with an entity type and then trying to determine its identity rule, we are often provided with an (implicit) identity rule, from which we have to work out what the entity type is. So let us explore the nature of identity rules further.

Logic of identity

There are three levels of identity:

1. True identity: this means that two things are exactly the same. Being exactly the same is what mathematicians call an 'equivalence relation', because it is:
   (a) reflexive   (A is exactly the same as A);
   (b) symmetric (if A is exactly the same as B, then B is exactly the same as A);
   (c) transitive   (if A is exactly the same as B, and B is exactly the same as C, then A is exactly the same as C).
2. Indiscriminability: this means we cannot tell two things apart. Whereas being indiscriminable is reflexive and symmetric, it is not transitive.
3. Pragmatic equivalence: this means that we are not interested in any differences there may be between two things. There is a discrimination process available, but we choose not to use it. Like indiscriminability, this is reflexive, symmetric, but not transitive. (Except that we might sometimes be able to arbitrarily impose a condition that would make it transitive, e.g. rounding to the nearest whole number.)

Just as an entity type must have an identity rule, so the existence of an identity rule implies the existence of an entity type or subtype, since identity only makes sense in such a context. (Indiscriminability and pragmatic equivalence also depend on such a context.)

Logic of non-identity

Similarly, there are three levels of non-identity:
1. True non-identity: this means that two things are not exactly the same. This is the logical negation of true identity.
2. Unrecognizability: this means we cannot tell when two things are the same.
3. Pragmatic non-equivalence: this means that we are not interested in any correspondences there may be between two things. There is a recognition process available, but we choose not to use it.

People usually do not bother to define a logic of non-identity as well as a logic of identity. This is because one is a logical consequence of the other. However, when we shift from true identity to other concepts, there ceases to be a clear correspondence.

Metaphysical and philosophical remarks

True identity and non-identity are ontological concepts, which means that they have to do with the nature of existence. Indiscriminability and unrecognizability are epistemological concepts, which means that they have to do with the nature of knowledge.

Our interest is primarily in pragmatic equivalence and non-equivalence, which are practical concepts. However, it is useful to compare and contrast these practical concepts with the ontological and epistemological ones, in order to understand their underlying logics.

Ethical remarks

Earlier in this chapter, we discussed the use of the word 'discrimination' in the sense of unfair treatment. This may sometimes be roughly expressed in terms of membership (If X is BLACK then X is not ELIGIBLE) or identity (BLACK is not equivalent to WHITE). It may sometimes be ethically necessary to ignore certain types of fact, in order to make just decisions. Thus we may choose to ignore differences between objects or classes, not only for economic reasons, but also for ethical reasons. We shall return to this in Chapter 6.

Rules depend on knowledge

A bank knows (indeed, must know) that the customer withdrawing £50 today is the same customer who deposited £100 last week. A supermarket does not know (has no mechanism for knowing) that the customer buying toilet paper today is the same customer who bought prunes last week. A recently privatized public utility company could know (if it chose to maintain the necessary records) which of its customers are also its shareholders.

Rules depend on purpose

For example, are Scottish pounds the same currency as English pounds? It depends why we want to know. If we are designing an automatic teller machine, which will dispense currency notes to bank customers, then we should be aware that the Scots have a one pound note, whereas the English have no pound note, but use a one pound coin. However, if we are using cheques, then this difference is irrelevant.

Is Swiss French the same language as Canadian French? If a Canadian company wants its letters, advertisements and other communications to be clearly understood by customers, the differences between Swiss and Canadian idiom and vocabulary may not matter. But if the company is concerned to appear friendly to the customer, then it might be a good idea to use Swiss French when communicating with Swiss customers.

Rules depend on space–time – plus ça change

For example, are Irish pounds the same currency as English pounds? They used to be, but they are not now. Or, for example, is Italian the same language as Latin? Presumably not, but there is no exact date when the common people in Rome stopped speaking Latin and started speaking Italian. Instead, there was a gradual shift; each generation of Italians could understand the previous generation. Thus we have a contradiction between the following two, equally plausible assertions:

- (The language spoken in Rome in year Y) is always equal to (The language spoken in Rome in year $Y+1$)

- (The language spoken in Rome in year *Y*) is sometimes not equal to (The language spoken in Rome in year *Y*+100)

The problem with Latin/Italian illustrates a class of similar problems, which result from development or evolution. If a small change in *X* leaves *X* the same, but a large change in *X* results in a new *X*, what about a large number of small changes? (Modelling of PRODUCT almost always requires this to be considered.)

In practical situations, we have not only to fix perhaps arbitrary rules about the number of small changes it takes to produce a large change, but also determine what counts as a CHANGE in the first place, and how to measure the size of one. Change management also demands we know when a change is 'the same again' – in other words, we need membership and identity rules for CHANGE.

Change and continuity

Heracleitus said 'It is impossible to step twice in the same river', and this is developed by Plutarch:

> Dead is the man of yesterday, for he is passed into the man of today; and the man of today is dying as he passes into the man of tomorrow. Nobody remains one person, nor is one person; but we become many persons, even as matter is drawn about some one semblance and common mould with imperceptible movement. Else how is it that, if we remain the same persons, we take delight in some things now, whereas earlier we took delight in different things; that we love or hate opposite things, and so too with our admirations and disapprovals, and that we use other words and feel other emotions and have no longer the same personal appearance, the same external form, or the same purposes in mind?[11]

If we took this view, however, we would be unable to use language altogether. John Doe would have to have a new identifier every day, or even every minute. But we *can* meaningfully talk about John Doe, without having to say which point of time we mean. John Doe is regarded for most purposes as being an unchanging person.

To talk of change itself means that something (some entity) must exist before and after the change, that is changed. What changes must, in some sense, persist. We have to allow that John Doe today is *for our purposes* the same person as John Doe yesterday. This is yet another reason why our purpose, or the nature of our interest in an entity, influences our identification of that entity.

Under what circumstances does the date or time of John Doe matter? When the entity type that is really of interest to us is not PERSON, but something much more transitory or abstract. Perhaps we are really interested in some role played by John Doe, or perhaps he serves to illustrate or test something only as long as he retains a particular characteristic.

In business, the continuity of an ASSET may be important for tax purposes. For example, if a company invests in computer equipment, which is subsequently upgraded, the availability of capital allowances against tax may depend on precise rules about whether the upgraded computer can be regarded as the same asset.

Identity across classes

If we want to identify this shareholder with that customer, this is only meaningful in the context of some entity supertype that encompasses both shareholders and customers. CUSTOMER and SHAREHOLDER might both be wholly contained within the entity type PERSON, or perhaps the union of the type PERSON with the type COMPANY. Of course, the identity rule for PERSON is not the same as the identity rule for COMPANY. But it should be fairly easy to construct a composite identity rule for PERSON-OR-COMPANY, subject of course to our being able to separate members of the type PERSON from those of the type COMPANY. And we often do not need to explicitly model any of the entity types PERSON-OR-COMPANY, PERSON, or COMPANY. They may remain implicit, buried within the identity rules for SHAREHOLDER and CUSTOMER.

Starting point

In some situations, it may be more appropriate to start with the assumption that things are different, until they are proved to be the same. In other situations, it may be more appropriate to start with the assumption that things are the same, until they are proved to be different.

The pragmatic choice between these options depends on the likelihood of things turning out to be the same, or different, and the probable difficulty of reordering one's knowledge when these discoveries are made; i.e. is it more effort to merge the facts relating to what now proves to be one object, or to separate the facts relating to what now proves to be two objects?

Error

The processes involved in discrimination can also lead to ignorance or error. If I fail to discriminate between the lengths of two lines, one slightly longer than the other, there is something I have failed to find out. If, misled by perspective, I judge one line to be longer than another, and they turn out to be of equal length, my would-be discrimination was incorrect. Failures of discrimination are cognitive failures.

A pragmatic question is how tolerant we can be of error. Marginal inaccuracies may be more trouble to eliminate than it is worth.

Anthropomorphism

If discrimination is a cognitive act, does it make sense for computers or socio-technical systems to discriminate? Metaphorically, yes. After all, we could speak of a window discriminating (in its response) between a feather and a ball. But if we saw the feather hit the window, and then saw the window shatter, we would be unlikely to accuse the window or the feather of error. It is really *our* discrimination (with the window as a measuring instrument), and *our* error.

There is a progression of technology, shown in Table 3.3.

Table 3.3 Technology progression

Naked eye	Normal sighted person can make direct visual judgement
Spectacles	Myopic person can make visual judgements
Telescope	Distant person can make visual judgements
Telecamera projecting images directly onto TV monitor	Person elsewhere can make visual judgements
Telecamera converting non-visible radiation to visible light, before projecting onto TV monitor	Person anywhere can make visual judgements of invisible phenomena (e.g. infrared or X-ray spectrum)
Telecamera feeding images to videotape	Person at a later time can make visual judgements, by watching the tape
Telecamera feeding data to computer	Person at an earlier time can make visual judgements, by programming them into the computer in advance

Some people might regard the last of these steps as qualitatively different from the others. The programmer could be dead, while the computer continued to discriminate. The other examples all require a live person to make the discrimination.

Use of models

A model is a partial representation of reality. The model is a structure of concepts, rather than objects. The lack of a simple one-to-one correspondence between concepts and objects was noted by Frege, and has been widely explored by modern logicians.[12]

True identity in the model may represent not true identity in the real world, but indiscriminability or pragmatic equivalence. (In other words, we may have a clear separation between entities in the model, whereas the corresponding separation in the real world is a lot less clear cut.) Nonetheless, we must have an equivalence relation within the model, albeit one that does not accurately reflect (ontological) reality, since the model is always an abstraction from the real world.

Thus we have an equivalence relation 'modelling' a non-equivalence relation. The logical consequences of this are explored by Williamson, and I shall not reproduce them here.[13]

3.4.3 Conclusion

In this section, we have considered difficulties associated with membership rules and identity rules. When defining entity types, the analyst should be sensitive to these rules, and should only define entity types whose membership and identity rules make sense. Starting from the rules, and using them to determine the correct entity types is often a good approach. An additional motivation for including this material is to demonstrate the power of information modelling, and encourage readers to deploy the same thinking for both simple and complex situations. Much work has been done in artificial intelligence, formalizing and automating fuzzy logics to carry out cognitive tasks. However, information science seems some way behind the latest theory and techniques. Models are built that rely on an unsophisticated logic. Membership and identity rules in these models are often inelegant, inaccurate or downright inconsistent. The position sketchily argued in this section is that it would be both feasible and useful to introduce concepts from philosophical logic, and techniques from artificial intelligence, into the business modelling practices of information science. Although the AI community has traditionally been remote from the commercial information systems community, we can expect increasing cross-fertilization of ideas and techniques, based on an understanding of the common logical structure of these kinds of problems.

Why is this material relevant to a pragmatic book on information modelling? Because it shows what difficulties ensue when the areas being modelled are complex, subjective and logically sophisticated. As information engineers move from traditional data-processing systems to more interesting problems, they increasingly encounter these 'fuzzy' situations. With proper attention to the definitions and identifiers of entity types, information models can be used as the basis for designing extremely sophisticated expert systems.

Even with traditional computer systems, some of the difficulties addressed in this section can easily arise, if the definitions are vague or ill considered. Modelling of time, currency, people, and other business concepts – these all need clarity of analysis.

3.5 Analysing entity state transitions

Considering the states and state transitions through which an entity may pass, between creation and destruction, often gives us further insight on the entity type, and on the processes that surround the entity type. The life history or lifecycle of an entity can be divided into a number of discrete **entity states**, which it is often useful to analyse in detail. Figure 3.1 shows the history of an office building. The life history or lifecycle of an entity extends from the first point in time when it may be meaningful or useful to talk of the entity, until it ceases to be meaningful or useful. This gives us the following paradox: that the entity may exist conceptually before it exists physically, and also after it has ceased to exist physically. Thus we can talk of a building before it has been constructed, and also after it has been demolished. In this example, the first state (*designed*) and the last state (*demolished*) are non-physical states, since the building does not physically exist in these states. It is extremely common for the first state of a physical entity to be a non-physical state such as *designed* or *planned* or *scheduled*. And it is also common for the final state of a physical entity to be a non-physical state, such as *dead* or *destroyed* or an unknown state, such as *lost*.

So it is not necessary for every occurrence of BUILDING to physically exist, since we may want to talk of past or future buildings. Sometimes a building never exists: the plans are drawn up, but for some reason or other the building is never

Figure 3.1 Entity states of an office building

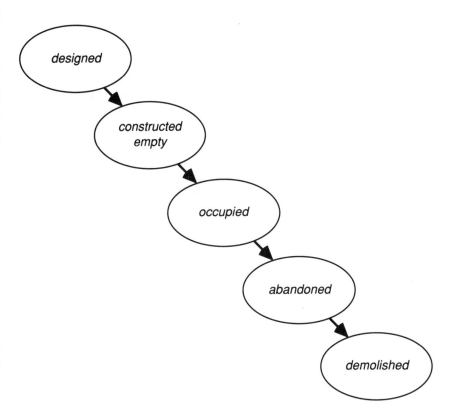

constructed. Yet even such totally non-existent buildings can have a conceptual existence: real financial costs can be incurred by them (including the architect's fee).

For business purposes, the final state of a person is often 'dead'. Of course, a person usually continues to exist as a concept after death. For a while, a dead person may still have property and debts, bank accounts and insurance policies, which may take months to transfer to the heirs. Eventually, a dead person is reduced to a memory, but even then may still exist as a concept, contributing perhaps to medical or actuarial statistics. This does not, however, mean that every person remains of interest until death.

In some cases, a person may even exist before conception. For example, an insurance policy or testament may refer to the future eldest child of a childless person. (This is a rare requirement.)

We spoke earlier of the life history or lifecycle of an entity type. These terms are commonly used in the literature. But we should avoid referring to *the* lifecycle or *the* life history of an entity type, in recognition of the fact that an entity type can have several independent lifecycles. An entity type can play several roles, and have a separate lifecycle for each role. The analysis of entity states has several different names. The word **history** implies a simple sequence (biography). The entity undergoes a standard series of crises (conception, gestation, birth, mid-life, death, or possibly fade away). The word **cycle** implies a loop or repetition (reincarnation). Some entities may repeat, but many do not. (Does a bankrupt CUSTOMER reappear under a new name?) There is an analogy here with the so-called product lifecycle, according to which products follow the sequence PROBLEM CHILD → RISING STAR → CASH COW → DOG. Do we then try to convert DOGS into PROBLEM CHILDREN? Should dead or dying products be reincarnated? Or would this be a strategic error?

So, because the words 'history' and 'cycle' are misleading, we prefer to call this analysis **entity state transition** analysis. This makes clear that we want to allow for sequence, selection and iteration in the life of an entity, and also avoids any implication of inevitability. It focuses our attention on the processes that transform (effect state changes) in the entity.

The steps of this analysis are as follows:

1. Identify **relevant** states of an entity, those that make some difference to the business, in other words that affect the logic of some process.
2. Decompose cumulative states. For example, SALES ORDER can progress through the following states:

   > Received (= ORDER exists)
   > Accepted
   > Allocated
   > Delivered (= DELIVERY exists)
   > Invoiced (= INVOICE exists)
   > Paid (= PAYMENT exists)

   This model imposes strict sequential rules on the business. Each state here implies $X(i)$ and not yet $X(i+1)$. Do we really want to enforce such strict rules? A more flexible model would separate these states into independent attributes.

   We may want to know when the order was allocated, or by whom it was accepted. This would require more information than is modelled by a simple STATUS attribute. We may want to model partial allocation or delivery or payment. This too cannot be done via a simple STATUS attribute. The method may therefore start by recognizing a life history of SALES ORDER, but we may want to refine the model, decomposing the status attribute into several independent attributes, or possibly additional entity types.
3. Determine whether the status is derivable from other information in the model. (For example, PAID is derivable from the existence of a PAYMENT.)
4. Decide how to represent the status – as one or more attributes (e.g. by code or status dates), or by reference to other (possibly additional) entity types (representing events or history). Like partitioning, an entity state may be determined from a state attribute, or otherwise.
5. Decide whether some attributes or relationships of the entity type only apply when the entity is in a given state. In this case, it may be appropriate to

represent the states as different subtypes of the entity type, using what is known as a **lifecycle partitioning**.

6. Check what state transitions are possible, and how these are triggered. An entity occurrence changes its state either as the result of a business process being carried out (e.g. SALES ORDER becomes *allocated* after the business process ALLOCATE SALES ORDER has been done) or as the result of an event (e.g. CHILD becomes ADULT on his/her 18th birthday).

   Some events (such as birthdays, or payments becoming overdue) are wholly automatic and can be predicted in advance. There is no new information available after the event, that was not available before the event. Therefore, the event does not count as a business process.

7. Analyse independent states. For example, each occurrence of VEHICLE can be in more than one of the following states at the same time:

   Owned
   Leased
   Roadworthy
   Awaiting repair
   Taxed
   Untaxed

In this example, we see that the renewal of the tax disk can fall due regardless of the physical status and location of the vehicle. Similarly, a company can negotiate a purchase or leasing contract, without any impact on the physical status of the vehicle. In this case, a simple STATUS attribute is not enough, since it would have several values at the same time; an entity may have several different (independent) statuses, which will need to be modelled as separate attributes (e.g. FINANCIAL STATUS, PHYSICAL STATUS, TAX STATUS). It follows that composite states ('taxed, insured and roadworthy') should be decomposed into independent attributes. This follows the principle that each attribute should represent only one fact.

For another example, consider the parallel states of LIBRARY BOOK. A book out on loan can be reserved by another reader. So can a book with a torn binding, that needs to be repaired before it can be borrowed. Thus the physical status (shelf/onloan/awaiting repair) is independent of the demand status (reserved/not reserved). But this example is more complex than the previous one. This is because the reservation refers not to the physical book itself but to the book title. (If the library has several copies of the same title, a reservation will be fulfilled by the first available copy.) Thus while physical status is an attribute of PHYSICAL BOOK, demand status is an attribute of BOOK TITLE. But this may not be enough. When a reservation is cancelled, does the demand status change to 'not reserved'? Not if there is a second reservation outstanding for the same book. Demand status cannot be adequately modelled by a single attribute, but requires a separate entity type : RESERVATION.

Thus we see that the analysis of entity state transitions forces us to reconsider the entity type itself. Although, in a typical model, many entity types are too simple to deserve such detailed analysis (since the simpler ones do not undergo any state changes at all between creation and destruction), there are usually some entity types for which this type of analysis is extremely useful.

3.6 Analysing distribution

The purpose of this section is to add a geographical dimension to an information model.[14] This may at first seem odd, since information might not seem to have a physical location. There are three answers to this: a philosophical one, a practical one based on time, and a practical one based on technology.

Communication can be regarded as moving information from one point in space–time to another. (Where the distance in time is much greater than the distance in space, it may be called memory instead of communication.) If we accept Einstein's demonstration, based on the finite speed of light, that instantaneous communication between separated locations is impossible, this implies that information always has a location.

Information needs may well have a physical location, in so far as the person or machine requiring a particular type of information will have a specific location in space–time. And if the information represents physical objects or events, then it is likely that the information will become available in the vicinity of the object or event, rather than remotely. Not only in theoretical physics, but also in practice, information takes time to travel from one location to another. Delays in the transmission and availability of information are caused not just by the finite speed of light, but also by the obstruction of people, procedures, technology and security controls.

If telecommunications were cheap and global enough, it would be possible to store all information at the point of source, and allow any interested person (or computer program) to access the information from this point. But technology has not yet attained that power. A designer therefore needs to know something about locations, in order to design procedures for shipping information around a network. The basic approach is therefore to produce a distribution model, usually expressed as a series of matrixes, which maps the information model (together with any process models) against the locations where the organization exists or acts or is represented.

3.6.1 Purpose

A distribution model can be used for planning development projects (since it can help determine suitable locations for project teams) or for the design and implementation of distributed systems (since it enables the telecommunications and data processing consequences of different design options to be calculated and compared).

Suitable project locations for each systems development project should be based on the following considerations:

- Source of changes to business requirements.
- Current location of managers who are to control the business system (e.g. steering committee members).
- Current location of staff with relevant application knowledge and/or who are to use the business system when it is implemented.
- Current location of staff with relevant technical knowledge.
- Current availability of appropriate development facilities.

Typical design goals for a distributed system are:

- Physical: to reduce technical complexity, increase technical reliability, flexibility.
- Logical: to reduce logical complexity, enhance data sharing.
- Psychological: to reduce perceived complexity, to enhance visibility, data responsibility.

Design and implementation of distributed systems should be based on the following considerations:

- Required/expected volumes, frequencies and usage patterns.
- Overall system requirements (e.g. security, service levels and system availability, response times).
- Technical feasibility and cost.
- Transition problems relating to the current location of systems and data.

Depending on the technology being used, it may be possible (although not always desirable) for the systems designer to make the apparent location of the data differ from the actual physical location of the data. The user of an information system does not want to be constantly bothered with the complications of telecommunications networks, and it should ideally be possible to alter the physical distribution as the technological factors (or the volumes, frequencies and usage patterns) change over time, without affecting the logical functioning of the system(s) or the human–computer interface. This is referred to as 'transparency'.

But it may not be such a good idea to allow the user to make false assumptions about the system, whether remote or local. For example, the user needs to know what level of physical security a terminal requires (depending whether it contains data, and whether it contains the only copies of data), and what could happen if he or she tries to operate it when disconnected from the remote system. Where are data backed up, and what would happen if he or she tried to restore data from a floppy disk back up? The architecture of the system should be visible.[15]

3.6.2 What is a location?

The analysis can be performed at different levels of geographical abstraction. Any of these levels may be valid in different situations, but it is important to be clear what exactly we mean by LOCATION. (The appropriate choice will depend on the number and diversity of locations.) Sometimes it can be done as a physical location (e.g. head office), sometimes as a type of location (e.g. regional warehouse).

Physical site

Location is an ambiguous word, it means both place and placing, in other words both the site itself, and the association of things with the site. A physical site can be an office building, or warehouse, or branch, or physical part of any of these. At a physical site, certain things (both abstract and concrete) happen or exist – that is what we mean by the physical location of those things.

Logical site

One physical site (e.g. an office building) may play the role of many logical sites. For example, the head office may also be the regional branch office for the region in which the Head Office is located. Thus, staff in the London office may have both national and regional responsibilities. Sometimes these responsibilities will be separated, but often there will be individual members of staff with dual or multiple roles. However, we should be able to separate head-office-related activities from regional-branch-office-related activities.

Physical movement of logical site

A travelling salesman moves from physical site to physical site. But we can define his logical site to be fixed, as wherever he happens to be. This spares us the problem of users travelling from one logical site to another, but may introduce further complexity, by giving us more logical sites to manage. There is a many-to-many relationship between logical site and physical site, both at a single point in time (if we take a dispersed team of salesmen to be a single logical location, which however we may not want to) and over an extended time period. What we want to know is how much users travel between physical sites, and what they do (or need to do) when away from their home base.

Access to entities

Where are the data used? Exclusively or mainly at one location? We need to consider what the partitioning of an entity type may be. Can we break the entity type into 'local' partitions, so that each access point needs access mostly or entirely to 'local' entity occurrences? A good example of this is in Directory Enquiries – the probability of an enquiry referring to Milton Keynes is much higher if the inquirer is a Miltonian Keynesian, than if the inquirer is a Basingstoker. What the designer wants to know, of course, is **how much** higher.

Partitioning

The key question to be addressed by the distribution analysis is whether we can predict *which* occurrences of *which* entity types are going to be needed *where*. This prediction may be based not only on the static predicates of the entity type (e.g. where you cash cheques depends partly where you live), but also on the behaviour history of the entity occurrence (e.g. where you will cash cheques is likely to be similar to where you have cashed cheques). This allows us the possibility of **dynamic partitioning**, whereby, for example, a customer record is held at a branch only if the customer has visited the branch in the last six weeks.

It may not always be possible to carry out this analysis to a high degree of detail and accuracy. But it is worth looking for a working compromise, to try to achieve an approximate picture of partitioning opportunities.

Psychological location

User departments want data, programs and processing to be 'here' rather than 'there'. This is related to their taking responsibility for data entry, accuracy, privacy and integrity. But for these purposes, 'here' and 'there' are more to do with the users' perceptions than with physical reality. This is not to say that users are fools, or can/should be fooled; simply that how they perceive the location of things is not completely determined by the physical location of those things.

3.6.3 Task structure of distribution analysis

An ideal task structure would be as follows (it is rarely possible to analyse distribution completely; instead, a reasonable attempt should be made to produce relevant and useful information):

1. Determine relevant physical sites.
2. Classify physical sites into types (e.g. warehouses, branch offices), and identify logical sites (i.e. site roles).
3. Associate site types with entity types and processes (e.g Warehouses need to update STOCK ITEM, need to execute CHECK STOCK QUALITY).
4. Associate site occurrences with entity occurrences (e.g. the Milton Keynes depot accesses information for Customer 4711 so many times).
5. Analyse these associations to identify location clusters, entity partitions and usage statistics (e.g. the London branches make 45 per cent of their accesses for customers in Greater London, 40 per cent for customers in the rest of the south-east region, and 15 per cent for customers outside the south-east).
6. Determine logical process groups (i.e. groups of related processes that business logic requires to be carried out at the same location, perhaps because the same physical materials are involved, or the same personnel skills and knowledge).
7. Estimate present/planned/possible volumes, frequencies and usage patterns for each entity type/subtype at each logical/physical site.
8. Document distribution options.

3.7 Presenting models to users

3.7.1 Introduction

In order to ensure active participation of users in the construction and confirmation of an information model, the model needs to be presented to these users in an intelligible form. In some circumstances, this presentation can be face to face; sometimes a written document needs to be produced, especially when the results of the analysis need to be circulated widely within an organization.

Users are frequently presented with work that has been done in the information systems (IS) department, and asked for their approval. This has always been problematical, and continues to be, even with the latest IS methodologies. The user may be asked to participate in the development of information systems, but this participation remains unequal, and is sometimes not as effective as it could be. This section explores the historical and current reasons for this, and suggests how it can be improved. In particular, we discuss the use of business and system models, as communication tools.

3.7.2 What should users understand?

What is an entity? What are relationships and attributes? Are these terms of computer jargon, inaccessible except to an elite of information engineers? Or are they terms that can and should be familiar to all? Is the information model an arcane technical construction, or a way to make a computer system more visible to its users?

There are two commonly expressed views about the relationship between the businessman and the business model. One view is that the model is a turn off. The model is a technical representation of the business, and is regarded by the businessman in the same light as any other piece of technical jargon. Only technically minded people can cope with the complexity captured in these models. Any attempt to discuss these models with non-technical people (especially senior management) is doomed.

The other view is that because the models represent the business, they must be easy for businessmen to understand. An appeal is made to pop psychology, with the common yet absurd assertion that diagrams are always easier to understand than text. (Some writers refer glibly to the left and right hemispheres of the brain, as if to suggest that the reliability of communication is improved by bypassing the vagaries of spoken or written language. But to repeat the quotation from Levinson: 'A picture is worth a thousand words only with some person or caption to explain it – only when framed in words.'[16])

Let us try to resolve this contradiction. Models (including diagrammatic models) can be valuable tools for sharing an understanding of a business and its system requirements. But this value must be worked at, does not come automatically, without effort. Which approach, the use of the models, the attitudes towards their construction and presentation – these factors crucially affect the acceptance, and therefore the success, of the models, in addressing a given situation.

If an information model is to be truly a tool for communicating an understanding of structure between users and information engineers, then it must be presented to the users in the most effective way possible. This may imply that the model takes on different forms and formats, other than the standard nth normal form that is most efficient for database design. It almost certainly implies that the model be presented in manageable chunks, rather than as an indigestible whole.

More crucial than the form or format of the information model, however, is that the users understand what the model is supposed to say. If users are to confirm a model as a correct representation of their business, then they must appreciate how the model is going to be used, what it is for. Then they can develop for themselves appropriate criteria of acceptance. Otherwise, their reviews will probably be unfocused and irrelevant.

3.7.3 User attitudes towards information models

Communication between users and information engineers has complex psychological overtones. The metaphor of the master–servant (with the user as master and the engineer as servant) clashes with the metaphor of Athenians and slaves (with the engineer as Athenian, controlling the workers and the machines alike).[17] Distrust and disrespect between the two groups is often thinly veiled; the presentation of work to users by engineers is a crucial interface point, where disguised hostility can emerge.

'If one man stands up on his own to address a crowd of other men, there is an implication that his status is in some way superior to theirs ... but in a presentation it is usually the other way around.'[18] This can be analysed through the metaphor of the child–parent relationship. In America to listen is parental, and in Britain to talk is parental.

> An Englishman when he is applauding another is indicating or signalling potential submission and/or dependency; when he shows off or demands spectatorship, he is signalling dominance or superiority; and so on. Any Englishman who writes a book must be guilty of this. For the American, the converse must hold. His boasting is but a bid for quasiparental approval.[19]

Similar cultural differences may be detected between users in America and in Britain.

In this book, we do not attempt to resolve these cultural, psychological and political differences. We merely state them, as a context for what are primarily technical suggestions. It is to be hoped, however, that by improving some of the technical aspects of the developer–user dialogue, the overall situation might be improved.

In the context of information modelling, several difficulties can be identified.[20] For the sake of alliteration, we summarize the problems as (1) political, (2) psychological, (3) participation, and (4) perspicuity.

Political

The identification and commitment of the user is itself problematical, and has political implications. Do we regard the line manager, or the clerk, or the middle manager, as 'the' user? What about staff management, professional and technical staff, people outside the organization itself. (For example, consider a computerized administration system developed for public clinics. Would the nurses' professional body want to participate in the development project as a 'user'? If the general public are to have direct access to the system, how would their needs be represented?)

Then the availability of the user also raises political problems. Sometimes there is no user at all, or none accessible. And in order to save money, or to enhance integration, systems may be developed jointly for several different groups of users, and their interaction may be politically fraught.

Psychological

The attitudes of users and information engineers, and their beliefs about each others' abilities and powers, cannot be ignored. A form of psychological warfare often takes place at the point where the users are supposed to review the work of the information engineers, which can almost amount to intimidation. The information engineers are human, and do not enjoy having their work torn to pieces. However loudly they reiterate the official message of the methodology, that feedback is essential and criticism is welcome, their manner will often contradict that message:

> We have spent X man-months (rarely person-months), using the XYZM structured engineering methodology, to produce these deliverables. We will give you this brief opportunity to spot any mistakes or misconceptions we may have made.

The users need a great deal of intellectual confidence to believe themselves able to make a valuable contribution under these conditions. Junior staff may be sensitive to the delicate egos of the information engineers, and can be reluctant to question better-educated, better-paid, higher-status co-workers or external consultants. Senior staff may be reluctant to get involved in details, or to contradict their colleagues and subordinates. All staff take every opportunity to avoid having to use their brains, having publicly to pit their inadequate wits against the 'scientific' XYZM methodology. It goes like this.

> SENIOR MANAGER: (aware that such-and-such is critical) How have you handled the such-and-such situation?
> ANALYST: Well, we spoke to so-and-so, and ...
> SENIOR MANAGER: (not wanting to know the details and/or to undercut so-and-so's position, (interrupts) Oh well, if so-and-so has been involved, I'm sure it's all okay.

Thus the user may refuse to listen to the answer to his/her own question, which was asked more out of duty than real interest. The intimidation can be mutual: sometimes a senior manager bullies his/her way out of making any serious effort, and the information engineer lets such a user get away with this evasion of responsibility.

Participation[21]

The task of systems design is complex. It has four inputs:

1. Subjective facts (e.g. targets, priorities, constraints, etc., obtained by interviewing key users and managers).
2. Objective facts (e.g. volumes and frequencies, obtained by direct observation and measurement).
3. Specific ideas (possible solutions to specific design problems, either invented or adopted/adapted from elsewhere).
4. Design methods and skills (based partly on the chosen methodology, but also depending significantly on past experience and present intuition of the participants).

Many information engineers regard user participation as extending no further than user interviews. And they regard interviewing users as a simple process of extracting knowledge, of types (1) and (2). Following the gods of what, why, how, when, who, where, how much and what else, they fire a series of questions at the interviewee. But the interviewee is not always told the relevance of the questions, nor is he or she given a chance to prepare answers. This means that neither the interviewer nor the interviewee can be sure that all the important facts have been uncovered. Many users worry, impotently, because they have imparted only a small amount of their knowledge to the interviewer, and do not see how a good design can come out of it. Thus there is a major problem, even with this restricted form of participation: how does the user know what it matters to tell you?

Full participation requires the user to be active in decision making. This means that he or she must understand the process as well as the end-result. This requires that the methodology itself, as well as its products, should be visible to the user. This visibility must extend to all stages of the methodology, not just to the current stage. Thus, for example, full participation in analysis requires, among other things, understanding of design. But we shall see below that this is still required, even if full participation is not the name of the game.

Perspicuity

Let us assume that you have found a user to review the models, you have nipped psychological warfare in the bud and established the right expectations on all sides about the right level of participation. Now how do the users evaluate a business model? What do they need to know before they can make the best contribution to the project? How do they know what is relevant? About the model and about the methodology?

If you ask people to evaluate a product, you must tell them what the product is to be used *for*, i.e. its purpose. This gives them the context to determine what is relevant. They do not need to know (although they may be interested) how you produced the product, not what you have done but what you are going to do next. Users want to know (and should not have to guess) how the deliverables are going to be subsequently converted into a working system.

Therefore, even if a user is not participating in building the model, he or she still needs to have an understanding of what the model means. A model is a simplification of the real world; it is obvious to the user that many aspects of the real world are not included. The user cannot properly judge whether a model is complete, without knowing what completeness would comprise, without having some guidelines as to whether the obvious gaps and simplifications are acceptable.

To take just one common source of conflict, the division between analysis and design, and the rationale for the division, may seem straightforward to an information engineer, with training and experience in the given methodology. To an uninitiated user, the division and its rationale may be difficult to understand.

3.7.4 Presentation techniques

Understand the purpose of the model

To understand a model, you have to understand three things: (1) what the model is of; (2) how the representation works, what constructs are being used and how they represent aspects of the situation being modelled; and (3) what the model is for. Thus to present, say, an information model to a group of users for review, you have to explain (1) what portion of the business is being modelled; (2) what entities, relationships and attributes are; and (3) why the model has been produced, what is going to be done with it, what decisions it will influence, and so on.

The scope of a business model usually needs to be broader than the scope of any system designed from the model, in order that the interfaces between the system and its environment be understood. (As a civil engineer surveys more land than just that bit on which her bridge will stand.) Thus the inclusion of an aspect of the business in the business model cannot itself be taken as a commitment to computerize it. On the contrary, it may be included so that any cost–benefit or human-factor arguments for not computerizing it can be made explicit.

The scope needs to be carefully explained. It will not, typically, coincide with the boundaries of any existing computer system or functional department. (It may be suspicious if it coincides too exactly.) Even the name of the model needs to be chosen carefully, to avoid false expectations of scope. The users must understand enough of the methodology to develop their own evaluation criteria. (The methodology may provide some guidelines, may help to develop criteria, but cannot provide them ready packaged.)

Dialectic approach

One of the most useful ways of presenting complexity, in all sorts of disciplines, is by stealth. We start with a simple, albeit inadequate model, and progressively complicate it.

1. 'Suppose we only had one branch and one warehouse. Then the model would look like this. But we already have several branches, and intend to have several warehouses. Therefore we have to have a more complex model, thus ...'
2. 'If we didn't allow our customers to have joint accounts, then we could have a model like this. But to model joint accounts, we have to make the model a little more complex, thus ...'

Meaning is use

One of the best ways to make an information model come alive for the users is to show how it supports the business requirements, in other words how it is used. Its meaning therefore becomes apparent through its use. Suppose we have the model, for a small car hire firm, shown in Figure 3.2. Suppose the business insists that the only person that can drive a rental vehicle is the person that signs the rental agreement. Then the *drives* relationship is redundant, and will not appear on the model shown to the users. On the other hand, if the business allows several people to drive the vehicle under the same agreement, then the *drives* relationship is not redundant. It is difficult for the user to see that the information model expresses this business rule via the presence or absence of a relationship. However, if the analyst talks through some business processes and information needs with the user, and shows how the drivers of rental vehicles are identified through the rental agreement, this makes the business rule visible to the user, who can then confirm or deny it.

Figure 3.2 Model of a car hire firm

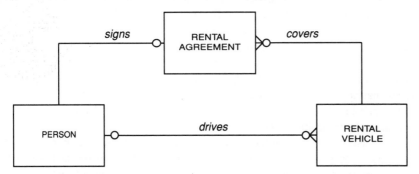

Note that the model should represent reality, not the user's wishes. Thus the user might like to restrict driving to the person that signs the agreement, and may indeed include such a restriction in the agreement itself. But if this restriction is breached by the customers, or if the rental company has to administer claims against accidents resulting from unauthorized people driving their vehicles, then the reality may be that the vehicles are sometimes driven by people who have not signed rental agreements. So the *drives* relationship is not redundant.

Subdivide model

The ease with which an information model can be understood depends in part on the number of entity types shown. To read a diagram of seven entity types, even an uninitiated user requires very little explanation of its structure (although the content of each entity type may always need considerable discussion). To read a diagram of twenty-one entity types, the uninitiated user will need some assistance navigating around. A diagram of forty-nine entity types will cause some problems even for experienced information engineers. And a diagram of over seventy-seven entity types will be of scant use to anybody (although such diagrams are popular as wall charts). Therefore, in order to make a diagram more useful, you may have to reduce the number of entity types and relationships shown. There are two ways of doing this: in this subsection, we discuss dividing an information model into parts; in the next subsection, we discuss hiding entity types by denormalizing the model.

The users should think of an information model in two ways: in terms of the information needs supported by the model, and in terms of the business processes represented by the information. For example, the SALES ORDER entity type is meaningful to the user both in terms of the sales analysis information s/he needs to make management and marketing decisions, and in terms of the order taking, delivery and invoicing processes that belong to the lifecycle of sales orders.

This gives us an approach for dividing an information model into parts. We take a coherent group of business processes (such as those concerned with the lifecycle of a sales order) or of information needs (such as those concerned with a particular set of planning decisions) or perhaps both. We then eliminate from the diagram all entity types and relationships that are not relevant to these processes or information needs. (The inclusion of two entity types should not force every relationship between the two entity types to be included.)

This gives us a **model subset**, which can be presented to one or more users. This can then be repeated for different groups of business processes or information needs. Not every user will necessarily be interested in every subset, but each subset should be of interest to at least one user, and each entity type should be included in at least one subset. Because of the way the subsets are defined, they will almost certainly overlap; indeed there may be a few entity types that appear in every subset. This approach therefore differs from that of Feldman and Miller, whose model clusters are not allowed to overlap.[22] This appears to be an arbitrary and inconvenient restriction.

Of course, the model presented to users need not be static. One widely used technique is to perform an accelerated development of the model in front of the users, starting with a few boxes and lines and progressing to a more complex picture.

Denormalize model

Other transformations on the entity–relationship model are also possible, and often desirable. They may be regarded as compromises on the pure, global, integrated, 'fully normalized' data model that is the goal of the data modeller and the data administrator, but they should be acceptable even to such purists, provided that they are for presentation purposes only, that they are properly controlled, and the compromised models properly mapped back to the pure, global, etc., model. I refer to all such transformations as denormalization, although strictly this title only applies to some of them.

1. Repeating groups, intersection entities and classification: everyone knows that repeating groups are anathema to the dedicated modeller. For example, an invoice, which may have many lines, may be represented as two entity types INVOICE and INVOICE ITEM. Similarly, many-to-many relationships often hide information, which requires an intersection entity type to resolve. However, for presentation purposes, such technical niceties often make the diagram more complicated. Within a given model subset, therefore, it is worth asking whether all repeating groups have to be broken down and normalized, or whether it would be more accessible to users if some of this structure was hidden.

    Attributes that classify or categorize entities are commonly pulled out into separate entity types. Thus CUSTOMER may be related to CUSTOMER CATEGORY. This entity type may be hidden in a subset (i.e. represented merely as an attribute) only if the allocation of customers to categories is clear, unique and non-contentious. However, if the customer can be categorized in several different ways, if the categorization is strategic to the business, or if there is any doubt about the consistency of this categorization, then it should be shown explicitly.

2. History, geography and audit: A complete information model may need somehow to represent time, which always introduces some complexity. A model may be easier to understand if the past and the future are excluded, and all information is understood in the present tense. Not every subset needs to show time explicitly. Accountants may fix time periods to which financially significant events (e.g. payments, stock movements) are allocated. However, to show an entity type ACCOUNTS PERIOD in each subset may be an unnecessary distraction. Similarly, it may be unnecessary, in a given subset, to relate every event to its LOCATION, to an ORGANIZATIONAL UNIT or COST CENTRE, and to the EMPLOYEE who authorizes it. Instead, this information may be shown to the users as if attributes of EVENT.

3. Different levels of abstraction: the users responsible for purchasing or personnel will see no similarity at all between the entity types SUPPLIER and EMPLOYEE, while the users responsible for making payments may see them as subtypes of a more general entity type called PAYEE. It may well make sense, therefore, to present different information models to the two groups of users.

    Information models for accounting purposes can always be expected to be more abstract than those for purposes elsewhere in the organization. This is because they are indirect models of the business, being in fact models of the accountants' models.

4. Derived information: the information model is a representation of information at its atomic level. But for most users, the atomic data are too small to be meaningful – their information needs are compounded from these atoms, sometimes in ways that they themselves do not understand. Thus they want to see preprocessed (i.e. derived) information shown in the models, rather than the raw unprocessed data. A technique for deriving these models, and for mapping them back to the main model, is described in Chapter 5.

Case examples[23]

Another technique for making information models more accessible is to provide worked examples or case studies, stepping the user through the occurrences of particular entity types, and examining their relationships to one another, and how they are transformed by particular processes. On some projects, libraries of case examples have been built up, each one named so that it can be referred to easily.

The danger of this method, however, is that a small number of typical or atypical cases may dominate the discussions, and other equally valid cases get ignored. This can lead to distorted models, and thereby to distorted systems designs. We have already discussed the difficulty in defining types and categories by pointing to examples. If this approach is adopted, it is essential to maintain the link at all times between the occurrences that are being described, and the entity types they are illustrating. Details should be avoided, in order to encourage generalization.

Prototypes can be placed into the same category, since a given prototype is a specific (and often partial) illustrative mechanism for a general business model. It is therefore important to make the business model, and its links to the prototype, explicit.

Coordinate reviews

Since we have several models (or at least, several model subsets) each describing a different area of the business, it will not be enough for each single model to be separately verified by one or more users. It will also be necessary to verify that the several models are simultaneously valid. Much of this verification can be done by information engineers, without burdening the users, particularly as the automated tools become more sophisticated, and able to handle more complex tie-ups between models. But the need will remain for some user participation in cross-model validation. In particular, the 'denormalizing' transformations must be valid for the business, as well as logically valid.

Establish trust

If the user is asked to trust the engineer in some areas but not in others, then s/he needs a very clear understanding of the boundary of trust. If the engineer wants trust, s/he must define it. Do not expect the user to 'take your word for it'. Most users now understand something about computers and computing, and many of them have used simple spreadsheet and database software on PCs. It is often difficult for them to understand why the information engineers insist on technical complexities.

The information modeller should respect the complexities of the user's business. Computing does not have a monopoly of arcane terminology and complicated machinery. If you expect to understand her job, allow her to understand yours. Be prepared to appear to bend the rules for the sake of the user. (But be careful – do not take risks with logic!)

Maintaining technical purity

The technical purist will object that this approach, although perhaps more user-friendly, may lead to an information model that cannot be implemented, or to a system that fails to have some important property. Information availability, data sharing, security, efficiency – these aspects of an information system are all ignored by the presentation approach.

Although it may be hoped to bring the technical specification and the user-friendly specification together into one document, such arguments suggest that this hope may remain unfulfilled, at least in the immediate future. In their framework for IS methodologies, the IFIP 8.1 working group explicitly allow for dual documentation: in their terminology there may be a **design product** which is technically pure, and a **user acceptor specification** which need not be.[24]

3.7.5 Impact of automation on the presentation of models

When information modelling was first practised, it was an entirely paper exercise. During the 1970s data dictionaries were developed, which enabled the definitions of entities, relationships and attributes to be captured. During the 1980s, analyst workbenches were developed, which enabled the entity–relationship diagrams to be drawn on a computer screen. During the late 1980s, CASE (computer assisted software engineering) tools became available, which would link the information modelling with the database generation.[25] With these tools, it is possible to maintain a much larger, more complex model than would be possible by hand.

Some automated CASE tools now give subsetting facilities. These are usually designed to allow analysis teams to be divided into subteams, so that each subteam can work on a portion of an information model on a different workstation at the same time. These subsetting facilities may not be designed for presentation purposes, but they can be so used or adapted. What is not yet widely available is the ability to define denormalized models for presentation purposes.

What is possible, on all CASE tools, is to define new models. Thus the information engineer may create information models for presentation purposes, and maintain manually the tie-up with the 'real' model. This practice will continue to grow, because it is at present the easiest way to satisfy the requirements of the methodology, and of the users.

3.7.6 Requirements documents

There is often a need to produce a report that will explain and communicate the business meaning of the information models produced by an analysis project, especially to top management, or to members of the wider business community who may not have the time to acquaint themselves with the concepts and notations of information models. There is also a need to maintain clear links between the models on the one hand, and the business benefits of development projects on the other, to enable effective project management and development coordination. This requires some sort of cross-reference between the business objectives and requirements, and the features or components of the information models.

A summary of the requirements can be presented as a table, with page references to more detailed description and analysis where appropriate:

1. The first column contains the business rules and constraints. Some readers of such a document may wish to read only this column.
2. The second column indicates briefly the data and process objects that have been used to represent the particular requirement. Complete definitions of these objects will of course be found in the information model. Extracts from the model definitions may be included in the requirements document.
3. The third column describes what is new about the requirement, and how the future business may differ from the present. This explains (and if possible quantifies) any business changes that are implied by the requirement.

Success measures will be defined and refined (in the third column) at the appropriate stage of analysis. At a later stage in the analysis, a fourth column may be added, to describe one or more design options, or to state the preferred or selected design option. Detailed cost–benefit analyses and other relevant data will be held as appendixes to the main requirements document, but will be referred to here.

The information model itself may be included as an appendix, drawn as a series of small subsets, each corresponding to one business objective, function or subject area, together with full or edited definitions. Diagrams and descriptions of the process model(s) may also be included.

3.7.7 Conclusions

A recent survey confirms the trend: 'Effective management of data as a corporate resource requires the participation of business managers.'[26] This participation, and especially the building of models, should be and frequently is a stimulating experience. Alexander reports similar fulfilment from users participating in architectural projects.[27]

If an information model is to be truly a tool for communicating an understanding of structure between users and information engineers, then it must be presented to the users in the most effective way possible. This may imply that the model takes on different forms and formats, other than the standard *n*th normal form that is most efficient for database design. It almost certainly implies that the model be presented in manageable chunks, rather than as an indigestible whole. More crucial than the form or format of the information model, however, is that the users understand what the model is supposed to say. If users are to confirm a model as a correct representation of their business, then they must appreciate how the model is going to be used, what it is for. Then they can develop *for themselves* appropriate criteria of acceptance. Otherwise, their reviews will probably be unfocused and irrelevant.

3.8 Reviewing quality of model

3.8.1 Introduction

In this section, we consider approaches and techniques for reviewing the quality of an information model. An inspection process may consider the structure of the model, and may test it for its ability correctly to represent all present and most future possibilities. Stability analysis considers the ability of the model to absorb likely future requirements without excessive difficulty.

3.8.2 Validation criteria

Complexity and adequacy

Table 3.4 Validation criteria

	True, adequate	False, inadequate
Simple, elegant		
Complicated, clumsy		

Which is the best model? Which is the best place to be on the matrix in Table 3.4? Top left, of course! But which is the next best place to be? Bottom left is better than top right.

Entity types

As we stated at the beginning of Chapter 2 'Concepts of information modelling', there are certain conditions that a class of things must fulfil, to be allowed as an entity type within the model. Now that we have introduced the concepts and terminology of entities, relationships and attributes, we are able to restate and explore these conditions:

1. There must be a clear boundary between the occurrences of the entity type, and the rest of the universe. In other words, if EMPLOYEE is to be an entity type, there must be no ambiguity as to who should count as an employee and who not.
2. The things that we are interested in *about* the entities must be reasonably alike, which then gives some structure to the entity type. We can define this structure in terms of the attributes of the entity type, and the relationships between the entity type and other entity types. Thus we can restate this condition as saying that the occurrences of the entity type are to have more or less the same attributes and relationships.
3. The entity occurrences must be identifiable in a standard way, and countable.[28] Countability is a consequence of identifiability – if you want to know how many entities of a particular type you have got, you have to be able to avoid counting one entity twice.
4. The number of occurrences of the entity type must be finite. This is because the method is pragmatic – infinite models may be theoretically interesting, but are of no practical value.
5. The entity occurrences must play similar roles in the business or organization. It is likely that a common set of business processes are associated with a single entity type.
6. The entity type must represent a single business concept. (In Chapter 2, we saw examples of **two-faced** entity types that failed to satisfy this criterion.)

Relationships and attributes

1. An attribute can belong to only one entity type. Thus two attributes, with perhaps the same name, but apparently belonging to different entity types, should be examined to discover whether they are in fact the same attribute (although it is not always a trivial matter to determine this).
2. An attribute can only exist once. Thus two similar attributes belonging to the same entity type. for example, STOCK LEVEL and INVENTORY QUANTITY should be examined to discover whether they are in fact the same attribute, under two different names. (Note: it is not enough for the two attributes always to have the same values.[29])

Finite knowledge

Here is an example of how the need for a finite model may affect the definitions of entity types and relationships. Suppose we have a many-to-many involuted relationship on PERSON, indicating that one person is a parent of another, as in Figure 3.3. Not everyone has children, so the relationship must be optional downwards. But everyone has two parents, so it would seem appropriate to make the relationship mandatory upwards. But although this conforms to biological theory, it does not correspond to what we know (or are capable of knowing). Not everyone has two **known** parents. Even if A knows that B was

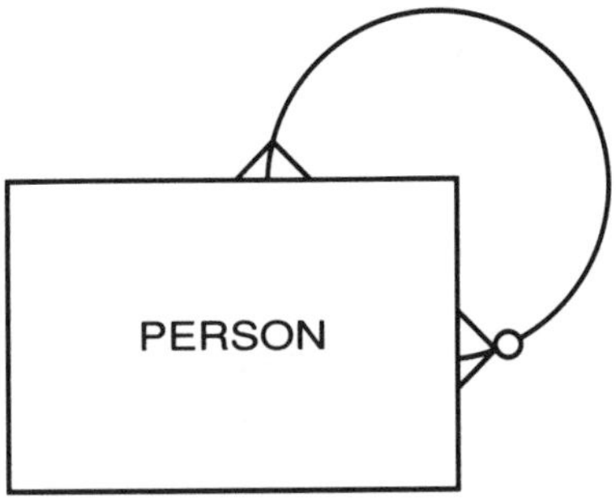

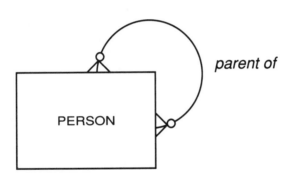

Figure 3.3 Many-to-many involuted relationship

parent of

PERSON

his ancestor, and B knew that C was his ancestor, it doesn't follow that anyone now can trace the line of descent from C to A. If you try to make the relationship mandatory, you cannot stop anywhere, you have to go all the way back to the apes (or angels, if you prefer). If you want to stop somewhere, then the first person in your model does not have an ancestor in your model, so Figure 3.4 is more accurate.

Figure 3.4 Modified version of Figure 3.3

parent of

PERSON

This illustrates two general points: first, that a model has to be a finite subset of the real world. We can only cope with a finite number of occurrences of PERSON. This has the consequence that some concepts (such as the *parent of* relationship in this example) do not bear their common-sense meaning. Instead, the restrictions of the model impart a subtle difference to what the concept means and how it can be used.

And the second point is that an information model, although it is not limited to what we happen to know already, is limited to what it is possible for us to know. (We may have to make some practical rules about the level of certainty that we require, to accept something as knowledge.)

3.8.3 Test cases

Introduction

This section contains guidelines for the critical review of an information model. It will be relevant to those performing quality inspections on entity–relationship models produced for strategic planning, analysis, or any other purpose. Although models for different purposes, at different stages of the systems development lifecycle, carry different expectations about the level of detail and the level of abstraction, similar principles and methods apply.

This may seem to beg the question of whether quality assurance is best served by external experts carrying out quality inspections. By external here we mean external to the modelling team, thus a person who was not involved in building the model. External inspections can be carried out by employees of the same company, while a consultant who played a significant role in the project is perceived to have played such a role and is therefore implicated in any weaknesses, is not external in this sense.

External inspections inevitably create an air of tension. It is never easy (although important) for the inspector to phrase criticisms in a positive way, to avoid irritating the modelling team. And it is not easy for the modelling team to remain cheerful and positive while its hard work is taken apart. If the inspections are to be carried out by such external inspectors, therefore, we can expect the modelling team to become defensive and the inspectors to become adversarial.

Full-time inspectors tend towards one of two possible demeanours: a fixed joviality or an unshakeable gloom. For this reason, it may be healthier to have part-time inspectors, who perform an occasional inspection interspersed with other activities, rather than professional critics. For the inspections to be successful, it may even be necessary for the focus of the inspection not to be predictable by the modelling team, lest it be possible to deliberately hide the dodgy parts of the model from the inspector. A degree of idiosyncrasy on the part of the inspector may therefore be worth cultivating. And if a mode is to be inspected several times during the project, there may be as much benefit in having a different inspector each time (who will uncover different problems) as keeping the same inspector (who will become familiar with the model).

Internal inspections, where the team itself carries out a structured walk through, may avoid some of the confrontation of external inspections, but despite this they may be less effective.

But it is not our intention here to analyse the psychology of criticism in detail, nor to prescribe managerial and motivational techniques for making one's criticism more palatable. Our intention here is merely to provide techniques for spotting potential weaknesses in an information model.

Reading and critiquing models

Many people find it very difficult to be objective about a model that they have not participated in building. They critique it by comparing it with the model they would have built themselves. This is a disastrous technique, and usually leads to complete rejection of the model by the inspectors, and complete rejection of the inspection by the modellers.

A much better technique is to try to understand what the model is saying. What would reality be like, if the model were true? What would the implications be? Is the model internally consistent? Thus, instead of going in heavy with both boots: 'Well, I wouldn't have done it like that, oh no. This bit is obviously redundant, and what on earth do you need that bit for?', the inspector should be able to achieve just as much with a softer approach: 'Gosh, you see the enterprise in much more complex detail than I do. I'd never have thought you'd need this bit. And to be honest, I'm still having difficulty working out what you are going to do with that bit.'

Entity definitions

As stressed previously, an entity definition should state two things clearly: a **membership rule** and an **identity rule**:

1. The membership rule defines when something counts as an occurrence of the entity type. For example, does the entity type EMPLOYEE include or exclude recruits, pensioners, free-lancers, women on maternity leave?
2. The identity rule defines when two things count as the same occurrence of the entity type, or where one occurrence stops and the next one starts. For example, does the A40 count as one occurrence of ROAD or several? Does the journey from London to Oxford count as the same ROUTE as the journey from Oxford to London? Does the journey from London to Oxford by train count as the same ROUTE as the journey from London to Oxford by road?

You need both the membership rule and an identity rule in order to count the occurrences of an entity type. Thus the ability to count occurrences is a good test of these rules. But the mere fact that the modelling team has estimated the volume of occurrences is not proof that their definitions are perfect.

To test the definitions, you have to come up with test cases. A test case for an entity type definition will be in the form of a candidate entity occurrence (i.e. an entity that may or may not be one or more occurrences of the entity type). A given entity may be a test case for more than one entity type – in other words, it may not be clear whether it is an occurrence of one entity type or another or perhaps even both.

A further criterion that a definition must satisfy is that the number of occurrences must be finite. For example, the entity type GEOGRAPHICAL AREA could have been defined as any continuous area of land. Or the entity type BLEND could have been defined as any possible mixture of raw materials, in any proportions. These definitions would not work, because there would be infinitely many occurrences. The business cannot be interested in an infinity of things. Even with finite sets, it is possible to define an entity type with an unmanageably large number of occurrences. For example, the entity type HUMAN GROUP could have been defined as any combination of living human beings. (This is a finite number: 2^n-1, where n is the number of living human beings. Such large numbers are effectively useless.) There must be some manageably finite subset in which the business is actually interested; thus what is often needed is some restriction on the definition, to identify this finite subset.

Model test procedure

The procedure is then as follows.

1. The inspector generates a test case.
2. The modelling team then says which entity type(s) the test case belongs to, and whether it counts as one occurrence or several.
3. If the modelling team shows uncertainty or disagreement, then this suggests that the test case has not been considered before. It may then be worth following the test case through the rest of the business model – are the relationships and attributes optional or mandatory, are the processes valid?
4. Even if the modelling team shows no uncertainty or disagreement, the answer should be compared with the definitions. If the definition is too simplistic or too vague, then it should be revised/expanded. It is always worth adding good test cases as examples.
5. If the modelling team claims that the test case is entirely outside the scope of their model, this should be documented and notified to development coordination. If the modelling team asserts or guesses that the test case has been covered in a different business area, then this should be checked against the model of that area.

Generating test cases

There is a problem here. How does the inspector generate the test case in the first place? Familiarity with the industry or function certainly helps, but is not absolutely essential. Here are some suggestions:

1. Look for entities playing several roles simultaneously. For example, subcontractors acting both as ORGANIZATIONAL UNIT and as SUPPLIER.
2. Look for the beginning and end of the entity lifecycle. What about people before they are employed, after they are employed? Are they covered in the entity type definition? Do they contradict the relationship and attribute properties?
3. Pay attention to the abstract entity types. Are their identifiers meaningful? Would you know where one occurrence stopped and the next one started? Is this clear from the definition?
4. Actual performance is likely to be compared with plans, budgets, forecasts, actual performance elsewhere.
5. Time and place are always difficult areas. Consider whether the model has established a sufficiently general and powerful set of concepts.
6. What are the obvious information needs for management and control of the area? How are these supported by the model?

Relationship and attribute definitions

The inspector must also examine the definitions of relationships and attributes, especially those where the meaning is not obvious from the name.

*   Every attribute called SOMETHING TYPE or SOMETHING CATEGORY needs to be defined. If there is a set of permitted values (as for example with SOMETHING STATUS) these may also need to be defined.
*   The definition of an attribute of an entity type should make it possible to state the value of the attribute for any given occurrence of the entity type.
*   The definition of a relationship between two entity types should make it possible to state, for any given occurrence of one entity type, which (if any) occurrences of the other it is paired with.

A test case for an attribute definition is therefore an entity occurrence (possibly hypothetical). The question then is what the value of the attribute for this entity would be. If the answer is unclear, if the attribute could take several values, or a value outside the defined domain, or (for a mandatory attribute) no value at all, then the attribute is problematic.

For example, consider an attribute that depends on a subjective assessment of the entity. Even for a well-known occurrence of the entity type, everybody might differ as to the value of that attribute. You could consider replacing the subjective assessment with a more objective measurement. The trouble with subjective judgements is precisely that there can be several of them, by different people at different times. If it is necessary to retain such a subjective judgement in the model, then either make it clear in the attribute definition *whose* judgement is to be captured, or define a separate entity type called, say, JUDGEMENT or ASSESSMENT.

A test case for a relationship definition is also an entity occurrence (also possibly hypothetical). The question then is what is paired with this entity under this relationship. If the answer is unclear, or if the answer conflicts with the properties of the relationship, then the relationship is problematic. For example, there might be a relationship between POLICY and PLAN, called *influences*. How do you define which policies influence which plans? Perhaps all policies influence all plans to some extent, so it is not a useful relationship. You should explore the plans influenced by a given policy, or the policies influencing a given plan, to discover what information really needs to be modelled.

Strategy versus detail

What is the difference between reviewing a strategic information architecture and an information model for analysis purposes? Should the same standards apply? Some might argue that the above procedures are too pedantic for strategic models. It all depends on what you think the strategic information architecture is for, and what the consequences are of getting it wrong.

The point of a strategic information architecture, in my view, is to identify opportunities for generalization and abstraction, so that analysis projects can be given clear and minimally overlapping scope. This means that the definitions of the major entity types should be thought out fairly thoroughly. Even if the entity type has no formal identifier, it should at least have an identifying strategy. (In other words, some thought needs to have been given to the kind of identifier that would be appropriate.) However, the relationships and attributes need not be defined in detail.

We could give many examples of inadequate thought during the strategic planning phase, causing serious problems for subsequent projects. Here is just one example. In the oil business, petrol is sold, not directly to motorists but to petrol stations. Some departments refer to the petrol station as the customer, while others refer to the motorist as the customer. In one oil company's information architecture, however, there was a major entity type CUSTOMER, completely overlooking this ambiguity. This caused problems for several development projects, and for development coordination. Such homonymy was too broad to be sorted out within the information model of a single business area, and should have been addressed at a strategic level.

Permutations and combinations

Where we have entity subtypes, or attributes with a small finite number of possible values, we can generate all the permutations of these values or subtypes, to check that we have considered every combination. A useful, albeit primitive, tool for doing this is to create a strip of card for each attribute (including the classifying attributes for subtypes). Onto each strip you write the possible values. Then the strips are placed parallel on the table, and slid up and down, to generate test cases. (Figure 3.5.)

Figure 3.5 Attribute permutations

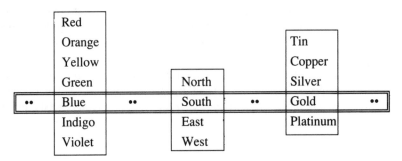

This technique can also be used to generate test data.

Conclusion

An information model develops through a dialectical process of example and counter-example. An external inspector contributes to this, with test cases against the model, and at the same time can assess the overall quality of the model by its ability to absorb such test cases. But our method is not dependent on external inspection; it is equally open to the modelling team, and to consultants attached to the team, to generate these test cases.

But the generation of such test cases is an art, not a science. There is no mechanical way of producing them. Their production requires a mixture of relevant experience, abstract models (e.g. general models of marketing intelligence, or of management control) and intuition.

3.8.4 Analysing stability of model

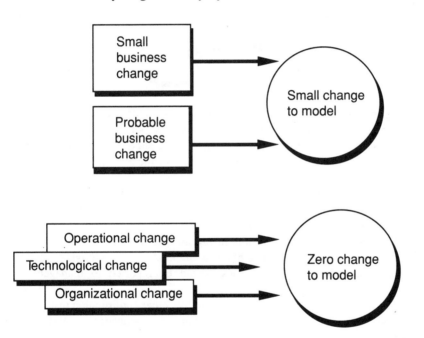

Figure 3.6 Desired quality of model

Figure 3.6 shows ideal model **stability** parameter. Stability means the ability to absorb shocks and turbulence. A stable model is one that will not require undue future modification – the maintenance should have a damping rather than an amplifying effect. Thus the goal of stability analysis is to confirm that small business changes will result at most in small changes to the model. (Some business changes may require no changes to the model at all, but this is not always possible, and should not be expected.)

The business model should be free of technological or procedural issues, and should be independent of the organization structure and division of responsibilities between departments. Thus any such changes should not require any changes to the model. For example, if a process assumes payment by cheque, then the model will be invalidated by a shift to electronic funds transfer.

Figure 3.7 Stability
analysis

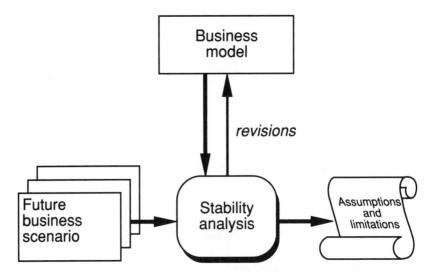

Figure 3.7 shows how stability analysis works. Future business scenarios are
constructed, e.g. possible changes in business policies and rules, possible
changes in the environment (including hypothetical legislation). These are
compared against the business model, to see how the business model could cope
with them.

We also need to assess the probability of each scenario. It may be worth
modifying the model to anticipate some of the more likely scenarios. It will be
impossible to anticipate all possible scenarios (i.e. catering for them in advance).
Stability analysis therefore results in revisions to the business model, but also
serves to clarify (i.e. make visible) the assumptions and limitations of the model.
These assumptions and limitations should be reported to management for
planning purposes.

But of course, like modelling itself, and like other confirmation tasks, stability
analysis is an infinite-discovery rather than a finite-construction task. In other
words, however much you do, you could always do a bit more, perhaps there is
an important fact still lurking undiscovered. Deciding when to stop is a
management judgement rather than a technical judgement.

Modelling the future

There is a trade off between flexibility and rationality – adaptation to present
requirements possibly impairs adaptability to future requirements. There is a
timing issue, about possible future requirements, either in function or
performance. If something is not required now, but may possibly be required in
the future, do you model it? In other words, do you complicate your model now
to make some modifications easier, e.g. to anticipate growth in data volumes?

To make these judgements, you need to understand what the modification cost
might be. With relational databases, especially with modern CASE tools, it is

easier to add new objects to a model than to alter the meaning or integrity conditions of existing objects. (With pre-relational databases, the opposite was true.) You also need to know how likely the future requirement is, how soon it may be required, and how clearly it can be specified. (If it is unlikely, distant or vague, forget it.)

Implementation and organizational learning

It is often part of the business strategy to introduce more systematic thinking about some aspect of management. Information systems (IS) development is deliberately used by senior management to educate middle and junior managers, and to force the organization as a whole to learn new concepts and practices. This has been used to introduce such concepts as project management, quality and cost control. An information systems methodology is used, not just to support changes in the way the organization works, but to encourage these changes.

Now this implies a period of organizational learning, while the business users gradually introduce more sophisticated and accurate measures, e.g. of performance and costs. The new information systems will enable these changes, but they cannot assume the changes have already been made. It would be wrong to make the completion of these changes a precondition for the implementation of the information system.

The information system does not have to automate the changes themselves. The change processes may be carried out by manual *ad hoc* procedures. But to design a good information system, that will enable the business to make the necessary/desired changes as smoothly as possible, the change processes should at least be understood, which means they must appear in the business model from which the information system is to be designed. Thus we must distinguish carefully between user-driven change and IS-driven change, in the context of our stability analysis: see Table 3.5.

Table 3.5 Different types of change

User-driven change	IS-driven change
Business uses new concepts	Business uses old concepts
Old system uses old concepts	New system introduces new concepts
New system catches up with business	But new system must also
Users can abandon old concepts quickly	support old concepts during user transition

Parallel information structures – options

You can always find some level of abstraction at which the old and new concepts are equivalent. This follows from the fact that we can, after all, replace one with the other. So there is a temptation to lump the old concept and the new concept into a single entity type or structure. But this is usually inadvisable. This is like saying 'we don't need to build a bridge across this river, because if you go far enough upstream, you can wade across'. If the new concepts differ from the old concepts only in degree, then it may well make sense to have a common information structure. But if the concepts differ in kind, then you risk confusing not only users but also IS staff, if you mix them up.

Example: we already have a concept of STANDARD COST, but it is too broad, it is calculated as an average of too many dissimilar events. We want to replace it with a more focused concept of STANDARD COST, where we pick a set of similar events and calculate an average. In this example, the concept of STANDARD COST arguably differs only in degree – we want to calculate it more precisely, and associate it with a smaller subclass of events. However, this subclass itself is probably a new concept, and requires a new process to create/ delineate it.

But for a substantial transition period, many of the occurrences of STANDARD COST will still be the old, unfocused values. One option is to leave these values outside the database, to be processed manually. (IS staff like this solution, because it simplifies their job, and they believe it gives the users an incentive to accelerate the transition to the new concepts.) Another option is to capture the unfocused values in the database, and provide some limited support for processing and using them. (User management like this solution, because it at least collects all the data in the same place, and enables the progress to the new concepts to be controlled. There usually needs to be some way of distinguishing the focused values from the unfocused ones.)

3.9 Conclusion

In this chapter, we have examined several techniques for building a model, and building upon a model. It is as important to acquire the skills in reading and interpreting existing models, as to acquire skills in building new models from scratch. We have considered some of the angles from which a model can be reviewed: we have offered techniques focused on the past and present, such as the creation of test cases, and we have offered techniques focused on the future, such as stability analysis. The aim is to produce a good model, as simple and elegant as possible without losing sight of the purpose. 'See simplicity – and distrust it.'[30]

Notes

1. M. J. Kirton, 'Adaptors and innovators: – why new initiatives get blocked', *Long-Range Planning*, vol. 17, no. 2, 1984, pp.137–43.
2. Genie Z. Laborde, *Influencing with Integrity*, (Syntony, Palo Alto, 1987, Chapter 5.
3. *Ibid*, p. 101.
4. William Olle J. Hagelstein, I. G. Macdonald, C. Rolland, H. G. Sol, F. J. M., van Asche and A. A. Verrijn-Stuart. *Information Systems Methodologies: A framework for understanding*, Addison-Wesley, Wokingham, UK, 1988.
5. Feature analysis was originally developed for use in psychotherapy, to allow a therapist to work out the structure of a client's beliefs.

6. This game, containing miscellaneous words and images to prompt lateral thinking, is marketed under the name ThinkLinks. However, when modelling a specific situation, blank cards should be used, so that the words written on them can be chosen to clarify that situation.

7. This section leans heavily on Timothy Williamson, *Identity and Discrimination* Basil Blackwell, Oxford, 1990.

8. W. V. Quine, *Word and Object*, MIT Press, 1960, Cambridge, MA, p. 29.

9. A. Kronfeld, *Reference and Computation*, Cambridge University Press, Cambridge, 1990.

10. J.-L. Borges, *Other Inquisitions 1937–1952* (translated by Ruth, L. C. Simms), University of Texas Press, TX, 1965.

11. Plutarch, 'The E at Delphi', in *Moralia*, translated by Frank Cole Babbitt, Cambridge, Mass, Harvard University Press, 1962, pp. 241–3.

12. M. Dummett, *Frege: Philosophy of language* Duckworth, London, 1973.

13. T. Williamson, *Identity and Discrimination*, Basil Blackwell, Oxford, 1990.

14. See F. Land, 'Organizational problems of implementing a distributed system' published in Infotech State-of-the-Art Report, *Managing the Distribution of DP*, vol. 6, *Invited Papers*, 1979.

15. R. Veryard, 'The role of visibility in systems' *Human Systems Management*, 6, 1986 pp. 167–75.

16. P. Levinson, 'Impact of personal information technologies on American education, interpersonal relations and business, 1985–2010, in Paul T. Durbin, *Technology and Contemporary Life* (D. Reidel, Dordrecht, 1988) pp. 177–91.

17. K. Robins and F. Webster, 'Athens without slaves … or slaves without Athens' Vol. 1, *Science as Culture*, **3**, 1988 pp. 7–53; D. Noble, *Forces of Production: A social history of industrial automation* (New York, Knopf, New York, 1984.

18. A. Jay, *Effective Presentation*, Management Publications Ltd, London, 1971 p. 5.

19. G. Bateson, *Steps to an Ecology of Mind,* Paladin, Frogmore, St. Albans, 1973, pp. 128–9.

20. For a more detailed analysis of these problems, see L. Bhabuta, 'Balancing system and organizational needs: User involvement in requirements analysis', UNICOM Conference 'Participation in Systems Design', London Business School, 7–8 April 1987.

21. Some of the material in this section is taken from Veryard, *op. cit.*

22. P. Feldman and D. Miller, 'Entity model clustering: structuring a data model by abstraction' *Computer Journal*, vol. 29, No. 4, 1986, pp. 348–60.

23. 'Hard cases make bad law', as the politician learns to his cost: Yet just is the artist's reproach–'Who generalizes is lost' (W. H. Auden).

24. T. W. Olle, J. Hagelstein, I. G. Macdonald, C. Rolland, H. G. Sol, F. M. van Asche and A. A. Verrijn-Stuart, *Information Systems Methodologies: A framework for understanding,* Addison-Wesley, Wokingham, UK, 1988.

25. See, for example Texas Instruments, *A Guide to Information Engineering using the IEF*™ Texas Instruments, Plano, 1988.

26. D. L. Goodhue, J. A. Quillard and J. F. Rockart, 'Managing the data resource: a contingency approach', *MIS Quarterly*, September, 1988, pp. 372–92.

27. C. Alexander, *The Timeless Way of Building*, Oxford University Press, New York, 1979, p. 453.

28. I use the term 'countable' here in a practical sense, namely the physical possibility of counting, rather than in the mathematical sense of a (possibly infinite) mapping to the natural numbers.

29. This is pointed out by W. V. O. Quine, in his essay on the individuation of attributes, in *Theories and Things*, Belknap Press, Harvard, 1981.

30. Alfred North Whitehead.

4   Reader exercises and solution hints

These questions and answers are written with more than one purpose. First, of course, they give the reader opportunities to test his/her understanding of the book so far, and to develop the skills of information modelling. The reader may therefore wish to spend some time thinking about the questions, before looking at the answers. Second, they give the teacher templates, from which to develop further questions and answers. Third, they give the author the opportunity to repeat and illustrate some of the concepts and techniques introduced in the previous chapters. (Thus, although there are no new concepts or techniques in this chapter, there may be a few new details.)

1. *Suggest at least three possible definitions for the entity type* MEAL *when modelling a restaurant. Discuss the implications of each definition:*

   (a)   That which is eaten by a single diner at a single sitting.
   (b)   That which is eaten by a group of diners at the same table at a single sitting.
   (c)   That which is ordered at one time from the waiter.
   (d)   That which is paid for together.

   Remember that food can be ordered but not eaten, or eaten but not paid for. Remember that some people may order (or even finish) their food before their friends have arrived. The number of meals eaten per day depends how these facts are accounted for in the definition of MEAL. Therefore, if the restaurant manager wants to know how many meals were served in a given day, the answer depends which definition of MEAL he is interested in, which depends in turn on what he needs the information for.

2. *Suggest at least two different ways of distinguishing between debit transactions and credit transactions. If they are subtypes of a general entity type, suggest a name for this entity type.*

   One way is to have a TRANSACTION TYPE attribute, set to 'DB' for debits and 'CR' for credits. Another way is to have TRANSACTION AMOUNT taking both positive and negative values, for debits and credits respectively. The entity type is presumably TRANSACTION.

3. *Suggest at least two different ways of distinguishing between full-time employees, part-time employees, casual workers and contractors. If they are subtypes of a general entity type, suggest a name for this entity type.*

One way is to have an EMPLOYEE STATUS attribute, with four possible values, corresponding to the four subtypes. (Remember: it is not necessary during analysis to abbreviate the attribute. It is a question for systems design, whether and how to reduce the attribute to a 1-character or 2-character field.) Another way is to relate each EMPLOYEE to several occurrences of CONTRACT TERMS, and deduce the subtype from the attributes of the latter entity type. The entity type may be called EMPLOYEE, provided this will not cause confusion. But if casual and contract labour is not commonly understood to count as employees, and if the analysts are not prepared to change this understanding, a more general word must be used, such as WORKER.

4. *What is the entity lifecycle of a library book?*

First we must resolve the ambiguity in the question. A library may have several copies of the same title. The term library book may refer to either book copies or book titles. A reservation relates to the book title, rather than the book copy, while a loan relates to the book copy rather than the book title. It is important to keep the entity state analysis for the two entity types separate, so do not include *reserved* as a state in the life of a book copy, and do not include *awaiting rebinding* as a state in the life of a book title.

(a) *Which is more important – book copy or book title?*

It depends on the purpose of the model. Consider some information needs. Why, for example, might you want to know how many books this library has?
(i)   in order to estimate the required shelving space – BOOK COPY;
(ii) in order to compare the coverage with other libraries – BOOK TITLE.

5. *Decide which attributes belong to which entity type in the model in Figure 4.1.*

Figure 4.1 Model of part of a hospital

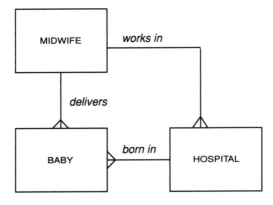

- *Name of mother*
- *Length of experience*
- *Number of beds*
- *Ward name*
- *Weight*
- *Location*

Name of mother, ward name and weight are attributes of the baby; length of experience is an attribute of the midwife; location and number of beds is an attribute of the hospital. However, it could be argued that the mother and the ward should both be represented as additional entity types, rather than having their names included as attributes of the baby.

6. *In a model for a theatrical casting agency, there are two entity types: actor and character. Each actor has the potential to portray those characters that are the same sex and roughly in the same age range. (In other words, a given 20-year-old actress can play Ophelia but not Lady Bracknell.) Think of some alternative ways of modelling this relationship between actor and character.*

Define an attribute of CHARACTER, called NOTIONAL AGE, as the normal age that an actor should appear when playing the part, and compare this with the actual age of the actor. The trouble with this model is that an exact match is probably rare between the age of the actor and the age of the character.

As above, but allowing the age of the actor to differ from the notional age of the character by up to ten years. The trouble with *this* model is that, just as different singers can sing a different range of notes, so different actors can portray a different range of character ages. (Thus while some 25-year-old actresses can plausibly portray teenagers, others cannot.)

Define an attribute of CHARACTER, called NOTIONAL AGE, as the normal age that an actor should appear when playing the part. Then define two attributes of ACTOR, called LOWER AGE and UPPER AGE, which are the minimum and maximum ages that the actor can appear, with the appropriate make up. Then an actor has the potential to play a given character, if the notional age of the character is within the LOWER AGE → UPPER AGE range of the actor. The trouble with *this* model is that in some plays the character is supposed visibly to age from one act to another.

Define two attributes of CHARACTER, called YOUNGEST AGE and OLDEST AGE, which indicate the age range that an actor will be called upon to portray in the character, during the whole play. This age range should be within the age range that the actor is capable of. The trouble with *this* model is that in some plays, a character appears as a child, as a young man, and as an old man. Sometimes it is impossible to portray the character with a single actor; sometimes a child actor is required to play the character's early years while an adult actor plays the rest.

Define the entity type CHARACTER, so that the child is not the same as the man, despite having the same name, and having a notional (albeit fictional) continuity.

A more complex model might recognize that the NOTIONAL AGE of a given character may depend on the perception of the director. In other words, in one production the director may want to portray Hamlet as a teenager, while in another production, a different director may want him portrayed as a 30-year-old man. Thus NOTIONAL AGE would be an attribute of an intersection entity CHARACTER BY DIRECTOR, rather than simply an attribute of CHARACTER.

Further complexities could easily be invented. The key question is: what goals would force the model to get more complex, or allow the model to get more simple?

7. *Employees receive a central London residence allowance in addition to their salary, if and only if their home telephone number starts with the central London prefix 071. How would this be modelled?*

The entity type EMPLOYEE could be divided into two subtypes, partitioned by the derived attribute HOME PHONE PREFIX, or by the function {if HOME PHONE = '071...' then LONDON else COUNTRY}

8. *Consider the following attributes of the entity type HOUSE.*
   (a). *ADDRESS;*
   (b). *MARKET VALUE;*
   (c). *RESIDENTS;*
   (d). *NUMBER OF ROOMS.*

What circumstances would force us to convert these attributes into separate entity types ?

(a) ADDRESS
     Can things other than houses have addresses? Is there any need to merge all addresses into a single entity type ADDRESS?

(b) MARKET VALUE
     Are we only interested in the present MARKET VALUE, or is there a succession of ever-increasing values, with different dates? Thus the same house can have more than one MARKET VALUE, over time. Different market values can also relate to different agents' assessments.

(c) RESIDENTS
     An attribute with a plural name is always going to arouse some suspicion. What possible values can this attribute have?
     • Yes
     • Three
     • John Smith, Jane Smythe and Thomas Anthony Smith-Smythe

     Whereas the first and second answers may permit RESIDENT to remain as an attribute, the third answer forces a new entity type RESIDENT. We remove it from the entity type HOUSE and introduce a new relationship between HOUSE and PERSON to represent residence. This may be a one-to-many relationship (each person lives in only one house); it may also be a many-to-many relationship (some people have second homes).

(d)   NUMBER OF ROOMS

The name of the attribute NUMBER OF ROOMS seems clear enough. But are we really only interested in the number of rooms, or do we need to distinguish bedrooms from reception rooms ? Do we need to know the size of the bathroom, or the fittings in the kitchen ? If so, we may need a separate entity type ROOM.

9.   *Consider the model in Figure 4.2, which depicts some aspects of property development.*

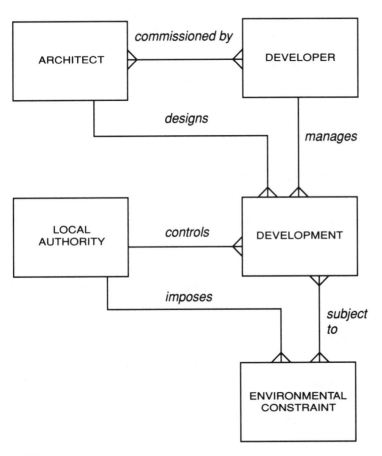

Figure 4.2 Some aspects of property development

(a)   *What assumptions would you have to make in order to remove as redundant either of the relationships* commissioned by *or* subject to? *How would you verify these assumptions?*

(b)   *Modify the model to allow for developments spanning the jurisdiction of more than one local authority.*

(c)   *Modify the model to allow for developments involving more than one firm of architects.*

(d)   *What happens if the local authority itself acts as developer?*

Many analysts would already have decomposed the relationship *commissioned by*, and introduced an intersection entity type COMMISSION. The redundancy of the relationship *commissioned by* now becomes a question of the equivalence of the entity types COMMISSION and DEVELOPMENT. Do all commissions result in developments? Are there other types of commission (e.g. surveys, interior designs) ?

The model shows that all environmental constraints are imposed by a local authority. Presumably this would be the same local authority as the one in whose jurisdiction the development falls. But if there was a hierarchy of local authorities, it could be that a given development is controlled by the district authority, but subject to constraints imposed by the regional authority.

If a large development spanned the jurisdiction of several local authorities, the crucial question would be whether all of the concerned authorities acted jointly, or whether each controlled separately that part of the development falling within its jurisdiction. In the former case, there would be a new entity type, such as LOCAL AUTHORITY SYNDICATE, representing the group of local authorities. The syndicate might have to reach a consensus about the constraints imposed on the development as a whole, which might not be the same as those imposed on developments entirely within the control of any single authority. In the latter case, the development would be divided into portions, such as DEVELOPMENT ZONE, each controlled by a single authority, and subject to different constraints.

Why would more than one firm of architects be involved? There are at least two possible reasons. One is that several proposals are commissioned, of which only one will be implemented. The other is that the development is to be spread across several firms, either because it is too large to entrust to a single firm, or because the developer wants a diversity of style. So we might have an entity type PROPOSAL, and/or an entity type DEVELOPMENT COMPONENT.

If the local authority acts as developer, it need not affect the model at all. The attributes and relationships of the two roles DEVELOPER and LOCAL AUTHORITY are different. Indeed, the two roles are likely to be represented by different departments within the local authority, to ensure the controls are properly exercised.

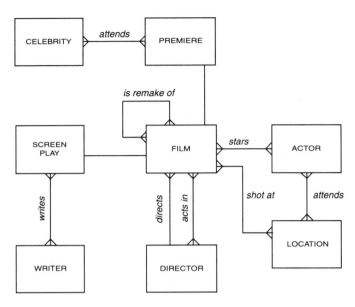

Figure 4.3 Model for a film studio

10. *Refine the model in Figure 4.3, which is for a film studio (e.g. Hollywood or Bombay).*

There are several problems with this model. First, there are several many-to-many relationships, and a few one-to-one relationships. Second, there are many overlaps between the entity types ACTOR, CELEBRITY, WRITER and DIRECTOR. (Consider Woody Allen or Raj Kapoor, who contribute in several ways to their own films, as well as appearing in the films of other directors.)

In Figure 4.4 PERSON now includes all contributors to a film, both in front of and behind the camera. It therefore lumps together the entity types ACTOR, DIRECTOR, WRITER, and CELEBRITY. ROLE corresponds to a line of credit – thus if a person both acts in and directs the same film, there will be two credits, and therefore two occurrences of ROLE. Actors who play several characters within the same film (such as Peter Sellers or Alec Guinness) will also have several credits, and therefore several occurrences of ROLE. Each SCENE requires the presence of several persons, playing particular roles, at a given location. Finally, the screenplay is either the plot, or the scene-by-scene shotlist; thus its attributes and relationships can be attached to the entity types FILM, SCENE or STORY.

Arguably, the arrangements for promoting the film (by circulating tickets to a première) are separate from the arrangements for making the film, and so the entity type TICKET should belong in a separate information model. But we have left it in anyway.

This model is an improvement in several ways. First, the many-to-many relationships have been resolved, and the overlaps removed. Second, the model is now more general, allowing everyone who contributes to a film to be included. And yet the number of entity types has not been increased.

Figure 4.4 Revised
model

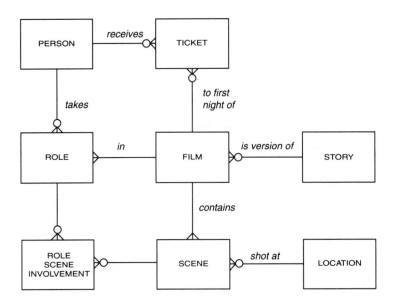

11. *Decompose these attributes of* PATIENT:
    (a) *PATIENT ALLERGIC TO PENICILLIN* (Y/N);
    (b) *PATIENT OPERATION DATE;*
    (c) *PATIENT DIAGNOSIS;*
    (d) *PATIENT UNDER MEDICATION;*
    (e) *PATIENT COMFORT* (ABLE)

An attribute such as PATIENT ALLERGIC TO PENICILLIN (Y/N) is **specific** because it specifies something (penicillin). Decompose into the relationship ALLERGIC TO, to the new entity type DRUG, or perhaps SUBSTANCE, of which penicillin is one occurrence.

An attribute such as PATIENT OPERATION DATE is **multi-valued** because a patient can have several operations on different days. This implies a need for an entity type OPERATION.

An attribute such as PATIENT DIAGNOSIS is **multi-valued** because several doctors may have different opinions. It is therefore multi-sourced, and requires an additional entity type DIAGNOSIS.

A status attribute such as PATIENT UNDER MEDICATION is **iterative** or **repeating**, because there may be several overlapping prescriptions. Thus the patient may be under medication twice at the same time. When one course of drugs is finished, it does not mean that the patient is no longer under medication, because he or she may still be taking other drugs.

A vague attribute such as PATIENT COMFORTABLE is **useless**, because it begs all sorts of questions. (Is there an adverb missing?)

12. *Imagine some counter-examples to the relationships in Figure 4.5. How would you find out whether these counter-examples existed? And how would you find out whether these counter-examples mattered?*

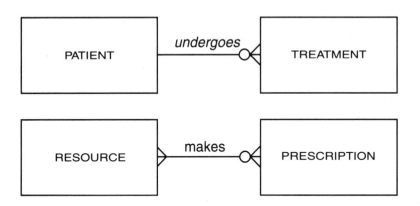

Figure 4.5
Patient–doctor
relationships

For patients undergoing treatment, consider group therapy. If several patients can undergo treatment in a common session, then this should perhaps be modelled as a single occurrence of TREATMENT rather than one per PATIENT. But what are the attributes of TREATMENT? Each PATIENT may have different objectives. Even if several patients are splashing around in the hospital swimming pool together with a physiotherapist, they are all there for different reasons, and so there may still be several occurrences of TREATMENT. But if the purpose of the model was to allocate resources (such as therapists, rooms, or other facilities) or to control costs, then a single occurrence of TREATMENT may be more appropriate. And if the model has to represent both concepts of treatment, then two different entity types, with two different names may be required, as in Figure 4.6.

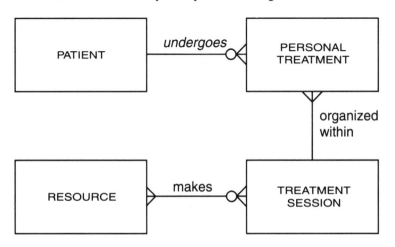

Figure 4.6 A revision of Figure 4.5

For doctors making prescriptions, consider second opinions. A patient may be reluctant to undergo some unpleasant chemotherapy on the say-so of a single doctor, or may ask for another doctor to confirm the dosage. What happens when the two (or more) doctors agree on the appropriate course of treatment for a given patient – is it the same occurrence of PRESCRIPTION, or two similar occurrences? Of course, you do not know in advance that the doctors will agree – if you did, then there would be no point asking for a second opinion.

The crucial question is: why do we care which doctor made a given prescription? Is it to assign credit or blame to the doctor according to the resulting change in the condition of the patient? Is it to find out which doctors are recommending the more expensive or risky drugs?

5 Modelling information needs[1]

In previous chapters we have described the building of an entity–relationship–attribute model, to describe the information structure of a business or business area. In this chapter, we discuss the analysis of information needs, and show how the information needs of the business (area) can be analysed top down and expressed by logical derivation from the information model. This can not only provide invaluable information to the database designer, but can also add quality and completeness to an inadequate information model. Furthermore, it provides a technique for extending data administration to full information resource management.

Most information modelling methods emphasize the need to test the information model, to check that it actually supports the business information needs. A standard approach is to 'navigate' around the information model as if it were a database. Our approach differs radically from this. Instead of starting from the basic data attributes (which can be regarded as the 'atoms' of information) and constructing the required information bottom up, we start from the business information needs themselves, which are to be derived from the basic data attributes, often in very complex ways, and analyse them top down until we have reached the basic, underived, underivable data, included in the information model itself. This process is illustrated in Figure 5.1

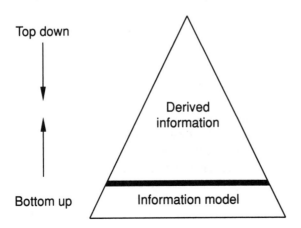

Figure 5.1 An information modelling model

The chapter is structured as follows. First we explain our approach, and we show by the use of simple examples how our approach works. We avoid a formal syntax, although it ought to be fairly straightforward to develop one, preferably one that can be easily implemented in an automated analyst workbench.[2] Then we briefly sketch two alternative approaches. Finally, we state what we believe to be the advantages of our approach over these alternatives, and what the implications of its adoption would be.

5.1 Need to describe information access

An entity–relationship–attribute model is a static description of the business. To obtain a dynamic description of the business, how it performs over time, we need to supplement the information model with a function or process model, which shows how the entities are transformed by the business processes. Then, in order that the information model be proved consistent with the process model(s), the information accesses required by each process must be shown to be fully supported by the structure defined in the information model.

Some details of these information accesses, including their logical structure and especially their frequencies, will be vital to the database designer, so that he or she can ensure a fast and efficient structure, with short-cuts where appropriate. (However, at least in our method, it will be for the database designer, and not the information modeller, to specify how information accesses are to be supported by a computer system, and what sequence of operations shall be used to navigate around the database.)

In addition to the information accesses required by the regular business processes, it is also necessary to explore whether the information model will support any general or *ad hoc* needs for information that the managers or other users may have, to the extent that these information needs can be predicted. (Analysis of the decisions made within the business area, and of the key performance measures, will help discover these information needs. Any paperwork currently used, including reports produced from existing computer systems, can be analysed to check that nothing has been left out.)

5.2 Automated support

As much of the analysis work as possible should be captured in an automated workbench or data dictionary, for use by both systems designers and users at all stages of development. It can prove invaluable for the management of management information systems (MIS), and for the creation of *ad hoc* reporting and analysis programs when the system is implemented (either by users themselves or by system professionals. (In some organizations, user access to information and information processing is promoted and supported by a group of systems professionals calling themselves an **information centre**.[3] Such an information centre will rely heavily on the documentation produced from the analysis described in this chapter.)

At the time of writing, no software product is yet commercially available that fully supports every type of information access described in this chapter, so the derivations and algorithms may need to be maintained manually, but this is a minor shortcoming which it is to be hoped that existing or future products will overcome. The author is aware of some promising research and development in this direction.

5.3 Method

A process involves two kinds of information access. First, to identify occurrences of various entity types (which may become READ operations in a database). Second, to amend the identified occurrences, and to establish new occurrences (which may become UPDATE, DELETE and CREATE operations in a database). As a check on the information model, we mainly need to verify that the identifications work; if they work, then the other accesses should also work. In addition to these process-driven information accesses, we need to analyse the information needs of the business. The technique described below caters for both.

The technique is as follows.[4] Start from an information model of the business area. State a particular information need as an information object, as if it were an object within the information model. It will usually be a derived attribute, or set of derived attributes. Define this object by derivation from one or more simpler objects. Define these objects in turn, and continue until all objects are fully derived from the basic entities, attributes and relationships of the information model itself. The intention is that all the required information shall be either contained in the information model or derived from it. The information model must therefore contain all underivable objects but need not contain any derivable ones. Any necessary object that cannot be derived from the model may have to be added to the model.

The syntax and semantics of the derivation logic are not formally defined in this book. We prefer to illustrate the idea by example.

5.4 Example: news archive information model

Let us suppose that a news archive, perhaps for a national newspaper, has been analysed, resulting in the following simple information model in Figure 5.2.

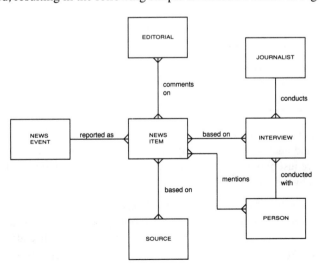

Figure 5.2 An information model of a news archive

In order to understand the examples, Figure 5.2 is not enough; you need some idea of what the names of the boxes are supposed to mean. Therefore the diagram needs to be supplemented by definitions of the entity types, given in Table 5.1. The table also shows some of the attributes belonging to each entity type.

This is a sketch of a model that for many purposes would not be detailed or precise enough. Furthermore, it fails to recognize many of the complexities of a real-life newspaper. However, for the purpose of demonstrating the information needs analysis, this sketch is adequate. (Remember: all models are produced for a purpose, which influences the level of detail. There is no standard level of detail, appropriate to every purpose.)

Table 5.1. Definitions of entity types in Figure 5.2

Entity type	Description	Attributes
JOURNALIST	A member of the newspaper staff, who conducts interviews and/or writes news items and/or editorials	NAME, SPECIALIZED SUBJECT, EXPERIENCE
PERSON	A public figure or other person mentioned in the news, or acting as contact for one or more journalists	NAME, TYPE OF PERSON, POSITION, ADDRESS, TELEPHONE, NAME OF PRESS OFFICER / AGENT / SECRETARY
INTERVIEW	A recorded discussion between a journalist (acting on behalf of this newspaper) and another person, on a given occasion, usually directed to a particular topic	DATE, PLACE, TOPICS COVERED, HOW RECORDED
SOURCE	A source of news other than direct interview, for example: Reuters news service, government press releases, etc.	TYPE OF SOURCE, LIBRARY ARCHIVE REFERENCE
NEWS ITEM	An article of news printed in a given edition of the newspaper on a given page, occupying so many words on a given news event	DATE PUBLISHED, NUMBER OF WORDS, HEADLINE, BYLINE
NEWS EVENT	A newsworthy story, perhaps running over several days, about which one or more news items may be published	TYPE OF EVENT, DESCRIPTION
EDITORIAL	A leading article may discuss the implications of several news items, usually of the same day's edition	DATE PUBLISHED, HEADLINE, NUMBER OF WORDS, NUMBER OF READERS' LETTERS PROVOKED

Let us imagine some information needs that the newspaper's editors or managers might have, and analyse how these information needs would be supported by the model we have just outlined. It may turn out that we can identify information needs not supported by the model, which could prompt us to revise and extend the model.

1. *Which journalists have interviewed the Minister of Education?*
   This question is about journalists. The entity type JOURNALIST has a derived attribute HAS-INTERVIEWED-THE-MINISTER-OF-EDUCATION. This attribute can be derived from the relationship HAS-INTERVIEWED <person>, as follows:

has-interviewed-X-WHERE X.POSITION = 'minister of education'
(X.POSITION means the job title of X or, more exactly, the value of the
attribute POSITION taken by the occurrence X.)

The *has-interviewed* relationship can then be derived from the existence of
an occurrence of INTERVIEW, which is both *conducted with* <person> and
conducted by <journalist>.

Note that the model supports the identification of the Minister of
Education as a person, rather than as a role. In other words, if there has been
a recent Cabinet reshuffle, interviews with the present Minister of Education
in his/her former job will be included, whereas interviews with the former
Minister of Education will not be included. This is because the information
model includes a PERSON (who may change jobs) rather than a JOB (which
may change job-holder). Continuity is always maintained through the entity
types in the information model. Note also that the model does not include any
interviews a journalist may have conducted before joining the paper. These
factors may or may not be relevant to the decision that the editor needs to
make, or to the situation that the editor needs to handle. Thus we have to
understand why the editor needs this particular information, in order to assess
whether the answer provided through the information model is adequate. Our
analysis may then lead us to revise and extend the information model.

But let us consider another example.

2. *Which journalists have interviewed soccer players?*

This question is also about journalists, but now instead of referring to a
single occurrence of PERSON, we refer to a single value of the attribute TYPE
OF PERSON. In the previous example we defined the derived relationship *has-
interviewed* <person>. We can use this derived relationship again. But
whereas in the previous example we ended up with a derived attribute
defined as follows:

has-interviewed-X-WHERE X.POSITION = 'minister of education'

this time we end up with a derived attribute defined as follows:

has-interviewed-X-WHERE X.TYPE-OF-PERSON = 'soccer player'.

Note that whereas there is only one Minister of Education, there are many
soccer players. This will be important to the systems designer using the
analysis results, and particularly to the database designer. But it should not
make a significant difference at this level; the structure of the two derived
attributes is broadly similar.

So far we have looked at simple derivation chains, where each object in the
chain is derived from the next object. And at the end of the chain, there is a data
object that is underived and underivable, included in the information model.
There is no theoretical limit to the length of the chain, although of course it must
be finite.

But to answer more complex questions, we need more than this. Instead of a
chain, we construct a tree. Here are some examples of this.

3. *Which journalists have interviewed any of the politicians mentioned in the coverage of this news event?*

We can divide the main problem into three simpler problems, which can be solved independently. The three parts of the solution can then be put together to solve the main problem. One part of the solution requires us to construct a derived relationship of the entity type PERSON called *mentioned-in-coverage-of* <news event>. Another part of the solution requires us to define the derived attribute IS-A-POLITICIAN of the entity type PERSON. And the derived relationship *has-interviewed* has already been discussed.

Figure 5.3 Access tree for question 3

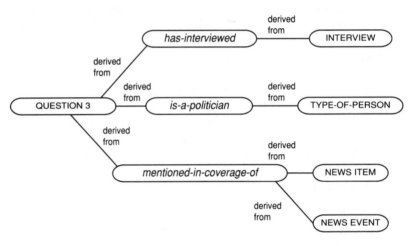

Thus, as we see from Figure 5.3, the information need expressed by question 3 is a derived attribute that is derived from three other derived data objects. We then separately define these three derived data objects from the information model. As we have seen before, each derived data object, once defined, can be reused. Thus it can contribute to satisfying several different information needs.

4. *Which journalists have interviewed any of the politicians mentioned in today's edition?*

Similar to the previous question, part of the solution here is for us to construct a derived attribute of the entity type PERSON called *mentioned-in-today's-edition*. Here we have a derived entity type, namely EDITION. An edition can be regarded as a collection of NEWS ITEMS with the same DATE PUBLISHED: see Figure 5.4.

5. *Which journalists worked on yesterday's edition?*

Again, this question can be divided into two parts: the derived entity type EDITION, and the derived relationship *worked-on*, between JOURNALIST and EDITION. The first we have dealt with above, but what of the second? What can we derive the relationship from? If we examine the entity–relationship diagram, we discover that the base information is missing. We know what interviews a journalist has done, but we do not know about the rest of the work: copytasting, fixing, writing, subediting, etc. The information model must be amended or extended, in order to support this information need. Perhaps we need a non-derived relationship PRODUCES between the entity types JOURNALIST and NEWS ITEM, added to the information model.

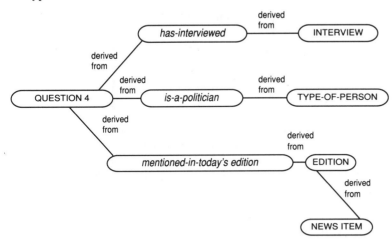

Figure 5.4 Access tree for question 4

So far, we have considered two types of information access: singular, in which attributes (or rather, attribute values) belong to a single occurrence of an entity type, and plural, in which attributes belong to several occurrences of the same entity type. In most programming languages, the plural ones are much more difficult to handle than the singular ones. Furthermore, it may be more difficult to design satisfactory screen and report layouts for the plural ones. But these are design issues, not analysis ones. In the analysis, the plural accesses are no more difficult to specify than the singular ones.

There remains a third type of information access: complex, in which attributes belong to occurrences of several entity types. These can be put together quite simply, as the sum of the accesses to the separate entity types. (Of course, this is not how a system would be designed, since there are usually ways of retrieving records from a database that require fewer physical database operations, but we must repeat that design considerations are irrelevant at the analysis stage.)

PC-based spreadsheets have accustomed managers to the notion that data can be presented as a two-dimensional matrix. This has infected some analysts, who try to analyse information needs as two-dimensional objects. For example, the editor might want to see how each journalist performed on different types of event. A system could be designed to display this as a simple table. But if the editor wanted to see how the performance of different journalists on different types of event varied over time, a more elaborate presentation would be required. Similarly, a sales manager often wants to see customer orders broken down by geographical region and customer type, as well as over time. Many business information needs, therefore, require a three-dimensional or larger matrix. But these are design issues, not analysis ones. It is outside the scope of this chapter to discuss how such matrixes can be most effectively manipulated and displayed. For the purpose of analysing information needs, it is enough to document the required combinations of data, which can be expressed as a vector. For example:

$$\begin{bmatrix} \text{JOURNALIST PERFORMANCE} \\ \text{TYPE OF EVENT} \\ \text{TIME} \end{bmatrix}$$

$$\begin{bmatrix} \text{SALES BY REGION} \\ \text{SALES BY CUSTOMER TYPE} \\ \text{TIME} \end{bmatrix}$$

The examples cited so far have been tactical information needs, rather than strategic ones. The same approach can be used to analyse strategic information needs, perhaps those directly associated with the critical success factors of the enterprise. There may be some additional complications, however, if these information needs span several information models.

5.5 Alternative approaches

There are several alternatives to the approach proposed in this chapter. One is a navigational approach, based on concepts of network databases. According to this, we carry out **entity actions**, such as READ, CREATE, UPDATE and DELETE, on occurrences of entity types. These entity actions are assembled with standard programming constructs of sequence, selection and iteration, into pseudo code or **action diagrams**. Action diagrams are supported by computer aided software engineering (CASE) tools, such as the information engineering facility (IEF™). Figure 5.5 is an example of an action diagram, to provide the information required by question 3, above. The vertical brackets indicate the extent of each repeating loop.

Figure 5.5 Action diagram for question 3

READ news event

  READ EACH news item WHICH reports news event

    READ EACH person WITH type of person = 'POLITICIAN'
                    AND WHICH mentioned by news item

      READ EACH interview WHICH conducted with person

        READ EACH journalist WHICH conducts interview

Another possibility is to draw numbers and/or arrows on the entity–relationship diagram, to indicate the sequence of entity actions, as the process traverses the information model. This explains why the procedural approach is referred to here as the navigational approach: see Figure 5.6.

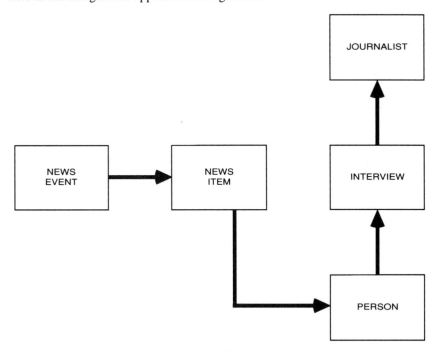

Figure 5.6
Navigational approach

Some writers prefer to analyse information access in a form that is closer to a relational database language such as SQL. For example, the data manipulation language DESPATH has been defined as an entity modelling corollary to SQL.[6] Simplifying the syntax a little, we might analyse question 3 as follows:

> SELECT journalist WHICH conducts interview WHICH conducted with person WHERE position = 'politician' WHICH mentioned in news item WHICH reported as news event.

This might seem heavily biased towards being implemented using a relational database. It is true that there is an easy transformation from this syntax into SQL. Since DESPATH allows relational views to be defined, the top-down analysis of information needs into derived objects is supported. Some analysts are more comfortable with this approach than writing sequential access paths in action diagrams. However, the syntax could also be used to design non-relational database structures.

There is already some automated support for this kind of analysis. Action diagram syntax has been extended to include SQL-like commands, to support the analyst who does not want to think as sequentially as a programmer. However, full support for the hierarchical derivation of data objects, and interchangeability between derived and underived data objects, is not yet automated. And recursive derivation (for example, information about organizational hierarchies or bills of materials) is still difficult to handle.

Analysis should define what, leaving the how to be specified in design. Thus it is not appropriate to specify during the information modelling how information accesses are to be performed by a computer system, nor what sequence of operations should be carried out to navigate around the database. Our analysis should only specify what information accesses are required. The derivational approach satisfies this requirement; other approaches do not. Thus to satisfy the criterion stated in a previous section, that analysis should not preempt design, we believe it necessary to eschew the navigation-based description of information accesses in favour of a derivation-based description.

5.6 Advantages of the derivational approach

There are several advantages of the derivational approach to information needs analysis, over the procedural or navigational approach.

1. Analysis is top down, starting with the desired end-result and working out how to produce it, rather than bottom up, combining things to see what you get. The combinatorial approach becomes increasingly difficult as the information model gets larger.
2. Adding an object to the information model does not affect analysis already carried out. Even removing an object from the information model does not cause any problems, provided that the removed object can still be derived from objects remaining in the information model. This means that the information modellers can change their thinking without undue hassle.
3. The way information needs are used to make decisions depends on their meaning, not on the source data from which they are calculated. For example, in a supermarket, restocking decisions depend on inventory levels. We want to be able to define and use the object INVENTORY LEVEL without specifying whether the inventory levels are calculated directly from data collected at the till, or estimated by looking at the shelf. If the restocking procedures were defined in terms of the source data, they would have to be redefined if the calculation procedure changed. The derivational approach allows us to make changes to the source of an object, without having to rewrite everything that uses the object.

    It also allows us to have multiple sources for the same derived object. Many of the difficulties of information processing at the higher levels of management are due to the difficulties of comparing compound data whose atomic structure differs. For example, rough estimates of the sales volumes of a company's competitors will be captured, and therefore modelled, differently from the known sales volumes of the company itself. Plans may be modelled differently from actual performance figures, because they may well be at a different level of detail.

With some approaches, this is dismissed as impossible, akin to comparing apples with mangoes. What this metaphor ignores is that we do compare apples with mangoes; similarly, businesses regularly compare their own results with their competitors. Our approach recognizes that an information need may have the same meaning, although it may sometimes be met by rough estimate and sometimes by accurate measurement.

4. Analysis of derived objects can be shared between several information needs. Whereas data administration usually concentrates on data sharing at the atomic level, the derivation approach provides an opportunity to make the use of non-atomic information consistent throughout the organization, even at the summary level (where much of the traditional misunderstandings and information clashes occur). It is particularly valuable to have consistent definitions of key performance measures, such as MARKET SHARE or BAD DEBTS or BACKLOG PERCENTAGE, which are often the subject of misunderstandings and politically motivated misuse by information users (especially in senior management positions).[7] Therefore we can and should extend the familiar concept of data administration so that it encompasses all levels of management information.

5. The database designer decides where to provide short cuts in the database, for performance or efficiency reasons, via controlled redundancy. A navigation-based definition of information access makes it difficult to maintain the correspondence between the analysis and the design, unless the database structure closely resembles the information model. If a database is denormalized for performance reasons, formal process specifications may have to be completely rewritten. But a derivation-based definition of information access is completely independent of database optimization. It is even irrelevant whether programs are written in COBOL or in a fourth-generation language, or generated by a CASE tool. This maintains the desired separation between analysis (defining what) and design (specifying how).

5.7 Conclusion

The point of building an information model of a business area is to prepare for better support of the business area by information. It follows that at least some of the analysis should be demand led. It is not enough to build a model of the data that are available ('these are the basic business events and transactions that we can capture, so let us build the model around them') and work forwards to see whether the contents of this model can be massaged into a form that might be useful and relevant to management decision making. It is also necessary to work backwards from the decisions that are being made in the business, and analyse the required information by decomposition, until a satisfactory algorithm can be determined for building up the business information from the available data. Using the top-down technique outlined in this chapter, we decompose each selected information need so that it can be defined from the entities, relationships and attributes in the information model. This tests the information model for completeness, and points the way for the business information needs to be satisfied by a database system that is designed from the information model. It also opens the door for corporate administration of information, not just of data; therefore this (or something like it) will be required to fulfil the oft-preached slogan, 'information as corporate resource'.

Notes

1. An earlier version of this chapter was published in the journal *Information and Software Technology*, December 1988.
2. A formal database logic would be a good starting point: see Barry E. Jacobs, *Applied Database Logic*; vol. 1, Prentice Hall, Englewood Cliffs, NJ, 1985.
3. Warning: in other organizations, the term information centre is used to denote something entirely different.
4. For a related technique, see D. W. Shipman, 'The functional data model and the data language DAPLEX,' *ACM Transactions on Database Systems*, vol. **6**, no. 1 March 1981, pp. 140–73.
5. Explanation of both action diagrams and data navigation diagrams can be found in James Martin and Carma McClure, *Diagramming Techniques for Analysts and Programmers*. Prentice Hall, Englewood Cliffs, NJ, 1985.
6. Wolfgang Roesner, DESPATH: An ER Manipulation Language, in Peter Chen (ed.), *Entity–Relationship Approach*, (IEEE CS Press/North Holland, Amsterdam, 1985.
7. See R. L. Ackoff, 'Management misinformation systems' *Management Science*, vol. 14, no. 4, December 1967.

6 Difficulties

This chapter addresses some of the tricky questions of information modelling, and challenges some of the simple assumptions prevalent among information modellers, such as:

1. An information model can and should represent the real (business) world.
2. To each modelling question, there is a single right answer.
3. All good information modellers adopt the same style.
4. Normalization guarantees a redundancy-free model with a consistent style.
5. All opportunities for data sharing should always be seized.
6. An information model is value neutral, and there are no moral implications.

If you believe these assumptions, then many of the problems of information modelling disappear, as if by magic. Many textbooks make these assumptions, or similar ones. If they were valid, however, then any idiot would be able to produce perfectly good models.

Even experienced modellers may be misled by the theoretical accounts of information modelling, and suffer because of their inability to deliver the level of quality and consistency demanded by the theoretical assumptions.

By challenging these assumptions, I am able to show why information modelling is difficult. This may provide reassurance for the person who has experienced greater practical difficulties in building models than the books and training led him/her to expect, and perhaps worries about his/her capabilities. But my primary purpose is not to provide psychological comfort but practical help. By analysing some of the genuine difficulties in information modelling, we may go a little way towards making them more tractable. And if we know the practical limits, we can set ourselves more reasonable (because achievable) goals.

Finally, the chapter contains some ethical issues that should be considered when modelling people.

6.1 Model status

An analyst produces a model of a business area, using constructs such as ENTITY, RELATIONSHIP, ATTRIBUTE, and perhaps ROLE. What is the status of this model? We can say the following things about it:

1. The model is less complete than the real world being modelled. The analyst will have overlooked some aspects of the real world, and will have deliberately discarded others as irrelevant. Superficial differences between fundamentally similar objects will have been ignored.
2. The model attempts to capture the **essence** of the real world. An aspect of the real world that is logically driven by the requirements of the business carries more weight than an aspect that depends on whim or fashion.
3. A different analyst would have produced a different model.
4. The model should make sense to other analysts, and to inhabitants of the business area. (Strictly speaking, we should say inhabitants rather than users, because we have not yet defined anything to **use**. The term user is a projection forwards to some system that will be designed from the model.)

A model is a representation or map of the real world. It comprises assertions which can be tested by interviewing or observing or other fact-finding. For example:

*   Each INVOICE is made out in a single CURRENCY.
*   Each EMPLOYEE is assigned to one DEPARTMENT, but may work on several PROJECTS.

The assertions in turn depend on precise definitions of the terminology:

*   Do casual staff count as EMPLOYEES or not?
*   Does a temporary transfer count as assigning the EMPLOYEE to the new DEPARTMENT or not?

The analyst starts with a framework of expectations, and systematically tests and elaborates this framework – by interviewing, observing, analysing current procedures and systems – to produce a detailed model. The framework is a theory about the real world.

Some writers distinguish between a theory, which is 'true', and a hypothesis, which is not yet 'true', because it has not yet been tested. This is an artificial distinction. All theories may yet be falsified; all theories are therefore provisional. There is no such thing as unrevisable certainty, either in physical science or information modelling.[1] For the pragmatist, the truth of a theory simply means that it works.

What exactly does the information model represent? What is the relationship between the model and the real world?

> It is often said that a data base models some portion of the real world ... It ain't necessarily so. The world being modelled may have no real existence. It might be historical information (it's not real now). We can debate whether past events have any real existence in the present. It might be falsified information (it never was real) or falsified current information (it isn't real now). Fraudulent data in welfare files: is that a model of the 'real' world? It might be planning information, about intended states of affairs (it isn't real yet). It might be hypothetical conjecture – 'what if' speculations (which might never become real).[2]

There are two further problems with the relationship between the real world and the model. One is that there is not always a one-to-one correspondence between concept and object.[3] Sometimes we can have several different names for the same thing, and only much later discover that the names all denote the same object. This complicates the relationship between the real world and the model.

The second is ghosts: that the destruction of an object does not result in the destruction of its representation. This is why people believe in ghosts – because they cannot accept that when loved ones die, their names and their memories no longer refer to anything – and because they cannot accept a similar lack of reference for their own ideas after their own death.[4] Ideas may carry on, but no longer refer to anything outside themselves. The life of a concept continues for longer than the life of the physical object. This is why the information model is sometimes referred to as a conceptual model, because it represents concepts rather than physical reality. So what is the 'reality' that is being modelled? We shall not follow the question into philosophical and metaphysical realms. Just remember (from Chapter 1): the map is not the territory. In other words, the model is not the real world.

The pragmatist is interested in the *meaning* of information, only as it is implied by its *use*. An information model should not go beyond what is meaningful at the time of modelling:

1. Model what makes sense to the business, not what might make sense in the future. What is modelled does not have to *exist* (it may be a future intention). It does not even have to make sense to all members of an organization. For example, senior management may formulate a policy, which requires a new concept to pervade the organization. (One High-Street bank has an initiative in progress to introduce the concept of PROJECT to the middle levels of management.) However, it must make sense to somebody!
2. Model what you are able to know – it is not useful to model theoretical facts that you are not practically able to discover (and there is no likelihood of becoming able to discover).

6.2 Is modelling uniform?

Information modelling is sometimes presented as if it consisted merely of a set of formal rules and simple diagrams. This leaves the analyst in the dark how to carry out the actual analysis, and how to arrive at the solution. Some methodologues dream of information modelling becoming uniform. In other words, that any two analysts, faced with the same situation, would produce the same model.

The basis of this dream is clear. It removes the seeming arbitrariness of today's models, and enables the modelling to be done by intelligent software, or even unintelligent people, instead of requiring any experience or flair. At present, the best CASE tools can only record the results of the modelling exercise, and perform simple consistency checks, but surely (so it may be thought) their role can be extended.

This section analyses the dream, to determine what it means and, whether it is a fantasy or a nightmare. It argues that the 'perfect' solution does not exist. Instead, there are usually several good solutions. Furthermore, there is no mechanistic path to a good solution. There is a creative element in information modelling that cannot be entirely eliminated.

6.2.1 Benefits of uniform modelling

The dream can be found in several contributions to a recent conference on information systems.[5] For example, a group of IEW users in the Netherlands see four benefits from the realization of the dream:[6]

1. Uniformity of modelling activities across large projects or enterprises.
2. Guarantee of quality for the models produced.
3. Partial or full automation becomes possible.
4. Straightforward guidelines and manuals, with effective training.

Other researchers also argue the same benefits: 'A method that can ensure a uniform solution to a given problem will lead to systems that have a good chance of dovetailing neatly even though they are produced by independent teams.'[7]

6.2.2 Meaning of uniform modelling

Let us explore in more detail what is meant by uniform modelling. A modelling approach can be evaluated in three ways:

1. The probability of always reaching an adequate solution to any given problem.
2. The probability of reaching the best possible solution to any given problem.
3. The probability that two solutions to any given problem would be the same or equivalent.

Each probability dimension spans a range from high risk to total certainty. The three dimensions are independent. It could plausibly be argued that any effort to increase (3) might serve to decrease (2); I am not aware of any conclusive demonstration that any modelling approach may achieve certainty on all three dimensions simultaneously.

To describe a modelling approach as uniform is to say that the third probability dimension reaches certainty: there is no chance element in the outcome to a modelling exercise. It is possible that striving too hard for this level of certainty would often lead to sacrificing the best possible solution, perhaps sacrificing the quality of one solution for consistency between solutions. Does this matter?

But this discussion raises problems of definition. What is meant by adequacy, best possible, equivalent? Without some understanding of these terms, some criteria by which they can be judged, the evaluation lacks meaning. Each model claims to be a representation of a business situation. So in what sense can two such representations be regarded as equivalent? Do the names of the entity types have to be the same? Do the definitions have to be the same? Must the integrity conditions be expressed in the same way? Must the scope be identical, and how would this be judged?

Perhaps formal definitions of these terms cannot be produced, yet it might still be argued that we understand them intuitively. Thus, even if we cannot prove that two models are equivalent, we may at least perceive that they are close. This line of argument greatly weakens the original dream, and makes uniformity a much rougher and less useful concept. Yet even this might be worth striving for.

6.2.3 Consequences of uniform modelling

One of the delights of modelling is the ability of the user to develop a new understanding of the business. New business opportunities emerge from the models, particularly where the model represents the relationship with the customer, or the interface with the environment. Uniform modelling could remove the creativity and serendipity of this activity, and replace it with a bureaucratic sameness. As Christopher Alexander points out, 'In most cases, design depends on the depth of the insights you have, and any investigation that you want to undertake preliminary to the design has to do with trying to deepen your insights.'[8]

If the users are to play a significant role in developing a model, then there should be a genuine possibility of their input making a difference to the outcome. The model is influenced by their conceptual framework, their priorities, their personal strategies as well as their interpretation of the corporate strategies. The way these are expressed, perhaps even the frankness with which they are expressed, will depend upon their personal relationships with the analysts. If this factor is to be eliminated from the modelling process, on the ground that it compromises the uniformity of solutions, there is a strong risk that valuable insights will be lost.

There is another side to this: one of the opportunities of information modelling is to break down the cultural barriers between information technologists and end-users, by allowing and encouraging users to take ownership of the models. This means that the users identify with and commit themselves to the models. This ownership may be endangered by an approach that attempts to impose standard solutions on problems, regardless of the local cultural variants, how people see things.

6.2.4 Example

Parenthood can be modelled in three ways:

1. As an entity type PARENT, with attributes indicating the number of children (which must be greater than zero).

2. As an attribute of the entity type PERSON, indicating whether the person has children.

3. As a many-to-many involuted relationship on PERSON, indicating that one person is a parent of another (Figure 6.1).

Figure 6.1 Model of parenthood

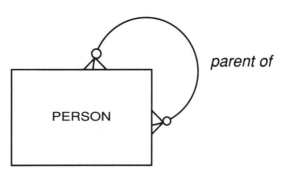

Some writers refer to our ability to represent similar meaning through several alternative structures as **semantic relativism**.[9]

6.2.5 Anti-uniform modelling

Of course, my argument can be attacked as partial. All experts want to argue that their expertise is special – inappropriate for automation, even invulnerable to the attacks of the automators. The expert always perceives subtle advantages of the human expert over the machine. The original Luddites were cloth workers, who argued correctly that no machine could replicate the fine quality of hand-carded material. They were overwhelmed by the economic argument, that a cheap imperfection (available to the masses) was better than an expensive ideal (only available to a rich elite).

6.2.6 Industry models and package solutions

Sometimes the dream goes further, to standard solutions of business situations valid across all businesses, within an industry or across all industries. Managers sometimes demand of experts in information modelling – surely people have modelled our industry before: so what is the solution? Can we buy it off the shelf?

We cannot expect two companies in the same industry to have the same models. I have seen the information architectures developed by three major oil companies; they are radically different. Part of the reason for this is cultural – each model or architecture is based on the conceptual habits and patterns of the given organization. Thus even an intelligent manager from oil company Alpha would probably find the model of oil company Beta more difficult to understand than Alpha's model (although I have not tried this experiment, for reasons of commercial confidence). Part of the reason is strategic – the activities and resources on which the business strategy is focused are likely to be centrally placed within the business model. And no two companies focus their business strategies in exactly the same way.

As computer systems come to dominate the modern enterprise, the source of competitive advantage increasingly lies in the quality and difference of the computerized information systems deployed by or on behalf of the enterprise. To have systems that are exactly the same as the competition may be a goal of the mediocre, of the second-rate, but it can never be part of a strategy of excellence.

However, it may well be that many of the support activities of an organization can be modelled in a standard way. Many organizations use packages or templates for applications as general ledger and payroll. Recently, even strategic applications have been traded between companies. For example, airlines that do not directly compete with one another have shared models for the administration of their Frequent Flyer programmes.

Furthermore, use of a template as a starting point may allow each company to develop its own additional sources of excellence, by adding richness to the template. We have discussed this use of templates in Chapter 3 'Techniques'.

6.2.7 Conclusion

Information models produced for different groups of users usually or always appear to be different. Even models produced for the same group of users by different analysts usually appear to be different. It is not clear whether these differences are significant. It could be argued that these apparent differences are superficial, and that the models must necessarily share a common 'deep' structure.[10] Even if the differences are not logically significant, they may be politically significant, since it may be embarrassing for analysts (especially when they represent the same consultancy company) to contradict one another.

Although there are many things that can be done to reduce unnecessary differences between different analysts' styles, it remains true that even the best methodology cannot entirely mask the personal style and flair of the analyst, and I do not think we should feel bad about that.

6.3 Attitudes to modelling

One of the apparent difficulties of information modelling is the fact that people think differently. Let us consider some of these differences, and explore the extent to which they cause genuine difficulties.

6.3.1 Lumpers and splitters

There are two types of analyst, who perceive the world in two different ways. It is a question of temperament and attitude. Some people see the similarities between entities more easily than they see the differences, thus they want to lump the objects being modelled into relatively few entity types, to gain generality. Others tend to see the differences more readily than the similarities, so they want to split the model, to divide the objects between a larger number of more narrowly defined entity types, to gain precision. For example, according to the lumpers, a subcontractor could be basically the same as any other supplier, and is therefore the same entity type, while the splitters would probably argue that there are significant differences between different groups of suppliers, justifying separate entity types in the model.

Some lumpers attempt to justify their position by elevating data sharing to an ideological principle. Wherever it is possible to define a common entity type, it is necessary to do so. Definitions should always be reused and generalized whenever possible. This offends against the pragmatic approach preferred in this book, since the costs of data sharing are sometimes greater than the benefits. The ideological lumper will nonetheless always insist on data sharing.

If a methodology warns you against any extreme, that is no reason to go to the opposite extreme.

Thus some care is needed in interpreting any guidance that methodologies may provide in such matters. If the developers of a particular methodology have concentrated on the dangers of 'splitteracy', then lumpers may be encouraged to get as generalized as they can. And if the methodology is full of warnings against excessive generalization, then splitters may feel justified in taking their approach to the extreme.

There is therefore, on many analysis projects, an unavoidable tension between lumpers and splitters, a trade off between generality and precision. There may be frequent arguments along such lines, although each argument should not be allowed to take much time. Such tension is healthy, because it prevents the model becoming either too detailed and specific, or too vague and universalized. It follows that a modelling team should balance lumpers with splitters. As a consultant, the author has had to play the lumper role on some occasions and the splitter role on other occasions, according to the temperaments of the other team members, to achieve the right balance.

In some cases, if the splitters disagree among themselves, then the lumper will win by default. For example, two splitters may both feel that there is an important difference between HOTEL and MOTEL. But when they cannot agree exactly what the difference is, then the lumper steps in and creates a single combined entity type. This is safer than basing a model structure on a disputed distinction, and still allows each splitter to create any partitions or subtypes that can be clearly defined, and whose relevance can be demonstrated.

The mechanism of entity subtypes can sometimes be used to maintain a compromise, since it allows these two opposite approaches to be (partially) reconciled. The similarities can be analysed and documented at the entity type level, the differences at the subtype level. Thus both lumper and splitter may be satisfied. (But even this mechanism does not always succeed in bringing peace to a strife-torn modelling team.)

Another possibility is to offer the lumper and splitter two different models, with a clearly defined mapping between them. This is appropriate where the lumper and splitter are associated with different business areas. For example, the accounts model of the business tends to be 'lumpy', with all sorts of things lumped into general entity types such as ASSET, whereas other areas of the business want to view different kinds of asset entirely separately. So we may have different data structures in the two different models, at different levels of abstraction, but constrained by some definite mapping between the two.

Finally, let us consider an analogy. Two artists sit down to sketch a scene. One tries to capture everything in a few freehand strokes of charcoal. The other uses a fine pencil to try and capture the scene in meticulous detail. Which is the better artist? Is this a sensible question? The first artist is a lumper, the second is a splitter. But if we magnify a portion of the second artist's sketch, it looks as rough as that of the first. Even the splitter cannot go on splitting to infinity, and for that matter, even the lumper cannot go on lumping.

What does this tell us about information modelling – or for that matter about any business modelling?

- That it is never complete – only completed. There is always more detail that could have been developed.
- That a small overlooked detail may have a broad impact (what has been termed the 'butterfly effect', since chaos theory claims that a butterfly with a perfect sense of timing may cause a hurricane, by flapping its wings just at the critical point).
- That we need better magnification (and demagnification) tools, so that every model, whatever its scope, has the same complexity.
- That we need a scientific but pragmatic way to tell us when it is reasonably safe to stop analysis.

6.3.2 Organization culture

An information model produced within a bureaucratic organization is very different to one produced within the opposite type of organization, sometimes called an 'adhocracy'. In a bureaucracy, there is a fear of the **arbitrary**. Everything may be specified in advance; rules and procedures are designed to ensure that decisions are rational, effective, efficient and fair. (This is not the place to discuss the degree to which bureaucratic rules and procedures actually achieve the goals for which they are designed, or the side-effects that they may produce. But it is important, since the word bureaucracy has acquired such negative connotations, to recognize the plausible and, to some extent, laudable motivations of the bureaucrat.) In an adhocracy, on the other hand, there is little fear of the arbitrary, and much greater fear of losing freedom. The adhocrat is reluctant to tie his/her hands in advance, and prefers to wait and judge each case on its merits. This makes an adhocracy open not only to innovation, but also to corruption and inefficiency.

An organization being bureaucratic or adhocratic is a very important aspect of its **culture**, and has a significant impact on the kind of information model we should expect to see. In a good bureaucracy, the definitions of entity types and other objects are likely to be static, fixed and visible. Membership rules and identity rules for entity types may be derived from existing policies, or formulated specially for the purposes of the information model, whereas in an adhocracy, it may be impossible to freeze the definitions of entity types, and inappropriate to try. Instead, it may make more sense to define entity types in terms of some dynamic learning process.

For example, whereas a bureaucracy may define PRODUCT as a combination of some fixed features, satisfying some fixed relationship to production and sales, an adhocracy may define PRODUCT to be anything the marketing department may, at any time, deem to be a product. This means the entity type membership rule refers to the set of decisions made at a given time, and these decisions cannot be exactly predicted.

Of course, no organization is totally predictable and bureaucratic, nor totally random and adhocratic, but somewhere between these two extremes. Thus it may be possible to identify some constraints on what may or may not be regarded as a PRODUCT, while it may not be possible to write a watertight definition. And within most enterprises, some functional departments are likely to be more bureaucratic than others. For example, some people might expect an information model for management accounting to be more bureaucratic than an information model for R & D. It is certainly true that flexibility of entity type definitions can be more readily tolerated (or even encouraged) in some areas than others. External auditors may be severe in their criticism of an organization that is vague about its assets; but if an enterprise has a rigid notion of who its competitors are, it may be in for a nasty surprise when its customers disappear to an unanticipated rival.

Just as organizations may be more or less bureaucratic, so may be the attitudes and expectations of the individual. So sometimes there will be a mismatch between the attitude of the information modeller and the culture of the organization he or she is trying to model:

1. The adhocratic modeller in an adhocratic organization will probably be careless about definitions, will spend little time on analysis, and complete the information model very quickly.

2. A bureaucratic modeller in an adhocratic organization will probably be frustrated at the inability to fix definitions, and find it hard to interest people in detailed analytical discussions of hypothetical or obscure contingencies. If the modeller controls the schedules of the project, it will never complete, and this will be blamed on the failure of the users to provide the necessary input.

3. An adhocratic modeller in a bureaucratic organization will be impatient to make progress, and may feel bogged down by the desire of the users to debate every last point. If the modeller controls the schedules of the project, these discussions will be guillotined, and the users will then disown the resulting model.

4. A bureaucratic modeller in a bureaucratic organization will be happy and fulfilled, since the users are as interested in the detailed analysis as he or she is. Good bureaucracies have rational and non-arbitrary task control

mechanisms to allow this kind of analysis to be at least provisionally terminated, in order that the models can be implemented, because they understand that it is better to have some rule or procedure in place, however imperfect, than wait, unruled and unruly, for the perfect procedure.

It may appear from this discussion that it is easier to model in an adhocracy than in a bureaucracy. This is not necessarily true. In a bureaucracy, there are many rules, but these rules are usually explicit and easy to identify. Where the analyst discovers a place where there could be a rule, but none exists, this is likely to create the desire to formulate a new rule to fill the gap. Thus the resulting information model is likely to be intricate, but closed and static.

In an adhocracy, there may seem to be nothing tangible to model. If, when you ask the marketing director what might characterize future products, he or she denies any definite knowledge and demands infinite flexibility, what can you do? If modelling a bureaucracy is like analysing complicated clocks, modelling an adhocracy is like modelling clouds. The model may be less complicated, but it has to be open and dynamic and flexible. The good analyst must understand the underlying real constraints and patterns, and build these into the model.

6.4 Resolving disputes

Since dispute is dialectic, the resolution may need to be dialectic as well. To illustrate this, this section is phrased in dialectic form.

Can an information modelling method answer all questions?
No. of course not. Even if we exclude entirely irrelevant questions, it is unreasonable to expect any method or methodology to do all your work for you. Information modelling is not a deskilling programme. As the ancient Chinese proverb puts it; 'Legless man cannot walk on stilts.'

Can the information modelling expert answer all questions?
An expert may or may not be equipped with a greater range of techniques, modelling options and leadership skills than most other people. But he or she cannot rely on always having the best ideas, and cannot assume that his/her intuitions are necessarily correct. Expertise in the business area being modelled is also required.

What the expert must provide to every situation is a clear understanding of the purpose and critical success factors of any given task or outcome, both in general and in relation to a specific project with specific goals. He or she must connect every specific judgement ('How do we model this?', 'How many models should we have?'), to the project's business goals and constraints.

Gimme an example.
A modeller comes to an expert with a problem. There are two alternative ways s/he can model something. (If he or she cannot think of any alternatives, then the expert's first task is to invent two or three alternatives for him/her.) Call these two alternatives A and B.

Either A and B are factually equivalent, or they are not. If they are not equivalent, that means there is some fact or proposition that is asserted by A and denied by B. For example, whether a given attribute is mandatory or optional depends whether all the occurrences of the entity type possess a value for the attribute – this is a question of business fact, and not a methodological question at all. The expert may help formulate a business question ('Do all your employees have driving licences/home phones or not?') and may even have enough business knowledge to guess the answer, but if the expert actually provides the answer, he or she is going beyond the methodology support role.

What if A and B are factually equivalent? In other words, there is no business fact that is asserted by A and denied by B. Subtyping provides many such problems – the model with subtyping is equivalent to the model without subtyping. Or perhaps a supertype is being considered. The two structures in Figure 6.2 may be equivalent, but they are clearly different. The choice between them can be regarded as methodological. But a methodology does not necessarily prefer one style of modelling to another. It merely defines the decision-making approach. You choose whichever better fits the project goals.

Figure 6.2 Two equivalent structures with different meanings

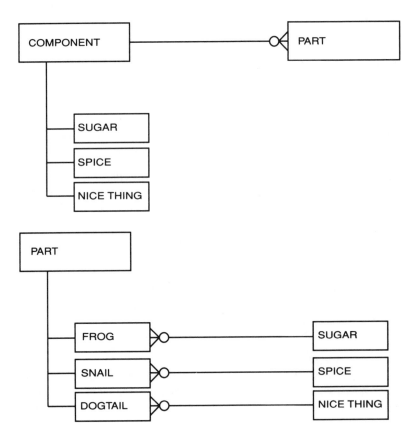

How do we decide which modelling option to use?
Why are we building an information model at all? Within a typical systems
development project, an information model of a business area may have five
critical success factors (in descending order of importance):

1. Supports the relevant strategies (as identified in the planning model or
   through other means).
2. Makes sense to the business users.
3. Enables the definition of correct process logic.
4. Enables the design and implementation of a working database.
5. Consistent style – similar solutions to similar problems.

Thus we ask the following questions, in the following order (each level
overrides subsequent levels):

1. Does A or B better reflect the strategies?
2. Do the business users prefer A or B?
3. Are the processes simpler or easier to analyse with A or B? Which of
   them makes it easier to maintain data integrity?
4. Do the database designers have a preference?
5. Are there similar situations elsewhere that have been modelled A-like or
   B-like?

When we reach a positive answer, stop. But if there is no identifiable impact at
one level, go to the next level. If there is no significant difference between A
and B *at all,* then toss a coin. (I am serious – do not waste time on such trivial
problems.)

What if the users/analysts cannot agree?
Consensus is nice. But sometimes there will be two camps of users who
perceive things differently. Or perhaps half the processes would be easier to
write with A, while the other half would be easier with B. Just suppose we
said that A and B were *both* right. We have two models instead of one.
Moreover, the two models are inconsistent, in the sense that they cannot be
merged into a single model AB without destroying either A or B. It is
sometimes possible, however, to design a single non-redundant database *D,*
which supports both A and B: see Figure 6.3.

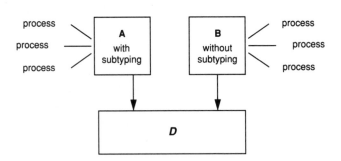

Figure 6.3 Non-redundant database for two alternative models

If A and B are well enough coordinated that this would merely require some tweaking at technical design, and if this separation of the two models makes the users happier, or greatly increases the development of process and procedure logic, then this is worth considering.

How do I know A and B are even compatible in this way without merging them into one model?
We do not have any general rules yet. But some specific cases are just going to be obvious.

How does development coordination work?
The role of development coordination is to control all the models A, B, C ... and to ensure that they are compatible *in all important respects*.

What do you mean – compatible?
Compatible does not mean identical, nor even identical within overlapping areas. **Consolidation** means creating a model AB, of which A and B are proper subsets - thus all objects contained in both A and B will be identical. However, if two data models A and B can be supported by a single integrated and redundancy-free database *D*, then they are fully **compatible**. If development coordination can satisfy itself that A and B are fully compatible in this sense, then the effort to consolidate A and B would be an unnecessary hassle.

What if the models are not quite compatible?
Here is the controversial bit. Suppose the database *D* is not quite free of redundancy, suppose that some technical fix is required, with some internal data overhead, to make *D* work effectively and to maintain data integrity. My assertion is that *sometimes* this will be acceptable, that the technical hassle caused by redundancy in *D* may be less than the organizational hassle required to make A and B fully compatible, and far less than the effort to consolidate them into one model AB.

So what is the bottom line?
Any technique is a means to an end, not an end in itself. Any methodology includes some technical generalities (*'X tends to cause Y'*). This does not mean that every time you want Y, you must do X, nor that whenever you want to avoid Y, you must eschew X. In a particular situation, X may not bring about Y at all, or perhaps X has other overwhelming side-effects, either desirable or undesirable.

So it is with the fear of redundancy in databases, or with slightly incompatible models. It may be argued that redundancy tends to cause problems – development, integrity, maintenance – and should therefore be avoided on principle. It is true that redundancy has these undesirable tendencies, and I agree that we should prefer to have less redundancy than more, but I am not prepared to elevate this from a guideline to a principle.

If engineers are allowed to justify actions according to technical generalities, this converts a methodology from a science to a religion or ideology. People should never do things just 'because the methodology says so'. A methodology should be used as a signpost, pointing people towards true justification, doing things 'to yield these specific benefits in this particular situation'. Information engineering, for example, is a business-driven methodology. Anything that is done out of habit, or by appeal to what 'everybody knows', can be dismissed as superstition, unless it scores specific business goals. The information engineer challenges every assumption, re-examines beliefs, questions the answers themselves. Of course, sometimes you have to simplify just to make progress, sometimes you have to put aside the intellectual challenge, and hope things work out okay. But you come back later, when the pressure is off, to think things through at leisure. A true science has no final answers, but a never-ending succession of better hypotheses. In that sense, a methodology, like life, has no answers at all. The final relaxation is death.

Consistency is contrary to nature, contrary to life. The only completely consistent people are the dead.[11]
(Aldous Huxley)

6.5 Language

6.5.1 Modelling in another language

English is a good language in which to analyse. We have a rich vocabulary, with a large number of synonyms to provide us with alternative names and descriptions for the same objects and activities. We can name and describe things at varying levels of generality or specificity. This feature of the English language is due to its origins, as a hybrid between Anglo-Saxon and Norman French, and is shared by few other languages.

For example, English contains the word *'cook'* in addition to the words *'fry,' 'boil,' 'bake,' 'grill,'* etc. This enables us to specify or to avoid specifying what type of cooking we are talking about. We have words for different meals – *'breakfast,' 'luncheon,' 'tea,' 'dinner,' 'supper'* – but we also have the word *'meal,'* which is at a higher level of generality. Other languages lack such general words, thus forcing the analyst to be too specific. A commonly cited example is that English only has one word for snow, although this can be made more specific by the addition of adjectives. In contrast, although the Eskimo has an accurate vocabulary for many different kinds of snow, he has no word at all for snow in general.

English is weak, however, when it comes to naming and describing abstract ideas. We can often only talk about intangible objects metaphorically. Systems themselves, for example, usually have to be named obliquely, by referring to their location. This weakness is not shared by other languages, such as German. In Turkish, apparently, nouns denote unqualified substance. Their primary concept is therefore not 'house' but 'house-ness' or perhaps 'dwelling space'. To speak of two, five or even one house, the Turkish grammar requires an extra term to indicate enumeration. The grammatical concept of singular and plural, which is taken for granted in most European languages, appears strange to the Turk. I do not know (but I should be interested to discover) whether this would make information modelling easier or more difficult for the Turk, especially for one who spoke only Turkish.[12]

6.5.2 Modelling in several languages

Many organizations operate in more than one language. Belgian, Canadian or Swiss companies may conduct all internal affairs in French, or then again they may not. American or Japanese multinational corporations may conduct all internal affairs in English, or Japanese, or they may allow and even encourage the use of local languages.

Organizations that are produced by international merger or joint venture may, for political reasons, need to operate in two or more languages. And international organizations (including the European Community, and the United Nations) may operate in a multitude of tongues.

Some organizations could select a 'master' language – say English – and then the other languages would be 'slave' languages. But often this would be politically unacceptable. Even the jargon 'master' and 'slave', though meaningful to computer scientists, would have unacceptable overtones to users.

There are two levels of problem that emerge when you try to produce a model for a polyglot organization. There are problems with the data values, and problems with the object names and definitions. First consider the data values. A simple attribute, such as NAME may be language dependent. Even a proper name like Warsaw is the English name for Warszawa. And textual descriptions, comments and even abbreviations are likely to be of greatest value if in the local language. Second, consider the object names and definitions. These, together with all descriptions and other textual commentary about the object, will be in one or many languages. If a master language can be selected, then it may be possible to maintain the model in the master language, with translations into the slave languages. Names in the slave languages of objects in the model could be treated exactly the same as synonyms. Translations of the object definitions and other descriptions could be made if wanted, and elaborate procedures may then be required to remove any translation inaccuracies and to resolve any disputes. If a single master language cannot be used, it may be necessary to maintain and coordinate models in each language. A polyglot organization may not only have problems with the modelling, but also with the technical administration of the models, since many workbenches and other tools are designed for single-language use.

6.6 Modelling ethics

There are a number of ethical issues that can arise from information modelling. There are three main issues: the responsibility of the analyst towards the organization (professional ethics), and the responsibility of the organization towards the data subject (data protection and privacy) and towards society (business ethics).

Who 'owns' the data? Does a company own the data it has collected about a person? Does the person himself/herself have any ownership rights over his/her 'own' data? The ownership rights, of course, entail an identity rule – in order to show that a record on a database belongs to me (i.e. that I have certain rights of access and correction to the record), I have to prove that it refers to me (and not to someone else with the same name).

There are three possible ways of capturing personal information, in database records for each PERSON:

1. A single occurrence of PERSON for each human being.
2. A single occurrence of PERSON for each human being in each (socio-economic) role.
3. Personal information aggregated into demographic or behavioural statistics.

One of the aims of the UK Data Protection Act (and of similar legislation in other countries) is to prevent the combination of data from several sources, for purposes other than that for which the data were originally collected. This means that (2) is preferred to (1). For some purposes, we are only allowed access to statistical aggregations of data, but not the raw data themselves. This means that (3) is preferred to (1) and (2).

Then the fun is to predict the behaviour of an individual from the demographic data, for example:

1. What is the probability that this person will respond positively to this mailshot?
2. What is the probability that this person will prove a good credit risk?

Thus it is possible to disaggregate and restore data, to return to the individual person from the anonymous totals and averages. Of course, this process introduces errors and inaccuracies. Does this benefit the person whose privacy is at stake? Hardly! Imagine: you are denied a loan because you live in a dubious district, or you belong to some demographic category that the statisticians depreciate.

6.6.1 Controlling the criteria by which you will be judged

Iranian women wear robes so they will not be judged by beauty but by less superficial qualities. To what extent is a person able to choose (or at least veto) the criteria by which they are evaluated? You cannot (or at least should not) introduce new criteria of relevance. (This is why retrospective legislation is frowned upon.) For example, if an employee is told that the criteria for promotion to the next grade are such and such, and then told (after struggling to attain the set standard) that the criteria have now changed (this is known as moving the goalposts), he or she may be disheartened.

Collecting additional information about employees' performance may inadvertently have this effect. Employees (and their representatives) can sometimes be very suspicious of additional performance measurement, because they expect it to influence and alter the existing criteria for promotion and remuneration.

6.6.2 Privacy

How much right does a person have, to keep his/her behaviour hidden? For example, does a person have the right to have a criminal offence forgotten (after a certain number of years have elapsed), or does the prospective employer have the right to know everything about the person? Does a person have a right to know the family medical history of her fiancé or his fiancée (which could affect the prospects of rearing healthy children)?

Information, at least as defined by computer programmers and bureaucrats, is intolerant of ambiguity. People are defined by a relatively small number of attributes, in a fixed way. A rash act at university, or in adolescence, can dog a man for life. You are what you have once done – this is a very dangerous doctrine. It labels people permanently as subversives, communists, homosexuals, drug addicts or whatever. (It was only in 1870, according to Foucault, that Carl Westphal transformed the practice of sodomy to the state of homosexuality: 'The sodomite had been a temporary aberration; the homosexual was now a species.'[13]) It may also be a logical error to classify people by their behaviour (see 3.4.1).

Under English law, certain types of information are excluded at certain stages of a criminal trial. Previous offences are not to be mentioned until the verdict has been reached, but may be considered in deciding the sentence. However, minor offences are supposed to be deleted from the record altogether after a set time period. This is a deliberate attempt to separate the individual from his/her historical behaviour. It allows an individual to be distanced from the past. Otherwise a criminal record can act as a millstone, preventing even the truly repentant criminal from ever going straight, because nobody will give him a straight job or a mortgage or an overdraft or decent housing or whatever.

It is a difficult moral decision. If A trusts B with the care of children, or money, or whatever, should A be informed that B has once been convicted of abusing a similar trust in the past? Or suppose that B has never been convicted, but has been tried and acquitted (thanks to insufficient evidence, or perhaps some legal technicality). Or suppose that B has never been tried, but has been questioned by police on several occasions, and there have been unsupported allegations in the press. What aspects of B's past history is A entitled to know, and what aspects is B entitled to put behind him/her? Should B be allowed to bury the past and rebuild his/her reputation?

My guess is that there would be wide sympathy for B being allowed to forget minor breaches of the law, committed many years ago and properly punished, provided that B has not lapsed since. And that it would also be considered unfair to repeatedly confront B with unproven and possibly malicious allegations and accusations. Thus the principle that *some* facts about B (and an allegation against B by C is a fact about B, although it may also be a fact about C) should be forgotten seems to accord with common sense notions of fairness. English libel law supports this: it is insufficient defence against a charge of libel that what is published happens to be true. Thus truth and honesty must be weighed against reputation. The American approach is different. Several candidates have been forced to drop out of the race for the Presidency, their reputations sullied by the uncovering of sometimes quite bygone indiscretions.[14]

6.6.3 Blacklists and whitelists

Blacklists are often used when vetting people for credit risk or for employment that involves some security risk. As a result of clerical error, bad luck or malicious misrepresentation, a person may be unfairly included on such a blacklist, causing that person to be refused employment or credit. In theory (although there are many exceptions), the UK Data Protection Act allows such a person to discover their inclusion on a blacklist, and appeal to have their name removed.

To evade such controls, some organizations now use whitelists. A whitelist includes everyone that is an acceptable credit risk or security risk. Exclusion from a whitelist has exactly the same effect as inclusion in a blacklist, except that there is no legal mechanism for redress. Implementing a whitelist solely in order to evade these controls is immoral. Any organization using either whitelists or blacklists has a moral responsibility to maintain the accuracy of the list, and to enable any valid correction process.

The ideal solution from an information modelling point of view, as well as from an ethical point of view, is to combine blacklist and whitelist into a single list, based on the entity type PERSON, differentiated by an attribute indicating whether he or she is acceptable or unacceptable. Furthermore, the evidence supporting acceptability or unacceptability should be preserved, to provide an audit trail enabling efficient and effective correction. There should also be a mechanism for deleting past misdemeanours, as discussed above.

6.6.4 Conclusion

A model is not merely a description of the real world. It expresses some intentions about the real world. When modelling people, therefore, the model expresses intentions relating to these people, including the intention to judge people according to particular criteria.

The inclusion of particular criteria in an information model, enabling particular decision or selection processes, therefore has ethical and legal implications. If people are judged according to inaccurate or inappropriate data, and if subjective assessments are mistaken for reliable facts, the information model shares some of the responsibility for this. The analyst cannot hide behind the convenient fiction of moral neutrality.

6.7 Summary

In this chapter, we have attacked some common misconceptions of information modelling, and considered some of the personal, organizational and wider social issues that may arise during a modelling project.

Notes

1. Imre Lakatos shows that, even in mathematics, theories may be revisited and revised: I. Lakatos, *Proofs and Refutations*, Cambridge University Press, Cambridge, 1976.
2. William Kent, *Data and Reality: Basic assumptions in data processing reconsidered*, Elsevier North-Holland, Amsterdam, 1978, pp. 16–17.
3. Gottlob Frege, *Über Sinn und Bedeutung* in *Translations from the Philosophical Writings of Gottlob Frege*, (eds) Peter Geach and Max Black, 2nd edn, Basil Blackwell, Oxford, 1960.
4. Félix Guattari calls these semiotic ghosts 'black holes'. See his *Molecular Revolution: Psychiatry and politics*, English translation, Penguin, Harmondsworth, 1984, pp. 93–4.
5. T. W. Olle, A. A. Verrijn-Stuart and L. Bhabuta (eds), *Computerized Assistance during the Information Systems Life Cycle*, North-Holland, Amsterdam, 1988 (sometimes known as CRIS 4).
6. S. Brinkkemper, N. Brand and J. Moormann, 'Deterministic modelling procedures for automatic analysis and design tools', in *ibid.*, T. W. Olle, pp. 117–60.
7. R. Stamper, K. Althans and J. Backhouse, 'MEASUR: Method for eliciting, analysing and specifying user requirements', in *ibid.*, T. W. Olle, pp. 67–115.
8. C. Alexander, 'The state of the art in design methods', *DMG Newsletter*, vol. **5** no. 3, 1971 pp. 3–7.
9. M. Brodie, 'On the development of data models', in M. Brodie, J. Mylopoulos and J. W. Schmidt, *On Conceptual Modelling*, Springer Verlag, New York, 1984 p. 39.
10. This approach could be taken by the philosophical realist portrayed in H. Klein and R. Hirschheim, 'A comparative framework of data modelling paradigms and approaches' *Computer Journal*, vol. 30, no 1, 1987, pp. 8–15.
11. Aldous Huxley, 'Do what you will', 'Wordsworth in the Tropics'.
12. My source for this detail is I. Illich and B. Sanders, *ABC: The alphabetization of the popular mind*, Penguin, Harmondsworth, 1989.
13. M. Foucault, *The History of Sexuality – volume I: Introduction*, Random House, New York, 1978.
14. In 1987, there was a Democrat who had cheated at law school, and a Republican whose son was born too soon after his marriage.

7 Case studies

In this chapter, we introduce four different case study exercises, based largely on real companies. Benson's Hotel is a simple problem of administrative information, but contains more than one stakeholder. Siva UK illustrates how a simple problem can develop into a more complex problem by growing the business and extending the objectives. WorldVis includes a broader range of types of information, not all of which may be simple to computerize. And Martimark Enterprises illustrates the complexities of information required for effective marketing in the competitive environment, at the strategic and tactical levels as well as the operational levels.

7.1 How to use the case studies

The traditional textbook approach to case studies is that the author poses some problems, and then publishes 'the' answers, perhaps as an appendix to the book, or perhaps in a separate book sold to the teachers. With many subjects, this is a good approach to enable the reader (or the teacher) to test whether the desired knowledge and skill have been attained. But with information modelling, this approach would give the reader entirely the wrong impression of what is required, and would fundamentally contradict the rest of the book. The skill of information modelling is not one of converting a written description into boxes and lines, but one of negotiating a structured set of concepts within a given business context. The ultimate test of your model is whether you can persuade other people to accept it. (I am aware of at least one company that used to test job applicants by asking them to draw an information model of a garage. This suffers from the same fallacy: the notion that information modelling is an activity that can be carried out as an isolated intellectual exercise, rather than as a process of discovery.)

Thus although some hints are given as to the kinds of object that could be included in the solution, complete solutions are not given. Therefore, the case studies should if possible be used as group exercises. These can be formal or informal. In a teaching context, the solutions can be evaluated by the teacher, not by comparison with a model answer, but against the quality criteria discussed in previous chapters. Some suggestions follow:

1. Formal role-play exercises. Each member of the group is assigned a different role within the organization being modelled, and thinks of the kinds of information required to fulfil this role.
2. Produce and compare independent solutions. Individually, or in small subgroups, several solutions are developed. These are then presented back to the whole group in turn, and critically evaluated.
3. Solutions are evaluated by experienced information modellers (using inspection techniques such as those described in Chapter 3).
4. In some situations, and given access to suitable technology, the solutions could be developed into working prototype systems. This would test the workability of the models.
5. Present the models to other people (possibly even people unfamiliar with information modelling), and see how easy or difficult it is for them to understand the models.
6. The group should not only discuss the solutions, but also the process. What has the group learned about information modelling in general, and how will this learning affect the way subsequent exercises will be tackled?
7. The isolated reader should find other people to discuss the models and modelling with. (They need not be people who have read this book.)

7.2 Benson's Hotel

7.2.1 Introduction

Benson's Hotel is a modest but comfortable sixty-room hotel somewhere in England. The restaurant and two bars are open to both residents and non-residents. Clock golf and croquet are played in the garden in summer, and there is a combined gymnasium and sauna; non-residents are charged for the use of these facilities. A ballroom and some smaller function rooms are available for hire. Business connected with the local university is encouraged, and there is a special weekend rate for the parents of undergraduates.

7.2.2 Staff

The senior members of staff are listed below, together with their areas of responsibility:

- *General manager:* overall.
- *Deputy manager:* food and beverage, conferences and banquets, gym and sports, etc.
- *Assistant manager:* reception, personnel.
- *Housekeeper:* upkeep of rooms and public areas, laundry and uniforms, first aid.
- *Head chef:* kitchen.
- *Night porter:* on duty from 11 p.m. to 7 a.m.

There are also several chefs, waiters, chambermaids, receptionists. There is a handyman who handles minor repairs and maintenance, and a part-time gardener. The total payroll varies between thirty and forty, depending upon season.

7.2.3 Front office

The reception desk is located to the right as you enter the hotel, with a small office behind it. It is the policy of the hotel that there should be at least two duty staff at the desk at any time, who are responsible for:

- Sale of rooms (reservation and registration).
- Dissemination of information to guests (concierge function).
- Telephone, messages and mail.
- Coordination of hotel services.
- Charting of room status reports.
- Maintenance, settlement and collection of guest accounts.

The following equipment is held behind the desk and in the front office:

- *Room rack:* an arrangement of file pockets that contain rack slips displaying room status and availability.
- *Folio well:* guest folios are arranged by room number.
- *Billing machine:* a cash register to record all cash transactions and issue receipts to guests.
- *Key rack:* a series of numbered hooks to hang the room keys on.
- *PABX telephone switchboard:* to control incoming and outgoing telephone calls and charges. The operator can monitor all calls if necessary.
- *Reservation rack:* contains information on advance reservations, arranged in date order.
- *Safe:* for guests' valuables.

7.2.4 Reservations

Most reservations are initially made by telephone, although for guests whose stay is to be invoiced to a company, the hotel requires written or telexed confirmation. The room rate is usually determined at this stage and agreed with the guest. The room rate depends on the room itself (i.e. on such features as size, view, quietness, washing and toilet facilities, TV and radio) and on the type of business. For any room, many different rates may be charged, including the following:

- *Standard rate:* normal undiscounted rate (also known as rack rate).
- *Commercial rate:* reduced rate offered to a frequent guest or to a company making frequent use of the hotel (also known as corporate discount).
- *Group plan rate:* reduced rate for a large group or convention.
- *Weekend rate:* Friday/Saturday/Sunday.

- *Package plan rate:* inclusive rate for a package, covering perhaps transport and entertainment as well as the hotel stay and some meals:
  - (a) bed and breakfast;
  - (b) full board;
  - (c) half board.
- *Daytime rate:* for daytime use only, e.g. for recruitment interviews.
- *House rate:* for the use of staff.
- *Complimentary rate:* a free room provided with the compliments of the hotel management.

After establishing the availability of a suitable room, the clerk records the reservation on a reservation slip (Figure 7.1).

Figure 7.1 Benson's
Hotel reservation slip

```
            BENSON'S HOTEL RESERVATION SLIP


Date of arrival:      15/03/89

Length of stay:       2 nights

Agreed rate:          £53.50 B&B

Requirements:         Single room, own shower, orthopedic
                      bed, prefer facing south-east

Name & address:       Mʳ G. Stayer
                      Amalgamated Sales Cᵒ
                      P.O. Box 43
                      London ECZ
                      071-234-5678 X 901

Status:               Guaranteed 3/3/89 - A.C.T.
```

7.2.5 Guest accounting

When a guest checks in to the hotel, an account is opened to record all charges he may incur during his stay. This account results in a bill, which is settled by the guest when he checks out, or signed for subsequent settlement by a company. The guest is only charged for the goods and services recorded on his account at the time he checks out. When guests take additional goods and services from the hotel after having checked out and paid the bill, the hotel often finds it difficult to obtain payment for the additional charges. Furthermore, if there is a delay in recording charges on the account, the hotel may lose its opportunity to collect payment for these. It is therefore vital to record all charges as soon as they are incurred and to prevent guests who have already checked out from receiving goods and services on credit. A floor limit is set by the hotel management from time to time. This is a limit to the credit that can be extended to each guest. The hotel manager must be informed when a guest account approaches or exceeds the floor limit.

Besides maintaining an account (or folio) for each guest, the hotel also maintains accounts as follows:

- An account for each room.
- Master accounts for groups of conventions.
- Accounts for non-residents.
- Employee accounts (for entertaining purposes).
- Control accounts for operating departments.

7.2.6 Agency bookings

Many bookings are not received directly from the guest or his company, but from a wholesaler or tour operator. A series of block bookings is received in return for a percentage commission. Most operators offer demi-pension; this means that dinner is paid for. In this case, the restaurant must offer such guests the *table d'hôte* menu (which is fixed price) and charge separately for drinks. Such wholesale bookings are usually paid for in full. The operator forwards the payment to the hotel on a monthly basis. Commission is calculated quarterly, and a cheque is sent to the operator. The hotel reserves the right to withhold all or part of the commission if the cancellation rate exceeds 15 per cent, according to an agreed formula.

7.2.7 Room management

It is the responsibility of the housekeeper to determine the status of each unoccupied room, which can be:

- Occupied.
- Guest departed.
- Out of order.
- Requires inspection (cleaned – not checked).
- Ready.

In order to assign rooms to guests, the front office requires this information to be passed to it as quickly and accurately as possible. If the housekeeper were provided with information about future reservations, it would be possible to plan more effectively such things as:

- Scheduling of housekeeping personnel.
- Central heating of rooms.
- Planned maintenance and redecoration.

Assignment 1. Develop an information model from the housekeeping perspective. Develop another model from the front office perspective. Compare and contrast the two models.

Assignment 2. Suggest what the business objectives of the hotel might be. Determine some of the critical success factors for the hotel (i.e. the things that must go right, for the objectives to be achieved). What information needs does this imply? Develop a model that includes these information needs.

Assignment 3. There are several commercial packages sold to hotels. If possible, obtain information about such a package. Analyse the data structure of the package, and determine the information model that is implied. Compare this with your own solution.

7.2.8 Management information

Regular operating and financial reports are prepared for the hotel manager by his staff, including:

- An analysis of the different room rates charged.
- A list of the guests who have exceeded credit limits (either the floor limit or the authorization limit quoted by the credit card company).
- An analysis of the business brought in by agencies, together with the commissions due.
- A daily analysis of profit and loss, based on the revenues and costs of each department.
- Guest arrivals/VIPs.
- Function/conference business.

Much of the information needed by the hotel manager and his staff is of an *ad hoc* nature, to support particular decisions. For example, information about the number of enquiries received after running an advertisement, and the amount of business resulting from it, would be useful in deciding whether to repeat the advertisement. Information is also useful in the preparation of budgets.

7.3 Siva UK car hire

The following (incomplete) example was developed by the author for training business users in information and process modelling techniques. It illustrates the typical content of a requirements document, and shows how the requirements document is further supported by the definitions of the entities and processes in the business model itself.

The core of the training was a hypothetical requirements planning exercise, based on a fictional car-hire company. This enabled the participants to build simple data and process models of the car hire company, and analyse the business implications of these models. The reason for choosing a car hire company as a training exercise was that the business would be familiar enough to the participants to enable them to understand the business issues, yet sufficiently distant to enable them to concentrate (for the purpose of the training) on the modelling issues.

Thus they were able to build simple models, and were shown how to progress from simple to complex models, instead of attempting everything at once.

7.3.1 Introduction and information architecture

This fictional car hire company presently operates in the UK only, but is planning to extend its operations into Europe. This will enable the participants to explore the business implications of transnational systems. The main subject areas of Siva UK have been identified as shown in Table 7.1.

Table 7.1. Subject areas of Siva UK

Staff	Vehicles	Hires	Customers
The employees of Siva, their skills and areas of responsibility.	The purchase and disposal of a fleet of cars and vans for hire to customers.	Reservation and hire of cars by customers.	Individuals who have hired vehicles from Siva, or who may do so in future.
Repairs	**Accounts**	**Billing and payments**	**Markets**
Inspection and maintenance of returned vehicles. Breakdown and recovery.	Historical and management accounts, with analysis of profits and costs.	Charging the customers for hire and other services.	Characteristics of customer demand, enabling advertising and other promotions.

Assignment 1. Develop an information model of the present car hire operations, with special attention to the billing and payments subject area. Make as many simplifying assumptions as you like. In particular, you should assume that all transactions are in sterling, and that payments are always in cash.

7.3.2 Requirements documentation

The information model itself is left as an exercise for the reader. However, the resulting requirements document, which was produced during the exercise, may be referred to (Table 7.2). (The document also includes some details of a process model.)

Table 7.2. Requirements document for Siva UK

Business requirements	Representation in model	Implementation considerations
Customers may be either corporate or individual.	There is an entity type Customer, which has two subtypes: Corporate and Individual.	At present, all customers are treated separately, as individuals. It is a new business initiative, to enable large customers to be billed monthly.
Individual customers must pay a deposit before driving.	For individual customers, the process Release Vehicle is dependent upon the process Receive Payment. The deposit counts as an occurrence of the entity type Payment.	
The deposit may be paid as cash or as an authorized credit card slip. Cash will be banked immediately; credit card slips will be retained until the car is returned (or is overdue for return).	Cash or cheque payments are handled by the process Bank Payment. Credit card payments are handled by the process Send Charge to Card Company, which is normally part of the vehicle returns function.	
When an individual customer returns a car, the actual amount due is calculated, and compared with the amount of the deposit.	The process Give Invoice to customer calculates the total amount due, and any outstanding balance, and notifies the customer. This usually takes place while the customer is still standing at the desk.	There is a business objective to speed up the processing when a customer returns a car.

Assignment 2. Siva UK has recently bought the German car hire firm Schmertz GmbH, together with some smaller firms in other countries, and now intends a consolidated operation across Europe. The new company will be known as Siva-Schmertz Auto Hire. Amend your model to allow for international operation.

Assignment 3. Some of the customers pay by charge or credit card. Where in the billing cycle do we send information to the card company? What information? Does your model support this? What information do we need from the card company? And what additional information might be available which would be useful to us?

Assignment 4. A strategic planning exercise for the company has identified some new objectives and action plans:
1. Quicker vehicle pick-up. 2. Better choice of vehicle. 3. Quicker vehicle returns. 4. Reduction of billing errors. 5. Consolidated billing for corporate customers. What changes are required to the information model to support planning, execution and monitoring of these business objectives?

Table 7.2. (Cont.)

Business requirements	Representation in model	Implementation considerations
The final amount due cannot be calculated until the car has been inspected for damages, and the fuel gauge checked.	The process Give invoice to Customer is dependent upon the process Inspect Car.	In the past, this rule has not always been strictly enforced, which has led to errors in billing.
		However, any delays when the car is returned, intended to reduce billing errors, may also annoy the customer.
		Thus the objective to reduce billing errors may conflict to some extent with the objective to increase customer satisfaction.
Revenue is counted from the time payment is received from the customer.	All payments from the customer, including credit card vouchers, are counted as occurrences of Payment. The subsequent receipt of the actual money (minus discount) from the credit card company does not count as an occurrence of Payment.	Credit card discounts and banking charges need to be handled outside this business area, presumably within the general ledger.
Corporate customers must have independent credit checks before doing business on monthly billing terms.		The credit check will be carried out periodically, *not* when the driver is waiting to take the car.
Corporate customers each supply a list of approved drivers. Only persons named on such a list may hire cars under the monthly billing terms.	There is an entity type Approved Driver, and each Corporate Customer may approve several Approved Drivers.	
	There are processes to add and delete Approved Drivers.	
	Each Hire is therefore driven either by an Individual Customer of by an Approved Driver on behalf of a Corporate Customer.	

7.4 Television news agency

7.4.1 Description of company

WorldVis is an international television news agency.[1] Newsworthy events are filmed by camera crews at various locations all over the world. This news coverage is transmitted via the WorldVis headquarters in London to various clients all over the world. Transmission may be by various types of communication link, e.g. satellite or landline, or physical transport of a tape cassette or film.

We are concerned here with assignment decisions, in other words the placing of journalists and crews at particular locations, each assigned to anticipate a particular newsworthy event. This is the responsibility of an editorial team in London which includes both senior journalists and management. (The managers are usually only present during normal office hours; the journalists alternate on a shift rota, so that there are always journalists on duty, 24 hours a day. This poses problems of consistency and continuity, as we shall see.)

The clients of WorldVis are mostly national broadcasting companies, who require foreign material for their news bulletins, which they obtain mostly from international news agencies such as WorldVis. There are many organizations around the world that deal with television news pictures. Besides agencies such as WorldVis itself, there are the big three US networks as well as local/cable broadcasting stations. Among these organizations are many alliances and rivalries, amounting to the sort of tangle familiar to students of diplomatic history. As a consequence of this, there are some 'friendly' organizations, with which WorldVis enters into cooperative deals, sharing resources and costs to get faster or better news; there are also some 'opposition' organizations, with which WorldVis regards itself as being in competition. For example, WorldVis has close ties with one of the three US networks, which usually rules out cooperation with the other two.

The value of a news story depends on the speed with which it can be delivered to the client. In some cases, there is a straight race between the rival agencies. (Thus it is useful to know where the opposition crews are located.) If the story is important enough, and the location difficult enough (e.g. a remote war zone), the clients may be prepared to wait days for the story, and the agency that gets the coverage out first, wins. But often a story is superseded by later events. (e.g. shots of the Pope getting on an aeroplane bound for Manila are of limited interest once shots of his arrival in Manila are available). Most news has a limited shelf life – it quickly ceases to be news at all.

There are many difficulties of moving news material from the source location to the clients, which may add to the cost or the delay. These include:

- Scarcity of satellite link ups (which have to be booked in advance, either for a regular transmission or for a single *ad hoc* transmission).
- War, weather, etc. (which may disrupt transmission).
- Censorship.
- Format differences, requiring conversion of video material from one standard to another.

Journalists often refer elliptically to 'stories', and it is usually clear from the context what exactly they mean. For our purposes, however, we need to use different terminology for each stage of the news-gathering process, and to distinguish carefully between the following entities:

- NEWS EVENT: this is a newsworthy occurrence, happening at a particular place and time. An event may be recorded on film or video by one or more camera crews, or be reported verbally, e.g. by participants or eye witnesses.
- NEWS COVERAGE: this is a sequence of video or film pictures (or 'footage'), shot by a particular camera crew on a particular occasion, covering a particular news event.[2]
- NEWS STORY: this is a packaged item of news, produced by editing, processing and adding commentary to news coverage. A news story may include several related pieces of news coverage, e.g. archive film from the library vaults may be included, or pictures shot at different locations may be juxtaposed. The same news coverage may be used in several stories, i.e. cut to different lengths for different purposes (e.g. a short report for the tea-time bulletin, and a long report for the late night analysis programme).

News coverage may be obtained by:

- Sending a staff crew to the expected location of a news event.
- Hiring a local crew on a freelance basis.
- Buying material from a 'friendly' TV organization.
- (In the case of unexpected events) buying material from any member of the public who happened to pass by with a video camera.

Producing news stories out of news coverage requires work by both journalists (editing decisions, writing commentary scripts, etc.) and technicians (format conversion, physical editing, transmission, etc.). This processing work is often partly carried out in the field (i.e. close to the location of the news events themselves, rather than back in the London studios) in order to utilize the local knowledge of the field journalists and to reduce transmission costs for unwanted coverage.

The exact nature, location and division of labour of this processing is of no concern here, except to note that it is the responsibility of the editorial team to ensure that it is feasible in any given situation. In other words, if there are any special problems that may cause deadlines to be missed, quality standards to be compromised, or excessive costs to be incurred, these should be recognized at an early stage. Often these problems are associated with the part of the world in which the news coverage is obtained (e.g. a war zone, or a country where censorship is rife). When the event itself is of marginal interest, the existence of such problems may persuade the editors not to assign the story.

The total output to the client is normally subject to time constraints. There are regular fixed-length output packages daily and weekly, each containing several stories and directed at several clients. There is no point making additional assignments if there will not be enough space to use any additional coverage. News coverage that cannot be used is a waste of money; it also harms morale. Cameramen get upset if they risk their lives for nothing.

To recognize and evaluate potential news stories requires knowledge of current affairs and 'breaking stories' (i.e. new or unanticipated areas of newsworthiness). This knowledge is obtained from a variety of sources. These include:

- Past coverage: the editors should be familiar with previous reports from the area, including reports by opposition organizations.
- Newspapers and magazines: ideally, the editors should find the time to read all of the British national dailies, as well as selected foreign newspapers and news magazines.
- Teletext and newswire: services such as ORACLE[3] and UPI provide up to date information on the events of the day. But they do not provide the journalists with a 'feel' of a developing political situation, since they are written in a very dry style without interpretation.
- People in the field: journalists, camera crews and other contacts (known as stringers) point out possible news stories to WorldVis. Their news judgement is often biased by their proximity to events and by their desire for work.
- Requests from clients: sometimes a client requests coverage of an event of interest only to itself (e.g. a state visit to Ruritania by the Freedonian President will be of interest only to Freedonian TV). A crew will be commissioned from WorldVis and paid for by the client. But sometimes these events turn out to be of more general interest (e.g. if the president is shot at).

7.4.2 Decision model

The decision whether to assign or not, or what to assign, depends on three factors: cost, benefit and risk. The aim of the editors is to maximize certain benefits, while minimizing the costs and risks involved. The calculation of cost is based on known travel and expense rates, and on charges for processing and delivery. Expense rates are negotiated according to the skill of the crew and the danger involved. This is the responsibility of the editor, who is the manager of the newsroom and a member of the editorial team. Most of the information required for the calculation is based on the experience of this manager, and is not documented.

The calculation of benefit is related to the size or importance of the story, which cannot be objectively measured without considering where and how the story will be used. How important a story is depends ultimately on how interested the clients are likely to be. Financial benefit to WorldVis depends on obtaining revenue from clients, but this revenue is mostly tied to long-term service contracts. WorldVis will gain or lose clients in the long run, according to how the clients evaluate the stories they are provided with. WorldVis must provide a better-quality, value-for-money service than the rival agencies: in crude terms it must have more scoops than the opposition. It follows from this that it is almost impossible to quantify the financial benefits from each individual story. Besides the financial benefits, there are also intangible benefits, including the job satisfaction of journalists and crews, and the prestige of WorldVis.

A calculation of risk is also required. When the editors are planning for the future, they do not know what newsworthy events are actually going to occur, but they should have a reasonable idea of where something interesting is likely to happen. This means they must think of potential stories rather than of actual events.

Assignment 1. Before reading any further, you are invited to try and draw an information model for WorldVis. Your aim is to model all the things that the editors and journalists in London need to know in order to make a s s i g n m e n t decisions. Start by identifying major subject areas.

For each potential story, the editors must estimate the chances of something happening, and the likely size or importance of the event. (For example, it may be reasonably certain that a particular demonstration will take place; what is uncertain is how many demonstrators will turn up, what the 'action' will be, and how much of the action will be captured by the camera.) There is also a risk of the coverage not reaching London within an acceptable time period.

As for the competition with rival agencies, there are two strategies that must be balanced. The low-risk strategy is to cover the same events as the other agencies, to prevent them getting exclusive coverage of anything important. The high-risk strategy is to cover different events, since this increases the chances of getting exclusive coverage. Because of this, each agency tries to conceal its plans from its competitors, but it is usually possible for an editor to make informed guesses about the locations of opposition crews.

7.4.3 Information model

There is a lot of information that is relevant to the assignment decision; much of it depends on subjective judgement and experience, and would be difficult to quantify. This does not affect the model, although it may affect the extent to which it could be represented on a computer. (In a later section, we shall see how it may be useful to model subjective information.)

My model (Table 7.3) identifies seven subject areas.

Table 7.3. Subject areas for WorldVis

Subject area	Relevant information
News events	Probability (in advance) of good coverage Size/importance Degree of likely interest (to each client) Location Type (e.g. war, diplomacy, sport, fashion ...) Danger to crew/other cost factors
Existing coverage	Quality, type, format, access rights Crew Duration and contents (i.e. detailed shotlist) Logistics of delivery to London - communications link - air freight (flight and waybill number) - expected time of arrival Cost - already incurred - required to complete processing

Table 7.3. (Cont.)

TV organizations	Client
	- value of business
	- contract renewal date
	- areas of interest/expectations
	- output packages received
	- usage of news (WorldVis/other sources)
	Ally
	- joint coverage arrangements
	(regular/*ad hoc*)
	- resources available for sharing
	Rival
	- strengths/weaknesses of crews
	- current/recent assignments
	- news coverage on offer
Journalists/crews	Home/base location, current location
	Mobility (e.g. visa problems)
	Terms and conditions of contract
	Costs per assignment
	Equipment and format
	- normally used
	- available if necessary
	Past history and experience
	Reliability, loyalty, inventiveness, guts
	Skills, specializations, preferences
	Languages spoken, local knowledge and contacts
	Morale (e.g. use made of recent coverage)
Locations	News budget for region or country
	Communications links to other locations
	Journeys to other locations
	- travel time and costs
	- geopolitical difficulties
	Living expenses (e.g. average hotel costs)
	Processing and editing facilities
	Local TV standards/formats
	Local language(s)
	Local contacts/stringers
	Censorship practices
Communications	Earth station capability
	Standards/formats
	Satellite advance bookings
	Cost and availability of satellite links

Assignment 2. Review your model against these subject areas. Do not worry if you did not guess all the details, but did you get the structure right? How would you put the remaining details into your model?

Table 7.3. (Cont.)

	- exclusive
	- shared with other TV organizations
Output requirements	Output packages
	- which clients receive which package
	- total length required
	- transmission deadlines
	- communications link
	Existing coverage to meet these requirements
	Documentary or archive library requirements

7.4.4 Discussion: use of model

Outside office hours, all editorial decisions are made by the most senior journalist in the newsroom, known as the editor of the day (EoD). He or she is authorized to make assignments on personal initiative, without consulting management, but subject to the following constraints:

- Assignments for today/tomorrow only.
- No moves across international frontiers.
- Not to exceed a specified cost limit.

The job of EoD is shared between the senior journalists in the newsroom, according to the rotation and alternation of shifts. This leads to problems of continuity and consistency.

First the incoming EoD needs to be brought up to date with the current state of affairs, including the assignments that have already been made (with the reasons for them, if not obvious) and the news that is in the pipeline. At present, this handover is in the form of a detailed written run-down of the present situation and any outstanding problems. Second, because of the differences of personality and experience between the journalists, their judgements of opportunity and risk will differ. The editor (who has overall responsibility for all editorial decisions) may have on one day to encourage a cautious EoD and on the following day to restrain an impetuous one.

Thus the assignment decision is made by a number of people, using a heterogeneous mass of information. Much of this information is soft, in the sense that it is dependent on the judgement of an experienced member of the editorial team, and cannot be accurately and objectively measured. However, this does not prevent such information being communicated. The decision itself depends on the recognition of an opportunity, followed by an evaluation of this opportunity in terms of its potential cost–benefit and risk. This is a classic form of decision making in business. Evaluation should not be based solely on personal experience and judgement; instead, a company consensus as to acceptable levels of cost–benefit and risk needs to be established and maintained.

The information model supports this in a number of ways. One possible use of the model is as a basis for improving the flows and storage of information in the newsroom. (Perhaps some wall charts can be designed to efficiently capture and communicate some of the information. Or perhaps some routine functions could be computerized.) Another possible use is to assess the readiness of individual journalists for promotion and additional responsibilities, since the basis for the decision is made explicit, and provides a yardstick to measure the individual's knowledge and experience. Training could be arranged to cater for specific gaps in an individual's knowledge.

This modelling of expert knowledge is regarded by technologists as a separate discipline, which they call knowledge engineering. Their view is that it serves to extract knowledge from experts and build it into expert systems, which may then make the experts themselves redundant. Our example, however, uses the simple techniques of information modelling to analyse the structure of the experts' knowledge, while staying clear of the rules and guidelines employed by the experts.

7.5 Martimark Enterprises

This commercial organization makes marketing decisions at strategic, tactical and operational levels. These decisions require information. Therefore Martimark will need one or more information systems, to provide information relevant to these decisions. How can we use one or more information models to help design and build such information systems? Marketing information can be more difficult to model than logistical information, because it is likely to be less stable in scope and requirements.

As an example of logistical information, let us consider the information required to manage a warehouse effectively and efficiently. Most of this information can perhaps be derived from the transactions that add stock to the warehouse or subtract stock from it. Observation of the warehouse operations will identify the basic objects: STOCK ITEM, SHELF LOCATION, DELIVERY ORDER, TRUCK, etc. Thus the scope of a warehouse entity model is (approximately) bounded by the warehouse walls.

In marketing, on the other hand, most of the information required for marketing-related decisions comes from outside the organization, not from the day to day business, and refer to objects not controlled by the business. Which objects we are interested in depends entirely what decisions we want to make. Information is of value not because it relates to an object but because it relates to a decision. A marketing decision may be affected by socio-economic trends, political factors, the sales tactics of the competitors, etc. Thus whereas the scope of a warehouse entity model is bounded by the warehouse walls, the scope of a marketing entity model has no natural boundaries. Therefore the only way to develop a reasonably stable information system (or collection of systems) is to analyse the decisions that the organization wants to make, preferably within the context of a systematic decision-making process.

7.5.1 Marketing information

The information of interest to Martimark's marketing department can be divided into market-related (customers and competitors) and external environmental factors, as shown in Figure 7.2

Figure 7.2 Marketing information

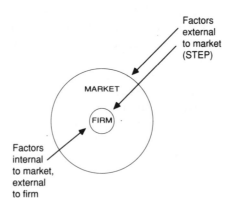

Some of the environmental factors are external to the particular industry or market. These are known as the **STEP** factors.

- *Sociological:* values, lifestyle, births, population, ageing, demography, self-employment, homework, part-time work, jobshare, second jobs, education, attitudes towards trades unions ...
- *Technological :* R&D, new products and processes, innovation, energy, IT, technological expectations ...
- *Economic:* level and volatility of GNP, economic growth, inflation, interest rates, currency exchange rates, monetary, energy prices, commodity prices, weather ...
- *Political:* slant and changeability of local and national policies, 'pendulum politics', parties, legislation, jurisdiction, executive power of government, planning permission, town planning and shopping centre development, attitudes of government: helpful/unhelpful re overseas business, other institutions (Trades Union Congress, Confederation of British Industry, Institute of Directors, universities and business schools, organized pressure groups, Consumers' Association, etc.) ...

There are also the factors arising from within the market itself:

Assignment 1. What are the subject areas for Martimark Enterprises?

- *Market definition:* what is it a market for? Substitute products/services, sub-markets (divisions and segments, relative importance of them), geography (local, regional, national, multinational, global), product differentiation (objective, subjective).
- *Size and growth of demand:* level and pattern of demand, number of potential/actual consumers, demand per consumer, product penetration, product life-cycle, maturity of demand, past trends, future forecasts, relevant STEP factors.

- *Costs:* fixed/variable/overhead costs, sunk costs, marginal production costs, promotion, distribution, economies of scale, learning effects, capacity, efficiency ...
- *Industry structure and competition:* how is market carved up: between a few major players or more widely? Number and size of firms (is each single market or multi-market?), volatility of market share, vertical integration (upstream, downstream), horizontal integration (product range, control over substitutes), competitor tactics, aggressive or gentle, new entrants, retaliation (by existing firms to new entrants or aggressive behaviour by existing firms), barriers to entry (absolute barriers, economies of scale, learning costs, government, product differentiation, switching costs, customer loyalty, patents and licences ...).
- *Bargaining power:* according to Michael Porter, competitive advantage can be obtained by improving negotiations with: (1) buyers; (2) suppliers; (3) capital; (4) labour; (5) management; (6) politicians. Therefore information is needed about the current balance of power.

Each factor should be considered from several angles:
- *Magnitude:* quantify any change
- *Timing:* when, how quickly, will any change take effect (long, medium, short-term)?
- *Probability:* how likely is any change? How accurate are any estimates of timing and magnitude?
- *Susceptibility:* can we do anything to affect the occurrence, timing or magnitude of any change? Can our competitors do anything? are they likely to?
- *Competitor perspective:* to what extent do our competitors view the market differently to us? Do they define the product/service differently, do they operate in a different geographic area, do they have competitors who are not ours?
- *Recursion:* the analysis may need to be repeated from the perspective of your bargaining partners, especially your customers, or *their* customers (e.g. a tin-can manufacturer may need to analyse trends in the food-processing industry, or the food retail industry).

The subject areas of marketing information could be as shown in Figure 7.3.

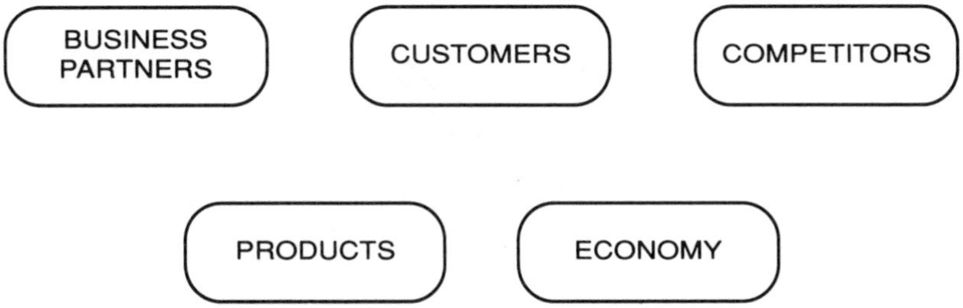

Figure 7.3 Subject areas of marketing information

They may be defined as follows:

Assignment 2. Identify some candidate entity types within the ECONOMY subject area, and produce a rough information model.

1. Business partners may include any person or organization with which a formal or informal agreement may be struck, including suppliers and sub-contractors, retailers, wholesalers, distributors and overseas agents, bankers and investors, trade unions, joint venture partners, universities and other research contractors, exhibitions and trade journals ...
2. Customers may include both the direct purchasers and the end-consumers of the products or services.
3. Competitors may include any organization offering equivalent or substitute products/services to the customers or any organization offering equivalent or substitute benefits to the business partners.
4. Products and services which the organization may provide.
5. Economic information includes general demographic, sociological, macro-economic, political and other external factors.

Note that all these five subject areas will include information that refers to a hypothetical longer-term future as well as the actual past and present and the planned short-term future.

7.5.2 Product marketing decisions

What is the information required for? Marketing decisions can be divided into four specific areas (known as the four Ps), which we can depict around a strategic core. (see Figure 7.4.) These areas may be defined as follows:

Figure 7.4 The four Ps

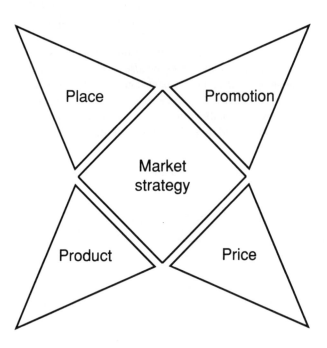

Assignment 3. Sketch one or more information models of the marketing four Ps.

- *Product* includes the packaging and differentiation of the product or service range, as well as an understanding of the features intended to be of benefit to customers.
- *Price* includes general pricing policies as well as the details of each price charged for each product within each market sector.[4]
- *Place* includes the distribution channels and tactics.
- *Promotion* includes sales tactics and general publicity.

Assignment 4. How does your economic information model interface to your product marketing model(s)?

The entity types could well be extremely abstract and generalized: FACT, DECISION, INFORMATION SOURCE, SURVEY, SCENARIO, etc. (A process model would probably be equally abstract and generalized, and could include such processes as OBTAIN FACT, COMMISSION SURVEY, EVALUATE INFORMATION SOURCE, CORROBORATE FACT, etc.)

7.6 Summary

In this chapter four case studies have been presented. This has given the reader the opportunity to experiment with information modelling techniques. Meanwhile, the diversity of the case studies is intended to demonstrate the variety of situations to which information modelling techniques can be applied. In particular, we have touched on the modelling of broad strategic information, and the modelling of complex knowledge.

Notes

1. The name is an amalgam of the two rival companies operating in London. This is intended to obscure which of the two companies is being described.
2. Virtually all coverage is nowadays on video, but the library archives are full of film coverage of past events.
3. This is a UK-based teletext service, unrelated to the DBMS (Database Management System) of the same name.
4. Good examples are to be found in C. M. Breath and B. Ives, 'Competitive information systems in support of pricing' *MIS Quarterly*, March 1986, pp. 85–96.

8 Difficult things to model

Part of the expertise of a skilled information modeller consists in knowing at least one (preferably more than one) solution to a wide variety of modelling problems. This chapter aims to give the reader a short cut to this knowledge, by discussing a wide range of the types of things that managers have to think about, from a wide range of businesses and services.

Some of the examples will be familiar to you from your private life as a consumer or citizen, rather than your working life (past, present or future). However, do not forget that, for some people, these areas dominate their working life.

8.1 How to use this chapter

8.1.1 Use as modelling resource

This chapter can be used as a modelling resource, containing standard and non-standard solutions appropriate to specific modelling situations, as well as hints, possible solutions, partial solutions and issues relating to a wide variety of business situations.

The examples in this chapter describe typical situations that an information analyst could encounter. For each situation, we have described one or more concepts or structures that could be used to model the situation. We have also tried to indicate how you would choose between the alternatives. What specific difficulties should you expect (or at least be alert to), and what kinds of questions should you ask?

Some readers may wish to browse at random within the chapter, while others may prefer to use the index to access specific topics. However, for the benefit of those readers that may wish to read the chapter from start to finish, there is an attempt to group related topics together, and to follow a progression from simpler entities (such as physical objects and people) to more difficult ones. (Some types of entity will crop up more than once in the chapter – this is to allow us to consider different aspects of the same thing.) The names for the entity types in this chapter are, of course, merely suggestions. You must find terminology that suits the organization you are modelling.

Some organizations may wish to use this collection of examples as the starting point for a more extensive library of examples, tailored to their own requirements.

8.1.2 Possible learning objectives

This chapter can also be used as a learning resource. Some of the things the reader may wish to learn from this chapter are:

1. An understanding of the possible ways of modelling specific objects, and of the specific issues that may need to be investigated when modelling these objects.
2. An understanding of the business issues relating to specific types of information and systems.
3. An appreciation how the same basic structure can often be used to model situations that at first sight seem completely different. The reader will gain more from each example by trying to think of further applications of the same structure, to model situations s/he is already familiar with.

Depending on the reader's background and experience, some of the examples will be easily recognized, while other examples will be unfamiliar.

Some of the examples are taken from particular functional areas of a typical business, such as manufacturing, marketing and personnel. Some readers may not be familiar with the problems faced in such areas, and the concerns of the relevant functional experts. Such readers are advised to persevere with these examples, since they stand to gain not only a better understanding of information modelling, but also a valuable introduction to business and administration. (This may sound arrogant, but it is not intended to be. Many information modellers, including the author, have gained much insight into business problems by expressing their information content as simple models.)

To get the most out of this chapter, you are advised to pause after each example, and try to think of some examples from your own experience, which the structure fits, and see whether you can apply our guidelines to your own examples.

8.2 Things

As an introduction to this chapter, we look at ordinary things and people, from the concrete to the abstract.

8.2.1 Physical objects

The unrefined and sluggish mind
*   Of Homo javanensis*
Could only treat of things concrete
*   And present to the senses.[1]*

The easiest class of things to model is that of physical countable objects. These are material bodies. Countable means that each occurrence is physically separate from every other occurrence. Entity types that belong to this class may include PERSON, PRODUCT, OFFICE BLOCK, VEHICLE, FURNITURE ITEM and HOUSE.

Each of these examples appears simple at first, but may reveal some hidden complications when analysed properly. For example, does a product include its packaging, does an office with two separate entrances count as two blocks, does a house include its garden, does a truck with trailer count as one vehicle or two, does a three-piece suite count as one item of furniture or three? (What about the cushions?) Despite these problems, concrete physical objects tend to be easier to model than abstract, conceptual objects. This means that modellers sometimes fool themselves; they pretend that what they are modelling consists of objective physical objects, when all they can really be sure of is subjective mental constructs.

We have already seen examples of this in Chapter 3, where the simple and natural interpretation of an entity type turns out not to be supported by the information available to identify it. And we shall encounter further examples in this chapter.

8.2.2 Persons

It would seem that the easiest entity type to define is that of PERSON and its various subtypes. There are however some complications, associated with the criterion of identity attached to people. A person changes continuously – in weight or opinions. But for it to be meaningful for us to say this, it must be the same person that used to weigh that or think that, and now weighs this or thinks this. A person can suffer amputation of a limb or breast, loss of hair or teeth, or any other physical alterations, while retaining his/her identity as a person. A person remains the same after a liver transplant, or a heart transplant. Even when a person is unrecognizable, thanks to cosmetic surgery, laryngitis and/or psychological transformation, we can discover, perhaps with surprise, that it is the same person ('old so-and-so after all!'), so this still implies continuity of identity.

But we would, I think, hesitate at brain transplants. Who is this person now, with a brain from here, and a body from there – does he or she 'inherit' the identity of the body or of the brain? What about transplants of only a part of the brain? It is in the West today that we commonly regard the brain as the location of 'personality'. In other cultures or periods, it may be the heart or liver. Descartes thought that the pineal gland was the seat of the soul. This illustrates that our choice of brain as the criterion of personal identity is to some extent arbitrary.

For most business purposes, it is not necessary to solve these philosophical puzzles, although if medical technology advances, some legal complications may emerge. Shall we sue a brain transplant patient for the debts of the brain donor (or, for that matter, the body donor)? In a paternity dispute, will it be the brain-father or the body-father that pays maintenance for the child?

Many business purposes can be satisfied with an entity type that represents people without requiring full lifelong continuity. There may be two or more occurrences of PERSON, representing the same person at different times.

One of the commonest entity types of a target organization is that of EMPLOYEE. What is the criterion of identity for an employee? For example, if a member of staff leaves the company and rejoins later, is he or she the same employee as before, or does the concept of employee imply continuity of employment? It may be easier to model EMPLOYEE as a continuous employment of a person, so that each employee only has one joining date and one leaving date. The number of people joining the company twice may be sufficiently low for it to become an acceptable simplification to ignore this altogether, so that such people exist as two or more occurrences of EMPLOYEE. You might need to consider how this affected pension rights.

Take another example: in a model of a university, does the former student have the same identity as the professor? In other words, does the 40-year-old professor have the same identity as the 20-year-old student she once was? To take a trivial consequence of this, does she have the same library membership?

8.2.3 Equipment

What is a computer? To the manufacturer, it may be a box containing a processing unit and possibly a hard disk. To the user, it may be a configuration including not only the box itself, but also a screen monitor, mouse, keyboard, various cables and connectors, and so on. Some people may not care to know about the distinction between hardware and software. If a manager requests a new computer for a new member of staff, she may well assume that it is a complete configuration, including all hardware and software accessories.

Many other types of equipment have the same ambiguity, having accessories that may or may not be included as part of the equipment, depending on the chosen perspective. To decide whether to model EQUIPMENT ITEM as the separate component, or the usable configuration, consider what information needs there are at each level. For example, at what level is equipment maintenance and repair carried out? Does the entire configuration have to be sent to the workshop, or merely the faulty component? At what level is planning and purchasing carried out? At what level do accountants want to calculate ASSET values and depreciation?

When equipment is leased, particular care is required in the definition, so that the leasing company knows exactly what it may repossess if the lessee defaults.

If there are some information needs at each level, then several entity types may be required, so that an EQUIPMENT CONFIGURATION will consist of several EQUIPMENT ITEMS.

8.2.4 Products

Here are the products of a beer company:

- Lager.
- Lager Brand X.
- Lager Brand X in large cans.

- Lager Brand X in large cans, packaged in sixes.
- Lager Brand X in large cans, packaged in sixes, with special promotional offer (e.g. price reduction, free gift, competition entry).
- Lager Brand X in large cans, packaged in sixes, as supplied solely to supermarket Y.

Which of these is the true entity type PRODUCT?

There may well be an existing product code, and it is worth knowing exactly what this code identifies. However, this is merely a fact about the current systems, not about the true business requirement. It may turn out that it would be better to model PRODUCT at a different level. (Implementing this new definition of product would, of course, require the design of a new coding structure, and a migration strategy to convert from the old codes to the new codes.) To discover the business requirement, consider the following types of question:

- At what level do you want to make marketing decisions (price, promotion, etc.)?
- At what level do you want to manage production and distribution?
- At what level do you want to monitor costs and profitability?

The possible levels include:

- Product group/type.
- Package type/size.
- Packages within packages.
- Special offers.
- Promotional give-aways.
- Customer-specific packaging.

The reason for some of the complications about PRODUCT is that a company does not want to manage every version and size of every product separately, but wants to analyse and control the business by grouping similar things together.

Product information model

Figure 8.1 is a possible model of the product structure. PRODUCT denotes the basic beer (or whatever), independent of packaging. PRODUCT BY CONTAINER TYPE denotes the packaged product. The attributes here include price. Customer orders specify quantities of these entities. And it is at this level that substitution rules can be defined, which define acceptable alternatives for particular products (e.g. when out of stock of Xs, deliver six times the quantity of Ys). Thus the ORDER specifies the product, independently of the product batch. However, the DELIVERY to the customer must contain specific amounts from particular brews. (This information must be retained in case of any possible quality problems.)

CONTAINER TYPE here denotes everything to do with the container – including its label. This implies that each special promotion involves different occurrences of CONTAINER TYPE . This is correct if we want to have different prices for the same PRODUCT in similar containers but with different special offers. The attributes

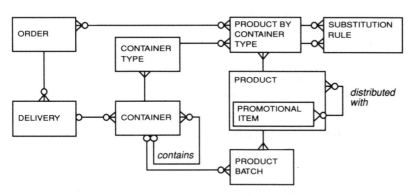

Figure 8.1 Product structure

include physical size (external), volume (internal), weight (both full and empty), as well as a description. There may also be standard cost details. A CONTAINER may directly contain product (more exactly, a quantity from a specific batch) or may contain smaller containers, or may be empty. A crate may contain empty bottles, or full bottles of one or more product. The CONTAINER can be identified by a code number on the label, from which we can deduce the contents (including the specific PRODUCT BATCH). The label may also include redundant data, if this is convenient for the production operations. Ideally, we should record exactly which containers have been delivered to which customers on which occasion.

Some types of container have permanent code numbers, which they retain when reused. Other types of container (e.g. bottles) have amnesia, and we cannot trace the history of an individual bottle from one use to the next (nor do we need to). It would probably be best to model empty bottles merely as stock items related to the container type; a bottle becomes an occurrence of CONTAINER only when it is filled and labelled and numbered. (Thus each time the same physical bottle is refilled, we get a new occurrence of CONTAINER.) The rule for allocating identifiers to containers therefore depends on the container type. Note: there can be ORDERS and DELIVERYS for other purposes, e.g. collection of empties or returns. Thus the relationships between the ORDER/DELIVERY subject area and the PRODUCTS subject area are optional.

New product development

More generally, new products usually emerge from a complex process of marketing and R&D. At what stage in this process can we start to identify a new product as such? When a customer casually mentions an unfulfilled need (PRODUCT OPPORTUNITY)? When the marketing department specifies the combination of features the new product would have to have (PRODUCT FEATURE)? When the R&D department builds the first prototype (PRODUCT PROTOTYPE)?

The crucial question is at what stage we can say definitely how many products we have. This is usually not finally determined until detailed market research is under way, and the product launch is being provisionally planned. This would therefore be the sensible place to create a new occurrence of PRODUCT. If earlier stages of product development need to be modelled, it may be safer to model these separately.

One-off products can be simpler than this. It may be valid to create a new occurrence of SHIP or BUILDING while it is still on the drawing board, since we can probably assume that one blueprint converts smoothly into one final construction.

8.2.5 Bill of materials

A product is manufactured from many components. Each type of component may be used in several products, or several times in the same product. For example, a bicycle factory may use the same type of spokes to build front wheels and back wheels, or bicycle wheels and tricycle wheels. One of the great innovations of Henry Ford was this standardization of products and components, which simplifies purchasing and assembly.[2] The fewer different components you need, the better. There is therefore a many-to-many relationship between PRODUCT and COMPONENT. Furthermore, there is the same relationship between a product and a subassembly, as between a subassembly and a basic component. This results in a complex network of parts; this network is commonly called a bill of materials.

In early days of information modelling and database, bill of materials modelling was regarded as the extreme of difficulty, and instruction in modelling techniques usually culminated in a triumphant demonstration of the standard solution to the so-called bill of materials problem. But although the modelling of bill of materials does present some features of interest, the solution is now widely known. Therefore this book does not expect the reader to gasp with amazement and admiration when the solution is revealed. In fact, we take the view that because the bill of materials represents purely technical information, it presents fewer difficulties to the information modeller than those aspects of the organization where people are involved.

Figure 8.2 Bill of materials solution

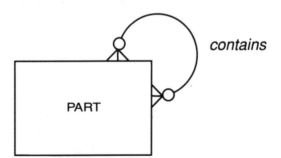

contains

PART

We have already seen that a many-to-many relationship can be resolved into two one-to-many relationships, by the introduction of an additional intersection entity type. This is also true of involuted many-to-many relationships. If we resolve Figure 8.2, we get Figure 8.4. It contains two entity types and two relationships: this is perhaps why some people think it complicated.

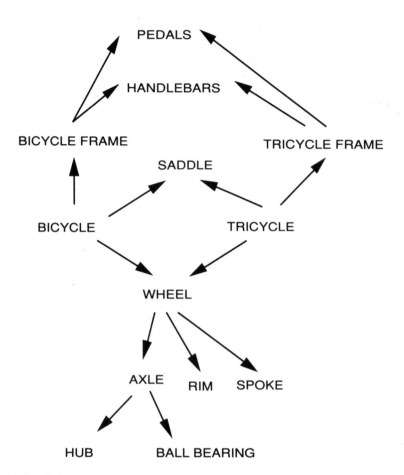

Figure 8.3 A bicycle and parts

In Figure 8.3, which shows the *contains* relationship, the arrow shows that the bicycle contains wheels which contain axles which contain ball bearings. Bicycles and tricycles share some common components (e.g. the same saddle is used), which is why the relationship is many-to-many and not one-to-many. What we cannot see on the occurrence diagram is that a tricycle requires three wheels, while a bicycle only requires two. Furthermore, a wheel requires a certain number of spokes, although the factory must allow for an additional number to be bent, spoiled and wasted. This information is represented as attributes of the COMPONENT entity type, as in Figure 8.4.

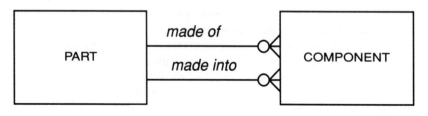

Figure 8.4 A component entity type

This can be illustrated as a table (Table 8.1), with the occurrences of PART shown as both rows and columns, and the occurrences of COMPONENT being all the non-empty cells in the matrix. (In the subset shown below, we have seven occurrences of PART and seven occurrences of COMPONENT.)

Table 8.1 Part–component matrix

PART made of / made into	Bicycle	Tricycle	Wheel	Axle	Ball bearing	Spoke	Saddle
Bicycle			2				1
Tricycle			3				1
Wheel				1		20	
Axle					40		
Ball bearing							
Spoke							
Saddle							

Herbert Simon[3] showed how hierarchical assemblage was more robust than unstructured.[4] If we imagine a watch-maker trying to assemble and align a complex mechanism, and being frequently interrupted, he will waste much less time if he only has to backtrack to the most recent subassembly, rather than to start from scratch.

But the division of a product into subassemblies is often arbitrary. The end-product may have a rubber tube joining A to B. Does it matter whether you attach the tube to A first or to B first? If the subassemblies A and B are produced by different man and/or machines, does it matter which of them has the responsibility for attaching the rubber tube? Could an expert determine from examining the end-product, what the sequence of assembly was? One or other sequence may be more convenient, but there may be nothing in it.

So although the atomic parts may be the same, and the complete product may also be the same, the intermediate subassemblies may vary. If we want this flexibility, it follows that the product cannot be identified bottom up, by its subassemblies.

8.2.6 Types and prototypes

When people talk of a particular car, or a particular flag, they are often speaking not of a real physical object: a heap of metal or a scrap of cloth. Instead, they are speaking of a class of physical objects, such as the Austin Mini, or the French tricolour. The Austin Mini is an occurrence of an entity type that is identified by manufacturer, make and model (and perhaps year and version); the French tricolour is an occurrence of an entity type that is identified by its pattern of colours and/or by the country or organization with which it is associated. Is it correct to call these entity types CAR and FLAG respectively?

The trouble with calling these classifying entity types CAR and FLAG is that we may also want to have entity types whose occurrences include particular instances, such as Michael Palin's mini, or the actual flag now flying over the Elysée Palace. In order to avoid confusion, therefore, we should reserve such names as CAR and FLAG for these physical objects, and use such terms as CAR MODEL and FLAG PATTERN for the types or classes. For this reason, it is common to find information models with several entity types called <something> TYPE. The real difficulty is not in naming but in defining these abstract entity types.

In a previous section (PRODUCT), we discussed the different levels of abstraction at which beer could be modelled. If we decided that the basic PRODUCT is the half-litre can of Brand X lager, then higher levels of abstraction, such as lager in general, or canned beer in general, may be referred to as PRODUCT TYPE. Such XYZ TYPE entity types need to be very carefully defined, since it is important to be clear exactly what level of abstraction is represented. Combining different kinds of classification into a single entity type is likely to be more confusing than useful – thus PRODUCT TYPE may be either entities like 'lager in general' or entities like 'canned beer in general', but not both.

Sometimes we want to classify our customers (and other external organizations), in various ways. Here again, the entity type CUSTOMER TYPE or COMPANY TYPE can be defined at several different levels of abstraction, but it is necessary to be clear exactly which level it represents in the model. A company can be a manufacturer, or a food manufacturer, or a frozen food manufacturer, or an ice cream manufacturer. What level of detail do you need in your classification?

Sometimes the selection of a specific level of classification is evaded by introducing a hierarchy on COMPANY TYPE. Thus the same company may be simultaneously linked to four occurrences of COMPANY TYPE: manufacturer, food manufacturer, frozen food manufacturer, and ice-cream manufacturer. This structure is clumsy, and should be avoided if possible.

8.2.7 Abstract entities

> The tendency has always been strong to believe that whatever receives a name must be an entity or being, having an independent existence of its own: and if no real entity answering to the name could be found, men did not for that reason suppose that none existed, but imagined that it was something peculiarly abstruse and mysterious, too high to be an object of sense. [5]

An information model will usually include both abstract and concrete objects. In simple terms, an abstract entity type is one that does not exist independently, but can only be understood as belonging to one or more other entity type. For example, CUSTOMER TYPE makes sense only as a classification of CUSTOMER, and so on.

Concrete objects are particular things that can be pointed at, or identified directly, such as historical occurrences, material objects, people and their shadows. Actions and events are concrete, in the sense that they can be directly observed, whereas qualities and properties, numbers and species are not particular entities, but either abstract entities or attributes.

It is not important to classify exactly which entity types are abstract. Philosophers might argue whether COLOUR was concrete (because redness can be directly perceived) or abstract (because redness implies the existence of something that is red). This debate is theoretical, and therefore of no importance to us. But what does matter to us here is that some particular difficulties arise, in defining and identifying abstract objects, over and above the normal difficulties of concrete objects.

Some analysts express hostility to any excessive proliferation of abstract objects in their models; they apply the principle known as **Ockham's razor** (named after the mediæval philosopher William of Ockham): 'Entities shall not be multiplied beyond what is necessary.' This principle is an attractive one to state, but a surprisingly difficult one to apply; what happens in practice is that as soon as something (however abstract) is put forward as a potential entity, it becomes very difficult to prove that it should not after all be included in the model. This bias, which makes it easier to add abstract entities than to remove them, has been nicknamed Plato's beard, since it is said to dull the edge of Ockham's razor.[6]

8.3 Substances

In this section, we consider the modelling of substances. A substance is an uncountable thing, whose quantity is a weight or volume or other measurement, rather than a number of occurrences; e.g., gasoline, salt, sugar, flour. (At grammar school, these would probably be called mass terms, which means that they do not have a plural.) The essential point about a substance is that it does not consist of discrete things. Of the substance itself, we cannot ask 'how many?', we can only ask 'how much?'. But for information modelling purposes, we need to find ways of representing substance with entity types that can be counted, associated with the substances themselves. This can be done in several ways, depending on the following question. What can we do with a substance?

Most of the discussion in this section is in terms of material substances, produced from such processes as mining and agriculture. However, the same approach may be taken in modelling non-material substances, such as energy or data or money. (Money is a classic substance: we always ask how much money, not how many monies.)

8.3.1 Quality

We can distinguish different types or qualities of the substance. For example, we may distinguish brown flour from white flour, or rye flour from wheat flour. This can be modelled using an entity type such as SUBSTANCE QUALITY, SUBSTANCE TYPE or often just SUBSTANCE.

Sometimes there may be several different aspects of quality to consider. For example, the quality of coffee depends on the region where it is grown, as well as the roasting and grinding. Thus if coffee can be from four different regions (say: Mysore, Java, Uganda and Nicaragua), can be roasted medium or high, and can be ground coarse, medium or fine, there are twenty-four (4 x 2 x 3) possible combinations of source, roast and grind, giving us twenty-four unblended occurrences of COFFEE. There is also an unlimited number of possible blends, since the unblended coffees can be mixed in infinitely many different proportions. Some of these possible blends might be occurrences of COFFEE. Which ones? Only those that are actively planned, produced or otherwise considered for some business purpose (and there can presumably only be a finite number of these).

With many agricultural products, the flavour may change from one year to the next, or from one part of a region to another. Wine is particularly distinguished by such characteristics. But with some products, the consumers may prefer (or may be thought to prefer) a standard and constant flavour. So there are sometimes professional blenders, whose job is to mix different substances to produce the same flavour, year in year out. These blenders can be found in cigarette manufacturers, tea importers, whisky distillers, and other such companies. In such situations, the central entity type may be SUBSTANCE FLAVOUR, since the blenders will be able to name and describe each one in some detail. (For example, a whisky might be described as follows: 'dark golden in colour with a lovely grassy / leafy / cut-barley aroma – very smooth with vanilla and slight marzipan notes'.) The information needed by the blenders are the relevant characteristics and the price or cost of each available batch of the input substance. This leads us to the next way of looking at substances.

8.3.2 Quantity

We can store a quantity of the substance in a container. This can be modelled using an entity type such as SUBSTANCE QUANTITY or SUBSTANCE BATCH. Alternatively, the quantity may be an attribute of the CONTAINER, but only if each CONTAINER only contains one type of substance (which would be a one-to-many relationship between CONTAINER and SUBSTANCE QUALITY). Note that although a container may only contain one type of substance at a given time, it may contain a variety of substances at different times.

Containers may be:

- Separately identifiable.
- Reusable but indistinguishable.
- Not reusable.

We have a problem if we try to model the identifiable ones and the non-identifiable ones in the same entity type. But there may be some processes in which the identifiable and non-identifiable containers play the same role. One option is to cheat, to pretend that all containers are identifiable (by giving them dummy ID numbers).

8.3.3 Moving

We can ship or move a quantity of the substance, from one location or container to another. This can be modelled using an entity type such as SHIPMENT or MOVEMENT: see Figure 8.5. Note that this is not the same as moving or shipping a container (empty or full) from one location to another. However, the movement of a container implies the movement of what it contains at the time.

Figure 8.5 Shipment or movement

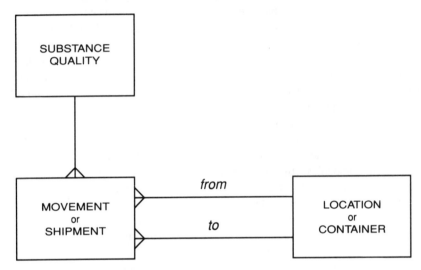

8.3.4 Measuring

We can measure a quantity of the substance. This can be modelled using an entity type such as MEASUREMENT. Remember that measurement may be inaccurate or unreliable. Thus two measurements of the 'same' quantity may give different results. We may for this reason be interested in the person responsible for the measurement, the date and time of measurement, and the tool or technique used; all of these could be attributes of MEASUREMENT (or relationships between MEASUREMENT and other entity types).

We can also measure the quality of a substance. For example, the specific gravity or sulphur content of a quantity of crude oil or other hydrocarbon. These measurements may also be inaccurate, so the same remarks apply as for quantitative measurements.

8.3.5 Dividing, mixing and separation

We may split a quantity of the substance into two or more quantities of the same substance. (We usually assume that this obeys the laws of arithmetic, i.e. that the weights and/or volumes of the resulting quantities add up to the weight or volume of the original quantity. But this may depend on how accurate the measurement is.) This may involve separate occurrences of SUBSTANCE QUANTITY, for the before and after quantities.

We may also merge two or more quantities of a substance into one quantity. If we assume that the qualities of the merged substances are consistent, then the laws of arithmetic will probably apply, as above. However, if the merged quantities are of different qualities, perhaps different substances altogether, then what will result is a different quantity of a new blended substance.

For example, if we mix one grade of gasoline with another grade, we get a grade that differs from both. (Separation of a blend into its components is sometimes possible, but may require rather more processing than the mixing. For example, to separate a gasoline blend into its components, you need an oil refinery. However, not all separation processes are as expensive and high-tech as this. For example, simple sieves can be used to sort small objects of different sizes, to separate stones from rice, or gold from river mud. Often the input substance is an impure mixture, and must be refined before it can be used. Wheat is separated from chaff by threshing, grape juice from grapeskins by treading, and so on.)

8.3.6 Transforming

The substance may change quantity or quality over a period of time. The weight of a bale of tobacco, or a sack of flour, depends on the humidity. The volume of a liquid depends on the temperature. Substances may leak, evaporate or ferment. Chemical or physical processes may be predictable or not, desired or not. If these changes are important, they can be modelled with an entity type such as SUBSTANCE TRANSFORMATION.

There may be many possible ways for substances, mixed in certain proportions, and subjected to certain conditions (e.g. temperature, pressure, vibration, radiation) for a certain length of time, to be transformed into other substances. Each of these ways can be modelled as a SUBSTANCE TRANS-FORMATION RECIPE, or just RECIPE. We could suppose that each RECIPE has several input substances, or INGREDIENTS, for each of which an input quantity is specified, and one or more output substances, or PRODUCTS, for each of which a yield quantity may be estimated. A planned or actual SUBSTANCE TRANSFORMATION may therefore be according to a set RECIPE: see Figure 8.6.

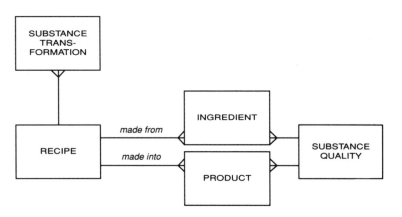

Figure 8.6 Substance transformation

Sometimes we will only be interested in recipes with a single product, or we ignore side-products and waste. This simplifies the model somewhat. Sometimes we will be interested in alternative recipes, with substitute ingredients (e.g. either so much honey or so much brown sugar). This might require an entity type called RECIPE VERSION. Each RECIPE has many RECIPE VERSIONS. Each RECIPE VERSION has a specific set of ingredients, without substitutions. Thus each RECIPE VERSION may be substituted for other RECIPE VERSIONS of the same RECIPE.

Sometimes we will be interested in intangible ingredients, such as various forms of energy; these can also be modelled as substances of a kind. A recipe may also require equipment or processing plant, and the use of a catalyst, which is a substance necessary to the process that remains unchanged by it.

8.3.7 Branding, buying and selling

We may sell the same physical substance under two different brand names, or different physical substances under the same brand name. Oil companies do this regularly, selling different mixes of gasoline in winter and summer from the same pumps.

Contracts between oil companies to buy and sell hydrocarbon and similar substances usually specify ranges of acceptable qualities (e.g. specific gravities, sulphur content, etc.) and quantities. Thus the purchaser does not know the exact qualities or quantities until the tanker arrives and is unloaded. The actual price to be paid may be calculated from these measurements. And yet materials planning must go ahead with the inexact or contracted quantities, with the flexibility to adjust the plans if necessary when the quantity can be measured.

The biggest problem with substances is to establish a criterion of identity. When is one substance the same as another? Sometimes the criterion of identity will be context dependent; thus the production department regard two things as different substances, while the marketing department regard them as the same substance. In some products, especially where colour varies slightly from one production run to the next (such as paint, knitting wool, wallpaper or cloth) the consumer demands that this confusion should be removed, and that the production run numbers (or equivalent) should be printed on the package, in order that the drawing room or pullover should have a consistent hue. (The consumer is here playing a similar role to the blender described earlier.)

We have been talking in this section about uncountable substances. There are often populations that are theoretically, but not practically countable. Thus sugar or sand is theoretically countable, grain by grain, but this is not an activity that appeals to practical people. Who wants to count the fruit-flies in a glass tank, or the trees in a forest?

8.3.8 Data/information

The English word 'data' causes grammatical confusion. Some people use the word as singular: 'the data is . . .' Others use it as plural: 'the data are . . .' Although one may count the number of bits and bytes in a parcel of data, common sense usage of the word is like a mass term, as the substances discussed in the previous section. 'A big library may contain a million books, and a floppy disc may contain a million bytes of data, but have you ever heard of a library with a million pieces of books, or a disc which can contain a million data? '[7]

Since it has become fashionable to preach the importance of information as a corporate resource, it has become necessary sometimes to model information as part of the information model itself. This sounds circular. Some people try to avoid this circularity; others embrace it. Let us explore some of the alternatives. One approach is to separate information from the other objects of interest to the organization. The information model of information is called a **metamodel**, because it represents the structure and semantics of the modelling language itself. This metamodel will perhaps look like an ordinary information model, except that the entity types will be information objects such as ENTITY TYPE, RELATIONSHIP, ATTRIBUTE and so on. From such a metamodel, a special kind of database is designed and implemented, called a data dictionary, encyclopædia or repository.

One of the problems with data is its easy reproducibility. This results in often having several versions of the same thing, floating about a data system. And then one version may be amended, enhanced, updated. Or perhaps more than one version may each receive a different set of amendments and updates.

8.3.9 Software and version

Data and information represent knowledge, which can be 'captured' into a model or into software. We shall return to the modelling of specific knowledge later; in this section, we are concerned merely with information as a kind of substance.

Software can exist in many different versions. This applies to all kinds of software: not merely computer programs but also books, films, music, TV programmes, etc. Information models themselves can be regarded as software, existing in many versions. One way of handling this is to distinguish SOFTWARE TITLE from SOFTWARE VERSION (or SOFTWARE EDITION). A version may have a specific date or purpose, and be written in a specific language. Different versions may be edited differently, be abridged or restricted (e.g. for demonstration purposes), or contain different bugs. A computer accounts package may exist in a number of versions which follow the local tax laws. One version of a foreign film may be dubbed into English, while another version of the same film may have English subtitles.

Distribution of software requires a physical medium (e.g. paper, disk, satellite transmission). Thus we may further distinguish SOFTWARE VERSION from SOFTWARE PHYSICAL VERSION or SOFTWARE VERSION FORMAT. For example, the same version of the same computer program may be available on three 5.25 inch disks, or two 3.5 inch disks. The same version of the same film may be available on Betamax or VHS. The same edition of the same book may be available in paperback or cloth-bound. A satellite transmission may or may not be encrypted. The distinction between SOFTWARE VERSION and SOFTWARE PHYSICAL VERSION is probably only necessary to support the duplication and distribution processes, and it may sometimes be possible to do without this distinction.

There may then be large numbers of physical copies of the software, represented as SOFTWARE PHYSICAL COPY. Protection of copyright requires control of the number of occurrences of this entity type, and/or rules for creation of new occurrences. Some copy protection routines require each SOFTWARE PHYSICAL COPY to be separately identifiable. When we require a copy of some software, we may sometimes specify which version we want, or we may merely assume we are going to get the latest or the local version. Thus an order may name a SOFTWARE TITLE, or refer to a SOFTWARE VERSION.[8]

8.4 Time and space

In this section, we look at some issues in the modelling of places (including addresses, locations, travel between locations, and geographical classifications), and time periods. We also consider how to represent the past as well as the present in an information model.

8.4.1 Address

In order to communicate with your suppliers, your customers, your employees, or the media, you probably need to know where they live. The simplest way of modelling an address is to regard it as an attribute of the person or company being addressed. But this approach has its critics. Some critics may observe that entities of several different types may have addresses, so that ADDRESS would have to be an attribute of CUSTOMER, SUPPLIER, EMPLOYEE and so on. Another observation is that the structure of an address is more or less the same regardless of whose address it is, so that each address consists of a street address, town or city, postal code or zip code, a telephone number, and so on. A third observation is that many people may share the same address.

Such observations may suggest the definition of a separate entity type, called ADDRESS, linked to whatever other entity types may have addresses. All companies or persons can have addresses, as well as such agencies as magistrates' courts or police stations. This is a common approach, but it now raises further problems.

1. Does anything uniquely identify an address, apart from the whole address itself? How do we specify that two people share the same address: is it based on the fact that the address details coincide, or is there a direct relationship between the persons involved?
2. What are the restrictions on sharing addresses? Two or more people can share the same address if they belong to the same household. Does that imply the existence of an entity type HOUSEHOLD?[9] (This would perhaps be

of interest to a company or organization providing service to households rather than to individuals, such as a bank that may offer a household budget service to manage household bills.) What about separate flats in the same house? If two companies have offices in the same building, do they have the same address? Do two employees of the same company, working in different departments, have the same business address, or is the department name included in the address?

3. Two companies (perhaps owned by the same holding group) may have the same street address, but maintain different post office box numbers. So does ADDRESS refer to the street address or to the postal address? In the UK we are accustomed to regarding street address and postal address as equivalent, but in other countries there is a clear functional distinction.

4. Does address include telephone number, telegraphic address, telex, telefax, electronic mail addresses and other codes, used for non-traditional forms of communication?

5. What happens if two people share the same postal address but have different telephone numbers? Is the extension number included in the telephone number? What about telephone numbers that are not associated with a fixed building, but are mobile (e.g. car phones)?

These questions will be answered differently, according to the particular reason(s) the business has for being interested in addressing people and/or companies. The answers to these questions might lead us to a more sophisticated definition of ADDRESS as being any set of directions that enables us to communicate with a company or person. Thus the postal address enables us to send mail, a telephone number enables us to make calls, a street address enables us to make personal visits, a telex number enables us to send telexes, a bank sort code allows us to send payments, and so on. So each company or person has several addresses, one for each mode of communication. This also allows alternatives to be captured: for example, both day-time and 24-hour telephone numbers.

Such a definition of ADDRESS may seem strange at first, but its advantage is its flexibility, being easily extended to new modes of communication. This still leaves some other modelling issues, whose solutions also depend on our reasons for being interested in addresses at all.

Often, all we are interested in is communicating a destination to the Post Office, to a travelling salesman, or to a delivery van. If our purpose is merely to send things in mail, or to give instructions for a personal visit or delivery (which may also include where to park, or which door to enter), there is no particular value in decomposing addresses into their constituent components.

Sometimes we want to plan or schedule sales or delivery activity. This requires us to group nearby destinations together, to make the activity more efficient (by reducing total distance travelled). Some distribution organizations define fixed or semi-fixed ROUTEs, which they follow on a regular basis, and they assign deliveries to customers to the most convenient route. This cannot usually be done from the address alone, but requires the address to be located on a map, on which the routes are marked. This also enables us to estimate the distance or travel time between two addresses. This is illustrated in Figure 8.7.

Figure 8.7 What can be derived from the address?

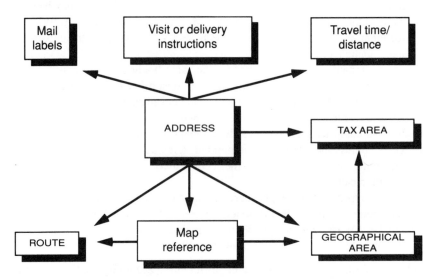

Some organizations have on-line computer support for finding locations on maps. This requires a very sophisticated geographical model, and is at present probably only cost-justifiable for such emergency services as police, fire brigade, ambulance, motorist rescue. These organizations need to recognize locations specified in many different ways (e.g. opposite pub, two miles from motorway exit, etc.).

Other organizations needing to model the content of maps are those that wish to change the environment. Digging up roads or creating new roads requires a knowledge of the roads that already exist (and the pipes and cables that run underneath them.) One of the modelling issues raised here is the identity of ROAD or STREET. Streets can have strange characteristics: they can be discontinuous, they can turn into pedestrian precincts and re-emerge the other side, they can have several names. For example, does Oxford Street denote the same occurrence of ROAD as Bayswater Road? (They are both part of the A40, running from Central London towards Oxford.)

Sometimes we want to divide/sort the world into GEOGRAPHICAL AREAS ('catchment areas'), for marketing or administration purposes. This is usually a means to an end – we want to associate a customer with an organizational unit responsible for the given area, or we want to associate sales in an area with an advertising campaign in that area, or we want to guess the social characteristics of a person from their address. This can sometimes be done by analysing the components of the address (town, district, county or whatever), but this is often inadequate. For marketing purposes, the most useful geographic classification may be based on the broadcasting 'footprint' of the local TV or radio station.

In the UK, the postal code is commonly used for demographic analysis and sorting. In the US, the first few digits of the telephone number can be used. In both cases, it is possible to obtain an algorithm that will convert the code into an approximate map reference.

Country or state may be needed to determine the applicable tax and excise rules – e.g. VAT or sales tax, or export restrictions. There may be other regulations that vary by country. There may also be an assumed relationship between COUNTRY and CURRENCY.

If an area is defined as a combination of addresses, how do we know which address is included in which area? If the new area is Devon-and-Cornwall, then perhaps the rule is: if the address includes the word Devon or the word Cornwall. But this will not work, because we should then include Devon Place and Cornwall Street. Then perhaps the rule is, if the address includes the words in the slot marked 'county'. (This assumes a common format for addresses – we shall return to this problem below.) But if the area is Tyne Tees TV Region, how do we know from looking at an address whether it falls within this area?

The information model should concentrate on what it is possible for us to know, as well as what is true. Thus the model has an epistemological as well as an ontological element. In this particular example, we cannot tell from the address whether a person can receive a particular television signal; this may depend on the power of their receiving equipment; it may depend on the weather. Nonetheless, advertising companies usually ignore these complications, and draw the approximate reception areas for each broadcasting company, which are accurate enough for their purposes.

8.4.2 Locations, routes and networks

When we want to know where something (or someone) is now, or where it was at a particular time, it is not an address we want, but a location. The trouble with LOCATION (as with so many other entity types) is determining where one occurrence starts and another finishes. Often this will depend on purpose. For example, during high-level forward planning, a factory or warehouse might be regarded as a single location. But for operational purposes, it may be necessary to identify specific locations within the factory or warehouse.

One approach to this difficulty is to avoid having a general entity type LOCATION altogether. Instead, we may have a series of specific entity types FACTORY, FACTORY SHOP, WAREHOUSE, WAREHOUSE BAY, STORAGE UNIT, with appropriate relationships between them. The advantage of this approach is that it is fairly concrete, and therefore probably stable. The disadvantage is that several of these entity types may play the same role, and we may end up with a large number of different but similar entity types.

Alternatively, we may have more generalized entity types that are however specific to the level of planning that refers to them, e.g. STRATEGIC LOCATION, TACTICAL LOCATION, OPERATIONAL LOCATION. This will result in fewer entity types than the previous approach, but because they are more abstract, and their definitions are dependent upon the planning processes, the model is more vulnerable to changes in the planning levels. Another disadvantage of the more abstract entity types is that they may be more difficult for people to understand.

In order to get from one location to another, we may need a route. A ROUTE can be regarded as a possible trip from one location to another, or as a set of directions to get from one location to another. How do we model ROUTE? A good way to start is by asking the following questions:

1. Is the route from A to B the same as the route from B to A? If all we are interested in is the distance or journey time or the expected volume of traffic, and if these are the same in both directions, then the answer may be yes. For example, a road plan (often printed as useful information in diaries) shows that it is 319 miles between Aberdeen and York, in either direction. However, if one wanted to know the times of trains or air-shuttles between Aberdeen and York, it would be necessary to specify the direction; thus for timetable purposes, the route from Aberdeen to York is a different occurrence to the route from York to Aberdeen: see Figure 8.8.

Figure 8.8 Route to and from a location

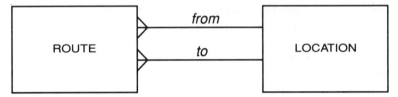

2. Is there only ever one route from A to B? That again depends what attributes of ROUTE interest us, why we are interested in routes at all. When planning the provision of public transport, for example, we should start with an estimate of the number of people that will want to travel from one particular location to another. These estimates are defined purely in terms of the FROM LOCATION and TO LOCATION; they are therefore attributes of an entity type ROUTE that is identified solely by its two relationships to LOCATION. (There may well be several estimates for each route, however, corresponding to different times of day or week).

   (a) If there can be several routes from A to B, what differentiates them? One may be a scenic route, or one route may be unsuitable for heavy vehicles, or unpassable in bad weather. Different routes may have different toll charges. Are we interested in such differences?

   (b) Or we may differentiate routes by the mode of transport: thus 'Aberdeen to York by road' and 'Aberdeen to York by rail' could be two different occurrences of ROUTE. Are we interested in more than one mode of transport?

   (c) Sometimes we need to distinguish between different types of road vehicle, e.g. small van versus large lorry. This may affect both the cost and the expected time to traverse the route (thus a motorbike can usually deliver a document through heavy traffic quicker than a car). However, these differences no longer seem to be associated with the route itself, but with the type of vehicle on the route. They are probably attributes of the intersection entity type ROUTE BY VEHICLE TYPE: see Figure 8.9.

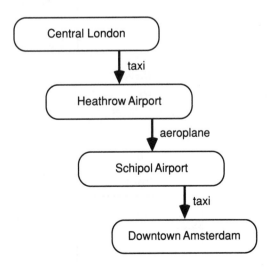

Figure 8.9 Route by vehicle type

ROUTE — *from* / *to* — **LOCATION**

ROUTE BY VEHICLE TYPE — **VEHICLE TYPE**

3. Can there be a route from a location to the same location? Consider circular sightseeing tours, delivery circuits, or test drives.
4. Are we interested in the locations that a route goes through or via, as well as the start and destination? If we are interested in ROUTE as a set of directions, then each step of the route may be of interest.

If we are interested in dividing the route into segments, then there are two possible approaches: either linking the ROUTE to a series of ROUTE NODES, which are the LOCATIONS through which the ROUTE passes, or linking a ROUTE to a series of ROUTE LEGS, which are the atomic indivisible steps from which the route is strung together. Thus in Figure 8.10 there are either three occurrences of ROUTE LEG (two by taxi and one by plane) or four occurrences of ROUTE NODE.

Figure 8.10 Route nodes and route legs

Central London

| taxi

Heathrow Airport

| aeroplane

Schipol Airport

| taxi

Downtown Amsterdam

There are therefore two alternative models for the segments of a route. Both would be redundant, since each could be derived from the other. Which of them to choose depends on what attributes of route you want to include in your model: see Figure 8.11.

Figure 8.11a
Alternative ways of
route modelling

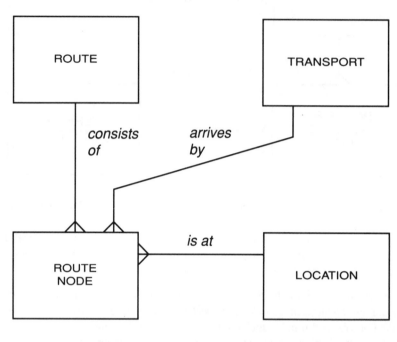

Figure 8.11b

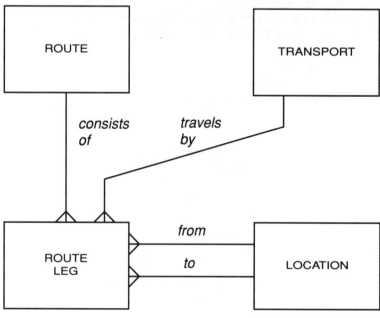

A route is a transport path for people, materials or data/information. A network is a collection of hypothetical or actual routes. Thus a road or rail system, a gap pipeline system and a telecommunications network all consist of routes, along which objects and substances can pass.

Operational planning is often carried out top down. In other words, when it may be decided to transport something from Aberdeen to York, we might have a rough route first, followed by a more detailed route in the later stages of planning. Or perhaps the exact route is left to the driver, with certain constraints.

The same may be true of network planning, where we start by comparing the present capacity and estimated future traffic for large segments of the network, for large occurrences of ROUTE, in other words. Broad plans can be laid down for enhancing the network, by providing extra route segments between particular nodes, or upgrading existing segments, where shortfalls in capacity are predicted. Then more detailed planning can take place, in which each segment is divided into its lowest-level parts, and the same comparison and development planning is carried out.

One of the complications of modelling this kind of forward planning is that because there is often a substantial time delay between planning and implementing major new developments or enhancements to a network, the calculation of future capacity must include capacity whose development has been scheduled, but whose completion date may be uncertain, thanks to project difficulties. And since some parts of the network may deteriorate beyond effective repair, calculations relating to a particular date in the future must also exclude capacity that is expected to have been taken out of service by that date.

In modelling regular transport schedules or timetables, care needs to be taken to distinguish the entry on the schedule from the actual journey. Sometimes you need two entity types. For example, for each route, there may be several occurrences of SCHEDULED FLIGHT, identified by the flight number (e.g. BA315, which is a daily 3.40 p.m. flight from Paris Charles de Gaulle airport to London Heathrow). For each occurrence of SCHEDULED FLIGHT there will be several occurrences of ACTUAL FLIGHT, identified by the flight number and the date (e.g. BA315 on 8 July 1990).

If we were modelling an airline, we should probably need one occurrence of ACTUAL FLIGHT for every day. This entity type would be related to other entity types to represent the physical aeroplane and flight crew, and other logistical information. But if we were modelling an airline user, our information needs would be more restricted. We might only want to know the occurrences of ACTUAL FLIGHT where we had booked a ticket. Thus ACTUAL FLIGHT might be related to EMPLOYEE TRIP, or to TRAVEL INVOICE. Perhaps the entity type ACTUAL FLIGHT becomes unnecessary, and we only need a direct relationship between SCHEDULED FLIGHT and EMPLOYEE TRIP. However, if an organization has a policy that limits the number of employees that can travel together on the same plane (i.e. the same ACTUAL FLIGHT) then this entity type may be required after all.

8.4.3 Geographical area

Bari is in Italy, Italy is in Europe. We can define Bari, Italy and Europe as occurrences of GEOGRAPHICAL AREA or GEOG AREA. There is clearly an involuted relationship, which we may call *contains*, from some GEOG AREAS to others. Thus Europe contains Italy and France, and also Rome; Italy contains Bari and Rome. This relationship is many to many; it is also transitive. (In other words, if A contains B and B contains C then A also contains C.) Mathematicians would call this a partial ordering. (We assume a GEOG AREA does not contain itself. Thus the largest GEOG AREAS are not contained by any other, and the smallest GEOG AREAS do not contain any other. The relationship *contains* is therefore fully optional.) Figure 8.12 shows the relationship between geographical areas.

Figure 8.12
Relationship between
geographical areas

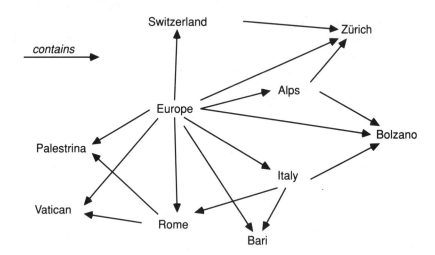

There is also a relationship between PERSON and GEOG AREA, called *lives in*. For example, Danilo lives in Bari. If a person lives in GEOG AREA A, and A is contained in GEOG AREA B, then it follows that the person also lives in B. Thus Danilo also lives in Italy, and in Europe. Therefore the relationship *lives in,* between PERSON and GEOG AREA is also many to many: see Figure 8.13. This way of modelling geography causes problems, because of the many-to-many relationships, and also because it involves much redundancy. So we should look for a more elegant model.

Figure 8.13 *Lives in*
relationship

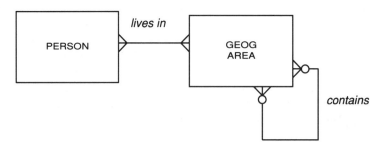

One way of resolving the problems is to classify GEOG AREA into subtypes, so that the geographical structure can be explicitly modelled. For example, COUNTRY contains STATE/PROVINCE contains CITY contains DISTRICT. It might be necessary to define the smallest unit of GEOG AREA, as (say) GEOG UNIT, although this structure may well be vulnerable to change. This is illustrated in Figure 8.14.

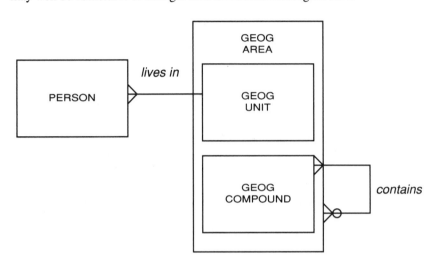

Figure 8.14
Geographical subtypes

When modelling geographical areas, we have to consider three things:

1. How the geographical areas are to be defined. Are we going to start top down, defining smaller areas by subdivision of larger areas? Or are we going to start bottom-up, defining larger areas as combinations of smaller areas?
2. How the geographical areas are to be redefined. Does the business need to merge or split areas, and how can the reallocation of addresses to the correct areas be managed in such a situation?
3. How the geographical information is to be used.

The modelling of geographical locations is linked to the modelling of ADDRESS. This is because the postal address of a person or company usually includes district, town, county, state, or whatever. In the UK, postcodes are allocated to addresses. Each code represents a small number of addresses, and marketing companies are able to pinpoint the social mix of each postal code area. In other countries, the postcode (or zip code) merely denotes the town (or suburb of a large city), and is a less accurate indicator of socio-economic status.

The trouble with modelling addresses is that addresses are not all in a common format. (Any European who has attempted to fill in a form designed by an American, or who subscribes to an American magazine, will have experienced this first hand. The European address does not fit into the form, and the address label produced by the computer is often quite garbled.) In the US, addresses are formatted by street, city, state, zip. In the UK, addresses are formatted by street, town, county, postcode. Can we generalize TOWN/CITY into a single attribute, or COUNTY/STATE/REGION? This will confuse the Americans, who have counties as administrative units, but do not include them in the address. Within the UK, do Scotland and Wales count as states? In some countries, it is common practice to lay out the address top down (i.e. with the largest area first: region, town, street). In other countries, bottom up is the norm (e.g. street, town, region). If you decompose addresses, you have to be able to reconstruct them properly: street number before or after street name?

Even within the UK, there are many different address formats. Addresses in Scotland may or may not include the word Scotland. People living in blocks of flats may have a flat number within a named block, or a flat name (e.g. basement) within a numbered block. People living in small villages may specify the nearest large town within the address. People living within housing estates may specify the access road as well as the estate name and the location within the estate.

What is the point of trying to model all this structure? Often there is no need to. Some organizations like to send 'intelligent' mail shots, that select a part of the address and repeat it in the letter. 'Dear Mr Retired, You will be the envy of all your neighbours in PO Box 4711 . . .' Even with strong commercial reasons for modelling addresses accurately, they rarely (if ever) get it 100 per cent right. Yet even in organizations with no such commercial reasons for decomposing the address, analysis projects may waste months trying to achieve perfection.

Some information modellers become concerned at the considerable amount of redundancy within the model. Once you know that a particular town is within a particular region, it seems wasteful to represent this fact repeatedly. If you 'normalize' the address, it gets decomposed into different entity types, representing the different components of the address. And we can imagine a computer system that validates addresses when entered, issuing warnings when a town is not recognized, or is placed in the wrong region. This would require some such information structure. This must cope with duplicate names (e.g. Kingston, Newcastle, Washington, . . .).

And if a town or street changes its name, or a county changes its boundaries, there may be a lot of work to bring all the addresses up to date. As for international changes (Pakistan, Yemen, Germany), there may be substantial complications to sort out (maintaining continuity of socio-economic statistics, for example).

But although many organizations need to respond to these events when they occur, very few need to anticipate them, or predetermine how they will deal with such hypothetical events. That is so far away from the business objectives, that it is not even worth analysing, let alone automating.

8.4.4 Time period

Is October 1917 the same month as October 1987? That, of course, depends how the entity type MONTH is defined. In some cases, it will be defined as a calendar month within a particular year; elsewhere, it will be defined as a calendar month regardless of year. Many organizations organize their accounts into months, but when these months are examined closely, it perhaps turns out that October 1987 started on the 28 September and ended on 30 of October. (This could be because the accountants want to avoid weekends.) Or perhaps October 1987 did not start until mid-October, because there were difficulties in completing the financial year-end (due at the end of September). In some organizations (especially multi-national ones), different groups of accountants may define different calendars, making the accurate consolidation of accounts impossible. (This may be a deliberate policy, designed to prevent the accounts being understood by tax authorities or shareholders, or may be the result of poor coordination.)

The reason I chose October 1917 for my example, together with a date approximately seventy years later, is that the Russian October revolution actually took place in November. This apparent tardiness was due to the difference between the Orthodox calendar and the Western calendar. This is an historical example of the same kind of confusion engendered by the accountants referred to in the previous paragraph.

Do we actually need to represent dates and times through entity types? Or are dates and times merely attributes? What is the significance of one date (e.g. DELIVERY DATE) being the same as another date (e.g. INSPECTION DATE)? Is there any significance in the set of orders that have the same DELIVERY DATE or INSPECTION DATE? (In other words, are there any facts common to all such orders, which would be attributes or relationships of a DATE entity type?)

A date is of course a special kind of PERIOD, usually a 24-hour period from midnight to midnight. (Complications set in when we operate across several time zones. It may be necessary to standardize on GMT or Eastern Standard Time.) Periods are arbitrary but sometimes useful concepts for grouping events and transactions, especially for planning, scheduling and budgeting purposes.

It is not necessary to maintain a calendar that states the number of days in each month, and where the weekends fall; it is one of the first exercises on many a programming course to write a little routine to calculate just this. A more difficult programming exercise (although not impossible) is to calculate the dates of Easter, as differently celebrated by the Roman and Orthodox Churches. However, even the cleverest programmer cannot calculate the dates of all public holidays in all countries; the need to know these dates usually provides the justification for maintaining a calendar, based on the entity type DAY.

But what shall we include in this entity type? How many occurrences shall we have? Do we need to have an occurrence for each of the 365 (+1) days in every year? Do we need to have an occurrence for each of the days in the current year only? Last year and next year as well? Do we need to bother about weekends, or can we make do with an entity type called WEEKDAY?

If all we need to know is whether a given day is a public holiday or not, then do we need to have the entity type DAY, or do we merely need the entity type PUBLIC HOLIDAY. The advantage of the latter is that it has far fewer occurrences, following the modelling principle of maximizing the utility of information represented by each object. (Another way of putting this is to say we have used Ockham's razor to prune out the normal working days as redundant.) If we are interested in the public holidays in many countries or states, then we may need the relationship *is a public holiday in* between the entity types DAY and STATE. We choose this relationship, rather than the relationship *is a normal working day in*, because it has fewer pairings, on the same principle as above.

8.4.5 History

There is a clash in information, between current and historical, affecting both attributes and relationships. Let us consider attributes first. If we are only interested in the name a person is currently known by, then NAME can be an attribute of PERSON. But people change their names, by marriage, deed poll or ennoblement. If we need to know the old name as well as the new name, then a second entity type may be required, holding attributes of the date, reason and legal status of the name change, as well as the name itself: see Figure 8.15.

Figure 8.15 Person known by many names

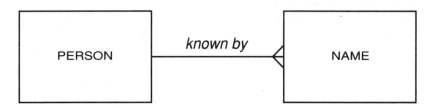

Now let us look at historical representation of relationships. Assume that a person lives in only one house at a time. To describe the current occupancy of houses, a simple model with two entity types is all that is needed. (Figure 8.16). However, this model does not tell us where a person used to live. Often, we will need the model to include historical information. For example, it may be necessary to produce forwarding addresses, for those people that have moved house in the last six months, say. An historical model would need extra information, to show not only who lives where but also when. A third entity type, RESIDENCE, holds these temporal attributes: FROM DATE and TO DATE. (Figure 8.17).

Figure 8.16 Person lives in many houses

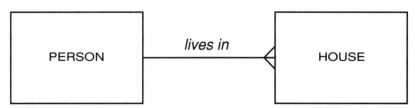

There is a danger that, in going to a more complex structure, we may lose the simple rule: that a person can only live in one house at a time (assuming this to be true). We may want to impose some integrity rule on this structure, to ensure that these dates are end to end, i.e. that a person starts living at one address on the same day as he or she stops living at another address – or we may not care. Most of the time, it is the current information that we are interested in, while the historical information is required rarely. The simple one-to-many relationship between

PERSON and HOUSE may be derived, when required, from the fuller structure shown. (Chapter Five has dealt with the definition and use of derived relationships.)

More generally, suppose an entity type X has several attributes A_1 to A_n, and several relationships r_1 to r_n. At a given time, each occurrence has at most one value for each attribute a_1, and is related to a well-defined set of other entity occurrences via each relationship r_1, see Figure 8.18. For example, a financial services operation may need to model several aspects of the financial and personal status of their customers. This could include their bank, savings and mortgage accounts, their current job title, employer and salary, the number and relationship of dependants and so on. If all or some of these relationships and attributes can change over time, and if we need to model these changes, we may have to add some complexity to the model to cater for the time-based information. One approach to this common requirement is to include a snapshot entity type in the model, representing an occurrence of X at a given point in time. Therefore the entity type X possesses the fixed relationships and unchangeable attributes, while the entity type X-SNAPSHOT possesses the transferable relationships and changeable attributes, see Figure 8.19.

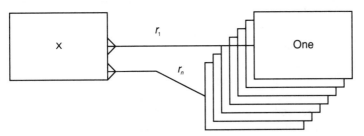

Figure 8.18 Entity with n relationships

This helps to explain why it is important to know whether an attribute value or relationship pairing could change once it was established. These facts about attributes and relationships need to be documented, not only for use by the system designer and database designer, but also to complete the understanding of the business, which the model represents.

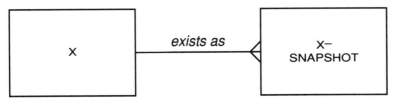

Figure 8.19 X-SNAPSHOT

For example, if X is the entity type PERSON, and the area we are modelling is a financial services operation, then a new occurrence of the entity type PERSON-SNAPSHOT will be required each time an individual person's financial or personal status changes. For example, when he or she opens a new savings account, or changes jobs, or acquires an additional dependant, there will be a snapshot to capture a complete picture of his/her current status, while the earlier snapshots remain for historical purposes: see Figure 8.20.

Figure 8.20 Historical snapshots

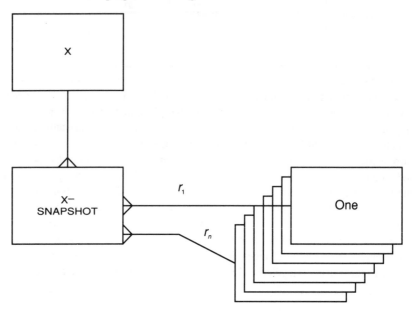

There are some problems with this approach, however. Each snapshot may be nearly the same as the previous one, which results in a cumbersome structure. It may be difficult to trace through the history to find out what has actually changed from one snapshot to the next. An alternative approach is to include an entity type in the model that represents, not the state of x between changes, but the changes themselves, as in Figure 8.21. Each can be derived from the other. Thus an occurrence of X-ALTERATION can be derived by comparing two successive occurrences of X-SNAPSHOT, whereas an occurrence of X-SNAPSHOT can be derived by applying a series of X-ALTERATIONs from a defined starting point. This, however, can result in a cumbersome information access structure. (Here is an example where there is a trade off between the simplicity of the information structure and the simplicity of the information access structure. We have considered information access in Chapter 5.)

Figure 8.21 X-ALTERATION

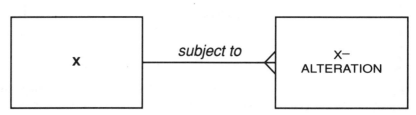

One way of making the model less cumbersome is to divide the history into sections. For example, suppose we are interested in both the credit status history and the personal history of a customer. Instead of having a single entity type CUSTOMER SNAPSHOT (or perhaps CUSTOMER ALTERATION), it may be easier to have separate entity types CUSTOMER PERSONAL SNAPSHOT and CUSTOMER CREDIT SNAPSHOT, both related to CUSTOMER but maintained independently. The analyst should review the business processes that alter an occurrence of CUSTOMER, the idea being that if these business processes are independent, then the histories can be kept separate. If there is a close dependence between the personal details and the credit status, such a separation may not be appropriate.

A situation that requires particular clarity and elegance is where one of the relationships r_1 is involuted, either directly or indirectly, e.g., where it is necessary to trace the history of reorganizations within a company reporting hierarchy.[10] The snapshot approach could require the entire hierarchy to be replicated even for trivial changes. The alteration approach, on the other hand, makes it tricky to determine the current organization structure. And if the reorganizations are phased rather than immediate, with perhaps a hand-over period from the old manager of a department to the new manager, does the intermediate structure also need to be modelled? Again, this will depend on the purpose of the model. (Note: the actual modelling of organizational structures will be dealt with below.)

(Successive redesigned versions of a product, with different part hierarchies in the bill of materials, should not cause these difficulties, since it should be clear which version of the product is manufactured at any time. It may, however, be necessary to include some indication of the design version when identifying the product. Thus, when you need a spare part for your car, you may need to specify the year that the car was manufactured, to be sure of getting the correct replacement.)

This leads us to a more general difficulty, where the changes are gradual rather than instantaneous. For example, the increase in the creditworthiness of a customer, or the deterioration in the external paintwork of a factory. Such gradual changes in an attribute can be modelled as if they were instantaneous, by measuring the attribute value only at fixed intervals, and acting as if the most recent measurement is the current value. (Note: measurements can be estimates as well as accurate readings – see the discussion on measurement in Section 8.3 on substances.) However, such a model is unstable because, in such cases, the measurement interval will always be arbitrary. A change in measurement frequency can significantly change the information quality.

This is particularly true where an attribute has a cyclical pattern. Let us suppose that to measure a person's wealth, we look at the bank balance. (This would be a rather simplistic measure, but it will do to illustrate the point.) Suppose the person is paid a monthly salary. Looking at the balance regularly at the beginning of each month (immediately after the salary has been paid in) could result in a much more optimistic opinion of the person's wealth than looking at the end of the month. And if we looked every week, we should get a different picture again: see Figure 8.22.

Figure 8.22 Measuring wealth by bank balance

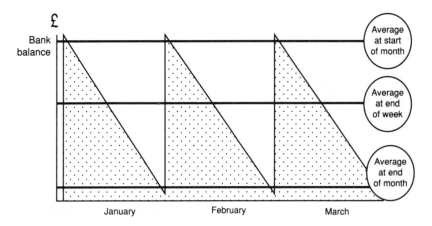

Structures similar to those described in this section are used to model the future, where the changes and the timing of changes are projected (expected or planned) rather than actual. Again, we have a choice between projecting the snapshot or projecting the alteration. But there are further complications with modelling the future, which we shall deal with below. We need to handle forecasts, which are passive predictions, differently from plans and schedules, which represent active intentions.

8.5 Incidents and adventures

This section discusses the modelling of things that happen, rather than things that 'merely' exist. We start with events, and look at particular kinds of events, such as actions and statements. Hypothetical future events may be regarded as scenarios for planning purposes, or as risks for insurance purposes. Finally in this section, we look at plans and actions from a more abstract viewpoint, and consider the modelling of intentions.

8.5.1 Event

An event is something that has, will or may happen. We include forecasts, but not plans. (Plans are treated below.) To understand events, let us return to the question of changes. There are six kinds of change: generation, destruction, increase, diminution, alteration, change of place. Alteration is change in qualification, in one or more non-quantified properties. An event can be regarded as a set of changes, to the same entity, or to different entities (of the same or different types). Some of the six kinds of change can be simultaneous for different aspects of the same entity – thus an event may shift an object to a warmer spot, causing it to expand, or another event may make a person both sadder and wiser. Of course, an entity cannot be simultaneously generated and destroyed, and an attribute cannot be simultaneously increased and decreased. But one entity can be generated as part of the same event that destroys another, e.g., a business contract or parliamentary act may nullify one or more previous contracts or acts. So we can have an event that involves different kinds of change to different entities but not every set of changes can be regarded as an event. There are two ways of grouping (clustering) changes into events:

1. Changes that occur at the same time may be part of the same event. But there are two difficulties with this definition. On the one hand, mere simultaneity is not sufficient – two changes may take place at the same time in different places by sheer coincidence, and we should not want to regard two unconnected changes to be part of the same event. And on the other hand, it may not be necessary for the changes to be exactly synchronized – we will often accept changes separated by minutes or hours or days to be part of the same event.

2. Changes that have the same cause may be part of the same event. This definition is also inadequate. For on the one hand, such changes may be far apart in space and time. In some cases, the generation and destruction of the same entity may have the same cause – for example, where a temporary arrangement is set up for a fixed duration, the starting date and finishing date may both be predetermined. And on the other hand, the concept of causality is itself difficult to pin down. We have an intuitive notion of causality as being something more than mere coincidence, but this has been challenged by philosophers from David Hume to the present day. We should not want our definition of what exists to depend on our beliefs on what causes it. Furthermore, 'nothing' can be a cause. 'The letter which you do not write can get an angry reply, and the income tax form which you do not fill in can trigger the Internal Revenue boys into energetic action.'[11]

How do we resolve this? The answer is that in order to understand the events of a business, we must understand the business processes. The information model is supplemented by a process model, which shows the interconnection between processes and events. An event is probably something that is either deliberately planned and executed as an event, or is recognized for some business purpose as an event. Some events and processes are of, performed by or undergone by entities such as material bodies. Thus a death is necessarily the death of a person, animal or other creature. Thus the entity type EVENT is usually linked to something else, that exists before and/or after the event itself. However, in some exceptional situations, there may be events that cannot be linked to anything else. 'But that a flash or bang occurred does not entail that anything flashed or banged. "Let there be light" does not mean "Let something shine". '[12]

8.5.2 Actions

Actions are particular types of event, which are carried out by persons or groups. Normally, the actions of a group of people are the joint and several responsibility of each member of the group. (This means that each of them can be fully blamed for any consequences.) Some organizations and institutions, however, can carry out certain actions for which their members cannot be held individually responsible. (Thus for example, neither the shareholders, nor the directors and employees of a limited company can be held liable for the company's debts.) For this reason, lawyers recognize companies as 'legal persons'. The actions of a part of such an organization are the responsibility of the organization itself.

Where a group of people is defined solely as the collection of its members, there will be problems with stability. Each time somebody leaves, or somebody else joins, we have a new group. How do we account for the actions of a group? We may be interested in acts carried out by the group as a whole, or in acts carried out by one or more individuals on behalf of a group, or in independent acts carried out by individuals who happen to belong to the group.

There are therefore relationships between the event or action, and the person or organization doing the action. The importance of actions is not to be underestimated: it is the businessman's main source of evidence about the intentions, plans, priorities, beliefs and fears of his competitors, his customers, his employees, indeed all persons and organizations with which he does business.

However, the information model has to be selective. It is neither appropriate nor possible to monitor every action, even of the most closely fought rival. Therefore, you are unlikely to have a general entity type called ACTION or even COMPETITOR ACTION. Instead, you are likely to have purpose-driven entity types, such as COMPETITOR PRODUCT LAUNCH or COMPETITOR PROMOTION, which allows you to capture specific areas of action in your model.

8.5.3 Statement

Each act of communication can be modelled as an EVENT, or more specifically as a STATEMENT. There are at least five types of communication that we might be interested in, listed in Table 8.2.

Table 8.2 Five types of communication

ASSERTION	To say something that may be true or false, or which may have a value associated with its probability	FACT, SCENARIO, ASSUMPTION, BELIEF
COMMITMENT	To pledge oneself (absolutely or conditionally) to some future action or policy	PLAN, PROMISE, THREAT
DIRECTION	To pledge someone else to some future action or policy	ORDER, PLAN, INSTRUCTION
EXPRESSION	To express an attitude towards, or an evaluation of something	OPINION, COMPLAINT, EVALUATION, ESTIMATE
DECLARATION	To declare something to be the case, i.e. it happens because it is said	VERDICT, AUTHORIZATION

Any of these statements may be modelled as entity types. (Some examples of entity types within each category are shown in the third column.) We can extract some general principles about each category, which the analyst can use to generate questions.

An ASSERTION usually stands independent of anyone asserting. Except for beliefs, the focus is usually on the content of the assertion, and perhaps the evidence for it, rather than whose it is. Sometimes a COMMITMENT belongs to the whole organization, in which case there is no point differentiating an owner. But often, commitments are made by individuals or departments, in which case there is almost certainly a need for a relationship between COMMITMENT and the committing entity. Although a DIRECTION involves two parties, one directing and one directed, it is rare for both to be of interest. With an EXPRESSION, it is common to ignore the source, but this is often a grave error, since it can lead to subjective opinions being taken as objective fact. Finally, a DECLARATION usually has to be linked to the author, which may be a person, a management role, a committee, or an institution (such as the Court of Appeal).

How are statements negated? Assertions are refuted, commitments are reneged, directions are cancelled, expressions are withdrawn, declarations are overturned. In most cases, a statement is negated by another statement of the same type. Thus, for example, a CANCELLATION is a negative DIRECTION.

There may also be more complex relationships between statements.

8.5.4 Scenario

A scenario may be a projected series of events and/or assumptions, usually hypothetical, constructed to test strategies and proposals, and to ask 'what if' questions. For example, a possible future construction project may be evaluated in four ways:

1. A financial evaluation compares the projected costs of the project with its projected benefits, and thereby assesses the investment value of the project. This may be expressed in such calculated values as the payback period, internal rate of return (IRR) or net present value (NPV).
2. A technical evaluation considers the practicality of the project, the probability of its being successful, the technical and environmental risks.
3. It may also be necessary to check that the proposed project conforms to any applicable policies and guidelines of the organization, any legal restrictions, prior agreements with other parties, etc.
4. A subjective evaluation considers how the project would be perceived by employees, customers, the media, etc., and confirms that the project will not induce any loss of goodwill.

To carry out any of these evaluations, it is necessary to make some assumptions. For example, the financial evaluation may depend on some economic forecasts (such as the rate of inflation, or the price of crude oil). And since the construction will be partly out of doors, it may be held up, incur extra costs, or even be made technically unfeasible by extremely bad weather; thus the financial and the technical evaluations may both assume good weather during the critical phases of the project. One simple way of modelling these evaluations, and the assumptions they depend upon, is to introduce an entity type called FORECAST, and to link each project with the forecasts that it relies upon. The evaluation itself (for example, the financial calculation of IRR or NPV) is modelled as attributes of the project. The set of forecasts against which the project is evaluation may be referred to as its scenario, but it is not necessary to model this as a separate entity type: see Figure 8.23.

Figure 8.23 A forecast

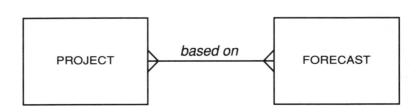

For large projects, a more sophisticated approach may be taken. It may not be enough to make a best guess as to the rate of inflation. The decision maker wants to know how sensitive the evaluation is to variations in the inflation rate. A given project may be financially viable if the inflation rate remains at the current rate, for example; but how much would the inflation rate have to rise before the financial evaluation became invalid? Sometimes the evaluation will be extremely sensitive, so that a mere half per cent rise would wreck the project; other times the evaluation will be less sensitive.

Instead of a single best guess, therefore, two or more guesses are made, spanning a range from the most optimistic to the most pessimistic. Thus each project may have several evaluations, each depending on a different combination of forecasts. (Figure 8.24). Here is where the scenario comes in (Figure 8.25). Because there may be a large number of possible combinations of forecasts, some of which may be mutually implausible, it is convenient to define a small number of scenarios, each representing a plausible combination of forecasts. Perhaps several projects will be evaluated against the same set of scenarios – this will be of particular interest where several alternative projects need to be compared. (For example, is it better to build an extension to our existing showroom, or to open a new showroom in the recently developed shopping centre?)

Figure 8.24 Project evaluation based on forecast

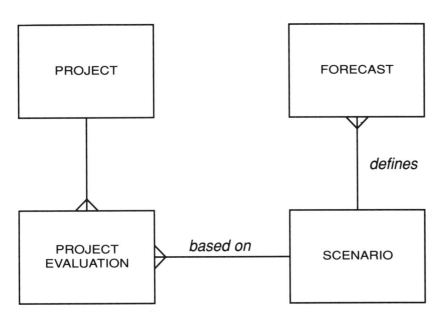

Figure 8.25 Project evaluation and scenarios

8.5.5 Risk and policy

Most organizations have some insurance policies, taken out for either commercial or legal reasons. Thus there may be fire insurance on the buildings, health insurance for the employees, and accident insurance on the vehicles. There may also be *ad hoc* insurance to cover shipments or specific occasions –organizers of outdoor events often take out insurance against being rained off. This section therefore discusses insurance from the perspective of the insured organization, and not from the perspective of the insurance company or underwriter.

The decision process usually starts with the identification of a RISK. We could attempt to define this as a hypothetical incident resulting in loss or damage. (The word 'accident' is probably too narrow, except in specific areas such as transport.) In other words, anything that could be insured against. For example, when a valuable item is borrowed from a museum for a special exhibition or event, there is a risk that it may be stolen or damaged. But this definition raises a few difficulties:

1. Loss or damage to whom? The organization may itself suffer loss or damage, or it may be subject to claims against it from other parties. For example, an employee may claim compensation after an accident at work. Or a victim of a car accident may claim compensation from the employer of the driver. But there must a boundary of interest – no organization is interested in all loss or damage, actual or hypothetical, to any party. Furthermore, the scale of the loss or damage is probably relevant. A power cut lasting a few minutes causes a small amount of loss, but not enough to be worth identifying. But a power cut lasting several days could cause great

loss, and may be a risk worth insuring against. We could define RISK as something we have insured ourselves against, but then we cannot use the model to support the insurance decision: which risks to insure, and which ones not to insure?

2. How many risks are there? Do we need to classify risks? Is the risk of theft the same as the risk of damage, or are these two different risks? Is the risk of water damage the same as the risk of fire damage? Perhaps we have a hierarchy of risks: (Figure 8.26).

Figure 8.26 Hierarchy of risks

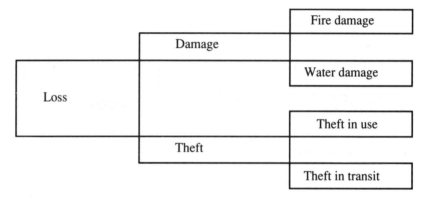

3. For on-going risks, we need to know when it starts and ends. Consider the risk of falling off a warehouse ladder and breaking a leg. Is the risk of breaking a leg on Tuesday the same as the risk of breaking a leg on Thursday? Probably yes. But if safety training took place on Wednesday, the answer might be no.

4. How specific is the risk? Does each warehouse employee have a separate risk of breaking a leg, or is there just one general risk that one or more employees might break a leg? (It may be that the probability of accident varies according to the age, with the young inexperienced and the old frail employees being most vulnerable.)

5. Is every risk associated with a specific incident? For example, there may be a risk associated with long-term exposure to a substance (e.g. asbestos, radium), without any single incident being identifiable. Claims for compensation may be received decades after the period of exposure.

Why is it important to separate risks? Because if the organization wants to be systematic about its management of risks, it needs to ensure that each risk that needs to be covered by an insurance policy is so covered, and that no risk is covered twice. For example, in the case of the item borrowed from a museum, fire damage may already be covered by a general fire and accident policy, and theft in transit may already be covered by the shipper's insurance, leaving only theft in use requiring cover. For another example, casual staff may need to be insured against accidents while on the premises, but managerial staff are insured 168 hours a week via a separate health plan, and do not need to be covered twice. The point is to avoid double counting of risks.

Legal disputes between insurer and insured often centre around the identity of a particular risk. Is this a recurrence of the same disease, or a new disease? (This may affect the payment of benefits.)

A single employee or a single vehicle may have a low probability of having an accident. But in a large organization, the cumulative probability of some accident occurring somewhere is very high. A company having a fleet of thousands of vans on the road is certain to incur many incidents each year. The larger the numbers, the greater the accuracy with which the number and cost of accidents can be predicted. There comes a point where it is not cost-effective to buy thousands of separate insurance policies from an insurance company, since the repair costs and other liabilities are certain to amount to less than the total cost of so many insurance premiums.

Another example of a situation where the risks may be spread within an organization is the weather. A company that relies on sunshine on a particular day (e.g. a product launch) may take out insurance to underwrite the event, but a company that relies on fine weather on at least 150 days in the year (e.g. for construction work, but it is not critical which days it rains) would not. If a company did hundreds of product launches a year, the risks could be spread internally, and an external insurance policy would not be needed, but it would be necessary to ensure that there were not too many events scheduled for the same day (thus concentrating the risk). Thus while a small organization may be sensible (if not legally obliged) to take out external insurance for a given risk, a large organization may be able to spread the risks within its own operations, and may therefore sensibly insure itself (if legally permitted) against these risks.

Having identified and evaluated a risk (how likely is it to occur, how often, what is the probable cost), a decision is taken to deal with it in some way. The risk may be insured externally, or accepted internally. (Sometimes, if the insurance premiums would be too high, the event or operation may be cancelled because of the existence of the risk. Thus the organization may not be able to afford to borrow that priceless item from the museum after all.)

Since the evaluation makes some assumptions, e.g. about safety or security measures, it may be possible to vary these assumptions. Thus several evaluations may be carried out, against several different SCENARIOs or sets of assumptions, as described in Section 8.5.4. This analysis may prompt various actions aimed at bringing about a more favourable SCENARIO, thereby reducing risk. Further occurrences of RISK REDUCTION ACTION may be required by the insurance company, as preconditions of the INSURANCE POLICY, or by government factory inspectors. Such actions may be single (e.g. fit security locks, mend fire escape), regular procedures (e.g. inspect kitchens, back up computer files) or rules (e.g. keep exits unblocked).

We start with a simple model, showing claims made by the organization against its own insurance policies: (Figure 8.27).

What this model does not show is claims against the organization by third parties (including employees and the victims of accidents) which may be covered by the

Figure 8.27 Insurance claims

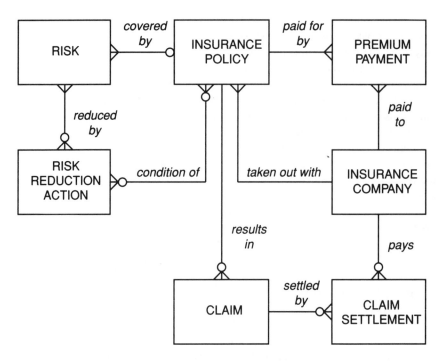

organization's insurance policies, and claims by the organization against third parties, who may be liable either for loss or damage incurred by the organization, or to cover claims made against it. Often there will be a chain of claims, with liability being passed from one party to another, until it reaches the 'guilty' party. Sometimes there is shared liability between two or more parties. Thus a more general model may show CLAIM linked to CLAIMANT, which may be a third party or the organization itself, and RESPONDENT, which may be a third party, the organization itself or any insurance company (not necessarily one with which the organization has any policy). Thus CLAIMANT and RESPONDENT would be role entities, probably with overlapping occurrences, and it may well make more sense to have a single entity type called CLAIM PARTY, including all interested parties.[13]

The claims are not directly linked together in the following model. Instead, they are linked indirectly, by referring to the same INCIDENT (Figure 8.28). This may or may not be adequate.

Figure 8.28 Incident–claim relationship

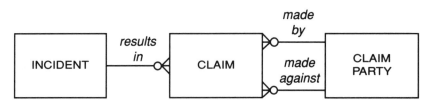

The level of sophistication needed to model insurance depends on the size and technological complexity of the organization. (Thus an energy company would probably have a large risk management and insurance department, because of the scale of potential liability in the event of disaster, while a clothing retail chain probably would not.) Validate your model against the kinds of risks incurred by the particular organization, as well as against the kinds of decisions taken. Although not all risks are hypothetical accidents, it is easier to find examples where a damage claim results from a single incident with a single cause. So you may well think of risks in those terms, but make sure that you can generalize your model to include other kinds of risk, and other kinds of claim.

> A person may take his umbrella, or leave it at home, without any ideas whatsoever concerning the weather, acting instead on general principles such as 'maximin' or 'maximax' reasoning, i.e. acting as if the worst or the best is certain to happen. He may also take or leave the umbrella because of some specific belief concerning the weather. ... Someone may be totally ignorant and non-believing as regards the weather, and yet take his umbrella (acting as if he believes that it will rain) and also lower the sunshade (acting as if he believes that the sun will shine during his absence). There is no inconsistency in taking precautions against two mutually exclusive events, even if one cannot consistently believe that they will both occur.[14]

8.5.6 Intentions and policies

Intentions can be positive (X shall occur), negative (X shall not occur), conditional (X shall occur if P happens), or policy (X shall occur whenever P happens). A policy is both a mental activity and a social process.[15] We may also include heuristics, which can be regarded as complex problem-solving policies.

PLAN and BUDGET (which are discussed in the following section) can be regarded as special types of INTENTION. If we regard an organization as monolithic, then modelling of such objects as PLAN, SCENARIO, STRATEGY, ESTIMATE, FACT, ASSUMPTION, etc., is fairly straightforward. We can assume all PLANs are compatible, all ESTIMATEs are consistent, all IDEAs meaningful, and so on. But often we need to recognize contradictions and tension within an organization, and make these explicit within the model. There may well be on-going discourse between individuals and organizational units, e.g. regarding the viability of various (perhaps alternative) PLANs, the appropriateness of various ESTIMATEs and EVALUATIONs, and the validity of various FACTs and ASSUMPTIONs. So we need to identify the ownership and status of each of these objects. If we model them as particular types of STATEMENT, they can be related to their owners, the logical relationships between them expressed, and their validity explicitly assessed.

One of the problems with intentions is that of specificity or vagueness. Consider the intention of opening a shop in either Bracknell or Basingstoke. One way of modelling this is to say that we intend to open a shop in a specific occurrence of TOWN and that the occurrence in question is the town Bracknell-or-Basingstoke. Another way of modelling it is to say that there are in fact two mutually exclusive intentions, one being to open a shop in Bracknell and the other being to open a shop in Basingstoke. Both approaches have their merits, although they may seem strange at first.

First let us analyse the pseudo entity Bracknell-or-Basingstoke. It may turn out to be a useful entity in its own right. Why do we develop the intention to open a shop in Bracknell-or-Basingstoke? Because the two towns are geographically adjacent and their residents share many demographic characteristics. So if we do not care whether a person lives in one town or the other, we may legitimately speak of the residents of the composite town Bracknell-or-Basingstoke. Therefore, the composite town may have a total population (equal to the sum of the populations of the two separate towns) and an average size of household. Many of the attributes of single towns (especially the numerical ones) may be valid for such composite towns.

One trouble with these composite pseudo entities is that there may be an infinite number of possible combinations. Another trouble is that the selection process often involves creating a shortlist, and then eliminating candidates one by one, until only one option remains. A model that uses pseudo entities would have to have a whole series of them.

Alternatively, the intention may exist before any shortlist has been created. We may want to open a shop anywhere in southern England. This can be modelled as the intention to open a shop in an **arbitrary** town, located in the right GEOG AREA, and with a range of possible attribute values (e.g. population size, average wealth). This follows the guidelines for **anonymous** objects, discussed in Chapter 2.

Is it a good idea to include these arbitrary towns as occurrences of TOWN? The attributes of the arbitrary town are **target** rather than **actual** values, and it is clearly important to distinguish the arbitrary towns from the real towns. But there is one major advantage in including both arbitrary and real towns in the same entity type: it allows the planning processes (which may have started before the final selection decision has been made) to continue uninterrupted. It may even be appropriate to keep the final selection decision secret for as long as possible, to prevent it leaking to your competitors. The town may continue to be referred to by a code name, rather than its real name.

8.6 Event management

The previous section considered the modelling of events. Here we look at the management of events. This is in the form of a loop:

plan → do → measure → control

So we start this section by considering how plans, measurements and control actions can be modelled. Then we look at the same loop from a financial perspective, where it becomes:

budget / forecast → do→ account → control

We finish this section with an examination of some specific issues relating to accounts and book-keeping.

8.6.1 Plan

Management control can be regarded as a loop, as shown in Figure 8.29. There are three possible ways to model the information associated with this plan–action–control loop. To illustrate the three possibilities, suppose we want to plan and control the duration and cost of operations of some kind. For example, the operation could be the repair of a machine of some kind, for which the two main resources required would be the time of a repair engineer, and the parts and materials used. In some hospitals, surgery to replace hip joints is managed in a similar way.

Figure 8.29
Management control loop

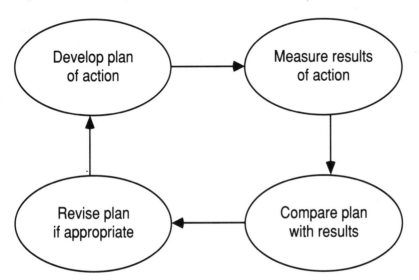

One approach is to regard the planned and the actual as successive states of the same entity. Thus we would have a single entity type OPERATION, with attributes PLANNED COST, PLANNED DURATION, ACTUAL COST, ACTUAL DURATION and so on. Until the operation had been carried out, it would possess values for the 'planned' attributes, but not for the 'actual' attributes. After the operation had taken place, the operation would be modified by acquiring values for the 'actual' attributes. This assumes that each operation is planned once, in other words that there is a one-to-one relationship between the plan and the outcome, justifying their being merged into a single occurrence of a single entity type.

Another approach is to regard the plan and the outcome as different occurrences of the same entity type. Thus we would have a single entity type OPERATION, with attributes COST, DURATION and so on. It would also need an attribute indicating whether a given occurrence represented a plan or an outcome, in other words whether the attributes were to be interpreted as planned values or actual values. An involuted relationship will usually be required to link the plans and outcomes together. (This need not be a one-to-one relationship; thus this approach is more flexible than the first.)

A third approach is to regard the plan and the outcome as occurrences of different entity types. Thus PLANNED COST and PLANNED DURATION would be attributes of PLANNED OPERATION while ACTUAL COST and ACTUAL DURATION would be attributes of ACTUAL OPERATION. Again, some relationship will usually be required to link the two entity types together. (As in the second approach, this need not be a one-to-one relationship.)

The first approach is not always enough, but it is the simplest. The second approach will be regarded by some people as the most elegant solution (partly because it requires fewest attributes to be named and defined), but will confuse most people (perhaps for the same reason). The third approach allows the plans and the outcomes to be completely separate, even incommensurate or incompatible, which often corresponds better with reality, and may be easier for the users to understand.

There is an additional problem with the modelling of plans. This is that plans are often aggregated, whereas results are specific. Thus the planning process may determine a total planned cost for a series of operations, instead of an individual planned cost for each operation. The control loop may be more complex, as in Figure 8.30.

Figure 8.30 Complex control loop

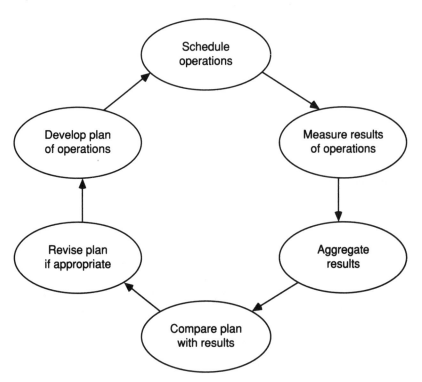

This may require the entity–relationship model in Figure 8.31, including the derived entity type (shown shaded) CONSOLIDATED OPERATION RESULT. (This entity type is derived, because all its attributes are derived by summary from the attributes of ACTUAL OPERATION). Note that whereas CONSOLIDATED OPERATION RESULT can be derived from ACTUAL OPERATION, PLAN OF OPERATIONS cannot be derived from SCHEDULED OPERATION, for two reasons. First, the plan exists before the schedule, and therefore cannot be derived from something that does not yet exist. Second, there are some attributes of the plan that cannot be decomposed into attributes of an individual scheduled operation. For example, each operation (let us suppose) either succeeds or fails. The target for each occurrence of SCHEDULED OPERATION would have to be 'success'; it would not make sense to attempt 90 per cent success on an individual operation. However, it does make sense to attempt 90 per cent success on a series of operations. Therefore if we want to set a target percentage success rate, it must be a non-derived attribute of PLAN OF OPERATIONS. (Actual percentage success rate, as an attribute of CONSOLIDATED OPERATION RESULT, can of course be derived from the actual success or fail indicator which is an attribute of ACTUAL OPERATION.)

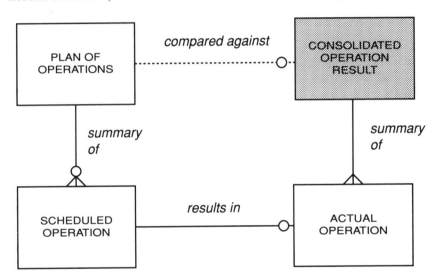

Figure 8.31
Entity–relationship model

Furthermore, hierarchies of plans cannot be derived from one another. If there are three salespersons in a sales department, the sales target for the whole department may be less than the sum of the targets for the individual sales-persons (on the grounds that you do not expect all the salespersons to achieve their targets, although you will not know in advance which will). And the inventory targets for the whole division will not be equal to the sum of the targets for each warehouse within the division.

Question: under what circumstances can the sales department target be greater than the sum of the targets for the individual salespersons? Answer: when the sales department is expected to expand, to take on additional salespersons during the period. Or perhaps when it is expected that at least one salesperson will exceed target.

8.6.2 Performance measurement

In archery, a target is a series of concentric circles. The nearer you get to the middle, the higher you score. The further from the middle, the greater the corrective action required: see Figure 8.32. In business, a target is usually a range of acceptable values. A delivery scheduled for 11 a.m. can be, say, twenty minutes late without anyone much caring. Between twenty minutes and two hours late is inconvenient. Over two hours late is serious. Over two days late is disastrous.

Figure 8.32 Archery target model

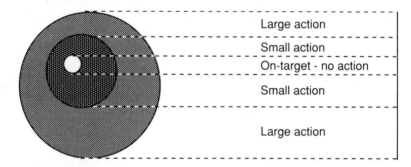

Note that, unlike in archery, the targets are not symmetrical: x minutes early is not equivalent to x minutes late. (For this reason, I have drawn the target off centre.) If you miss a train because it leaves the station five minutes early, and the next train is not for another hour, then five minutes early is equivalent to fifty-five minutes late. The impact of an early arrival depends on the **policy**. Some delivery firms will wait until the appointed time if they arrive early and the customer is not there; some leave and return later; some leave altogether and you have to make another appointment.

Performance: single-loop system

The simplest view of performance control is to assume the targets are fixed outside the system. This gives us a simple loop, as in Figure 8.33. We assume

Figure 8.33 Simple loop

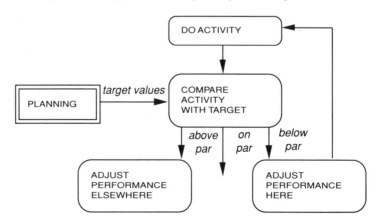

the measurement of an activity is contained within the activity itself. We ignore here any requirements for audit controls (e.g. double checking and verification).

If the performance is on par, we do nothing. Worse, and we need to take some corrective action. Much better, and we may want to see if there is an opportunity to improve performance elsewhere. (Note: please translate golfing metaphor into archery metaphor, or perhaps your own favourite sport.) This model applies both to operational performance targets, and to strategic performance targets (sometimes called 'goals' – yet another sport!). There may be hierarchies of targets contributing to higher targets.

Performance: double-loop system

A more sophisticated system, as in Figure 8.34, includes the process of setting the target values. However, the things that are measured are still fixed (here shown supplied by the planning function). This gives us a secondary loop, which may be on a longer cycle than the primary loop. (Some organizations have a policy that target changes must wait until next year. The process structure is still the same; but there is a built-in delay.) Not shown here is the third level of sophistication, where the very choice of measures is dynamically controlled within the performance monitoring system.

Figure 8.34 Double-loop system

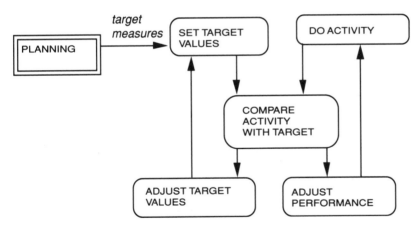

This usually requires a higher level of measuring, to test whether the operational measures are providing good predictions of profitability or customer satisfaction. (For example, are our formal measures picking up all the things the customers typically complain about? This implies more than one data source, to enable the measures to be compared – perhaps an informal survey to complement the formal measurements. Otherwise, we may not be aware that our customers are complaining at all.)

A good system should not only be able to add measures that could be more useful than the existing ones, but also be able to drop the measures that prove less useful. Bureaucratic systems tend to be asymmetrical in this respect – it is much easier to add than drop, so the paperwork goes on increasing. And the only way to prevent it increasing seems to be to resist any new measures, however useful.

The third loop should normally be on a rather slower cycle than the first two. (We do not want to change the measures so often that the first and second level control becomes unstable.) For strategic performance measures, the third loop may take some years.

In implementing new measures, there may be organizational resistance if the relevance of a new measure is disputed. The best way to prove the relevance of a measure is to demonstrate that it is strongly correlated with an accepted measure (e.g. profitability or customer satisfaction). There may also be resistance based on the perceived fairness of the new measure (e.g. is my bonus or promotion vulnerable to decisions made by other people, outside my control or influence?). Testing a new measure (either by actual pilot or by 'what if' analysis) belongs to the third loop.

Thus change implies informal *ad hoc* execution of the third loop processes, but it is probably not possible to model this systematically until the organization has experienced this a few times. Figure 8.35 is a simple generic information model of the performance targets. Each performance target may be of a different type, but all can be expressed as a single range of acceptable values, or as a series of nested ranges. Sometimes a resulting CONTROL ACTION may be associated with a range that represents off-target performance.

Figure 8.35
Performance target
information model

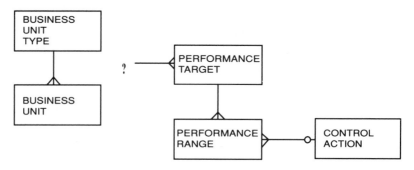

At what level are performance targets defined?

The attributes of PERFORMANCE TARGET would be the type of target, and the period (date/time) to which it applied. Note that targets for the same business unit need not be end to end. A business unit could have one target for weekdays and a different target for weekends. You could either model this as different target types, or as different target periods. (In the latter solution, of course, a period may be discontinuous, and cannot be defined merely by start date and end date.)

The attributes of PERFORMANCE RANGE would be the upper and lower values of the range, together with an attribute to indicate the units of measure. Note that several occurrences of PERFORMANCE RANGE may by coincidence have the same values. However, they belong to different business units, or different periods/types, and result in different CONTROL ACTIONS. The main attribute of CONTROL ACTION would be a description of the action.

A slightly more sophisticated model would allow several possible CONTROL ACTIONS for each PERFORMANCE RANGE, where each CONTROL ACTION would also possess an attribute to describe the condition or context when the action would be appropriate. A very sophisticated model would represent the actions and conditions not as descriptions but as formatted data, enabling them to be automated. The entity type CONTROL ACTION would then need relationships to other parts of the model. This solution would be required for a full process control environment, but is not advised here. It may be appropriate to assign performance targets to individual business units, or to classes of business unit. Either or both relationships could be drawn in, depending on the business policy.

Each business area would of course require specific processes to compare the actual performance with the targets, since although the targets may be generic, the actuals will be derived from information all over the model.

Performance: service levels

Let us take delivery as an example of a service to the customer: see Figure 8.36. When the delivery is completed, the customer signs a piece of paper that may specify some aspects of the service (e.g. quantity delivered) and not others (e.g. time delivered).

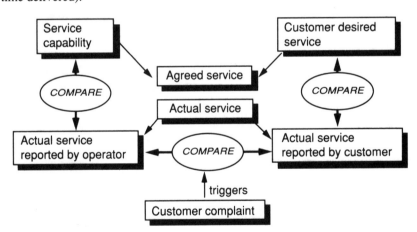

Figure 8.36 Delivery service model

The delivery can result in a COMPLAINT, if the actual service falls short of the agreed or expected service. The delivery can also result in a DISPUTE, if the complaint refers to some aspect of the delivery that is not signed off at the time. In other words, the operator's report of the delivery may differ from the customer's report. We tend to discover that there is such a difference of opinion only if there is a complaint in the first place. If the customer does not complain, we will probably assume that he is happy, and that he views things the same way we do.

The debriefing from the operator when he returns from a delivery only covers some aspects of the delivery. If there is a complaint about some other aspect of the delivery (e.g. excessive noise), then you may have to go back to the operator to get his side of the story.

Sometimes the customer may request a higher service than is specified in the contract, (e.g. next-day delivery, when the contract only promises 48-hour turnaround). Or the customer may desire a change to an already agreed (and scheduled) delivery. Does an agreement under these conditions carry the same penalties on default as a normal agreement? (We do not have to answer that in the information model, as long as we have the information to reconstruct the different situations.)

The contract may specify a cumulative service level (e.g. 98 per cent of deliveries shall be on time). This means that we monitor performance, not only at the event or transaction level, but also at summary levels, over given periods of time.

Figure 8.37 Delivery service targets

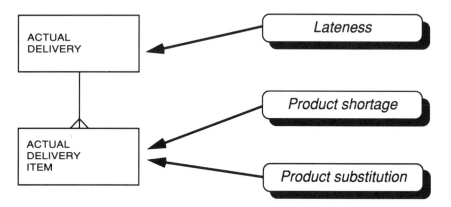

Another issue with performance monitoring is whether to include over-achievement as well as underachievement. If we want to include over-achievement, then the information model must contain enough information to identify the overachievement attempts. If we are consistently achieving a 98 per cent service level, should not we go for further improvement? Figure 8.37 shows delivery service targets. Some of the delivery targets refer to the lateness of deliveries; other delivery targets refer to the completeness or accuracy of deliveries. Time is an attribute of the whole delivery; product and quantity are attributes of the delivery item. Table 8.3 is an example of a semi-satisfied customer.

Table 8.3 Job analysis

Requested delivery	11 a.m.	120 cases	Original WANT
Suggested delivery	11 a.m.	240 cases	Revised WANT
Scheduled delivery	11 a.m.	240 cases	
Actual delivery	11 a.m.	200 cases	
Promised delivery	3 p.m.	40 cases	Is this a second SCHEDULED DELIVERY?
Actual delivery	4 p.m.	40 cases	

There are several ways this situation can be assessed. What is probably important is that the whole series of events can be recalled for comparison. This means that the information model would have to support all these events, including the iteration on CUSTOMER WANT (caused by negotiation and interaction with the telephone salesperson).

There are a whole number of possible performance measures/targets:

1. Number/volume/value of late deliveries.
2. Number/volume/value of late delivery items.
3. Average lateness of deliveries by volume/value/number.
4. And so on.

Performance measures assess the quality of decisions made by the relevant manager. The key question is whether the manager is encouraged or discouraged to make decisions leading to customer satisfaction or profitability. For example, do we prefer to disappoint one customer a lot, or many customers a little? Would a customer prefer 80 per cent delivery of every item ordered, or full delivery of 80 per cent of the items ordered? If we think the former to be preferable, from a customer satisfaction point of view, we should measure delivery performance so that this gets a higher 'score'. Figure 8.38 shows a delivery service information model.

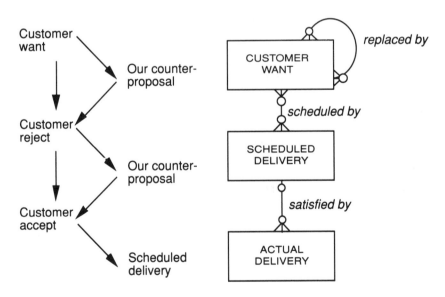

Figure 8.38 Delivery service information model

The CUSTOMER WANTS are influenced by the sales process. The telephone salesperson may make counter-proposals, for a number of reasons:

1. Large differences/omissions from previous orders made by same customer.
2. Non-availability of desired product, or policy to push new product.
3. Unreasonable delivery demands.

This negotiation continues until the customer and the salesperson think they have reached an agreement. The negotiation may result in several delivery dates being agreed, each for several products. Present systems do not capture what the customer wants or expects, but only capture what we have agreed with the customer.

What if there is no schedule, but an *ad hoc* delivery is made? It is always possible to cheat, by creating an instantaneous SCHEDULE, which is immediately satisfied, but this could distort the performance. (This makes the relationship *satisfied by* mandatory, but only by having false occurrences of the entity type SCHEDULED DELIVERY.) Otherwise there perhaps needs be a way of linking the actual delivery back to the customer want, if we want to measure the true value to the business (in terms of satisfying the customer). This may apply particularly to special kinds of customer wants, such as delivery of empty bottles back to the depot, which may be scheduled, but often is not. Note: I have not modelled all the intermediate stages between CUSTOMER WANT and SCHEDULED DELIVERY (e.g. ORDER) because I do not know what they are, and because in any case they are probably just steps towards the goal, which is delivery. At least, that is the customer's goal. Our end-goal is to receive payment. But we are here interested in the customer service levels.

8.6.3 Budget and forecast

A BUDGET is usually an amount of money allocated for spending on a particular purpose. It is a particular kind of PLAN or INTENTION, related to a future COST. The modelling of BUDGET is very similar to the modelling of PLAN. BUDGETs often form a hierarchy, in which different levels of budgets do not necessarily add up. This is for the same reason that hierarchies of PLANs do not need to add up. Thus a divisional manager may control a budget of which 80 per cent has been allocated to the department managers, and 20 per cent is retained in reserve, to cover unplanned contingencies.

In some companies, the allocation of a BUDGET is separate from the AUTHORIZATION to spend the money. Thus although the department manager has a budget of £50,000 to spend on equipment, each equipment PURCHASE may need to be separately authorized by a more senior manager.

A FORECAST is a prediction of costs and/or revenues. Usually the distinction between budget and forecast is that budgets emerge from a formal planning process, and may be fixed annually, whereas a forecast may be a more accurate (because more recent) calculation. For example, there may be a training budget of £25,000; however, because of abnormally high staff turnover in recent months, we shall probably need to spend over £35,000. Managers may compare actual costs both against the original budgets, and against revised budgets or forecasts. From an information modelling point of view, there is very little difference in structure between BUDGET and FORECAST. The difference is in the process that creates them, and in their status.

8.6.4 Cost

Costs: purposes

There are several reasons why a business needs to have a fairly good idea about its cost structure:

1. To predict expenditure for planned operations
2. To calculate minimum price-level for profitable operations.
3. To identify opportunities for saving costs (e.g. emulation of best practice).
4. To motivate managers to save costs.
5. To quantify cost–benefits of proposed changes.
6. To analyse cost–quality trade offs.

How profitable is each depot? How profitable is each product? How profitable is each category of customer? Which are the factors that have the greatest impact on costs (and thus on profits)? What trends can we identify? What would be the impact of a projected increase in operational volumes? What would be the impact of a proposed change in operations?

If we think our load planning and scheduling is really efficient and effective, we may create a new business, selling this service to other distribution companies. In order to do this profitably, we have to know exactly how much the service costs us. Similarly, we may want to compare our internal costs of performing a given task with the cost of subcontracting that task out. We need to know the cost implications of agreeing any given service level to the customer. This enables intelligent negotiation – how much can we offer before the service becomes unprofitable?

Cost model: fantasy

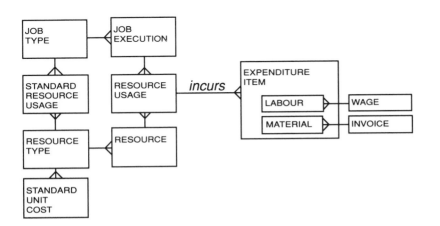

Figure 8.39 Cost model: fantasy

Costs are incurred by using resources on jobs (Figure 8.39). For example, a specific delivery uses two human resources (driver and mate), one physical resource (truck) and a consumable resource (fuel). What we really want to do is add up all the costs actually incurred by that delivery, and compare them with how much the delivery should have cost. e.g. this delivery ought to have taken so many hours, driven so many miles, consumed so much fuel. (This is the STANDARD RESOURCE USAGE.) And the driver should cost so much per hour, the lorry should cost so much per mile, the fuel should cost so much per litre. (This is the STANDARD UNIT COST.) Actual costs are what appear (in summary form) on the profit and loss accounts. Labour costs must correspond somehow to the payroll; material costs must correspond to the purchase ledger.

But you do not pay for things at that level. The driver is probably on a weekly wage, rather than on a fixed payment per trip. The cost of the lorry covers tax and insurance, regular cleaning, periodic replacement of tyres, occasional repairs and service, as well as depreciation, which is an accountant's jargon word for saving up to buy a new lorry. Even fuel is usually bought by the tankful. (And if some of the fuel in your tank was bought this week, and some last week at a different price, how do we calculate the cost per litre?)

Information about expenditure is obtained from such sources as supplier invoices. For example, when the tyres of the delivery lorry are replaced, an INVOICE is received, containing one or more items of expenditure to be paid for. The cost of the tyres is probably greater than the cost of a single delivery trip. Fortunately, the tyres do not need to be replaced after each delivery. Each delivery incurs a small fraction of the tyre replacement cost.

One EXPENDITURE ITEM (i.e. the tyre replacement) is therefore partially incurred by many RESOURCE USAGES (i.e. delivery trips). This is a many-to-many relationship. Thus we cannot determine the actual cost of a specific delivery by simply adding up numbers on invoices. If one RESOURCE USAGE can be completely isolated from all others, then direct calculation of costs may be possible. This may be necessary in some situations, but has the disadvantage of preventing the enterprise from reusing any resources, or exploiting any economies of scale.

But since it is in most cases impractical to break expenditure down into small enough pieces, actual costs cannot be directly determined by adding expenditure items. To compare actual costs with budgeted or standard costs, the actual costs first have to be calculated indirectly, by apportioning EXPENDITURE ITEM according to a formula or algorithm. For example, if the tyres need replacing after 1000 deliveries, then 0.1 per cent of the tyre replacement cost is added to the actual cost of each delivery. (This simple formula of course assumes that each delivery wears out the tyres an equal amount. Clever modellers may want to develop a more complex formula, but should only do so if the business really needs such levels of accuracy.)

Cost model: practical approach

Instead of trying to decompose individual EXPENDITURE ITEMS, the usual approach is to group them into COST ACCOUNTS, group the RESOURCE USAGES into

COST CENTRES, and then share out (or apportion) the total amount incurred within a COST ACCOUNT between the applicable COST CENTRES, according to some algorithm. So we end up with some bridging structure between RESOURCE USAGE and EXPENDITURE ITEM, that allows the incurs relationship to be indirectly approximated, instead of being precisely specified.

I have not shown the relationship between RESOURCE USAGE and COST CENTRE in Figure 8.40. This is because most companies simplify their cost accounting by defining the COST CENTRE at a higher level, e.g. by JOB TYPE (broken down by LOCATION or ORGANIZATION UNIT or whatever). Thus the COST CENTRE may turn out to be equivalent to one of the other entity types already shown, or to an intersection between one of these entity types and something else. There are many different options here, and the information model should represent the chosen accounts policy.

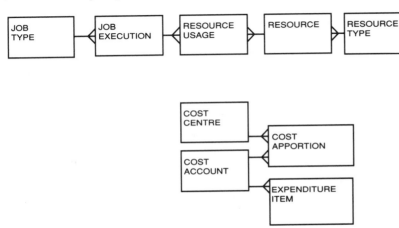

Figure 8.40 A practical cost model

Another complication not shown here is the fact that many companies want to analyse costs at different levels of summary. There may be hierarchies of COST CENTRE or COST ACCOUNT. You may think that upper levels of these hierarchies are redundant, because the actual costs at the upper levels can be derived from the costs at the lower levels. There are two reasons why the upper levels are needed. Cost allocation is often performed top down. This means that the inaccuracy is greater at the lower levels. There will often be other non-derivable information, such as budgets, at the upper levels. The strategy is to start with broad cost centres, covering ranges of activities and expenditures. Then gradually introduce refinements, at whatever speed the organization can assimilate them. Concentrate on costs that can be influenced.

Costs: general approach

In the previous section, we described a practical approach using specific entity types as examples of cost groupings. This section sketches a more generic approach, usable whatever the cost groupings are.

Figure 8.41 Costs: general approach

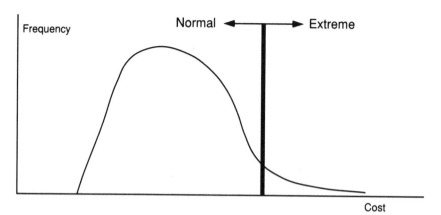

1. Group similar expenditures
2. Obtain standard costs. Where do standard costs come from? There are two approaches:
   (a) the descriptive approach. Calculate standard cost as average for group either for all cases (i.e. the average of actual historical costs, with no exceptions, or for all except extreme cases (i.e. the average of actual historical costs, not counting extremes and disasters). This of course means you have to have a way of identifying the extremes, e.g. only if the extreme can be associated with a good excuse (e.g. freak storms); anything more than, say, double the lowest cost; or automatically discount the most expensive 10 per cent. See Figure 8.41.
   (b) the normative approach. Calculate standard cost from the lowest in group (the cheapest we have ever done this, under ideal conditions). Sometimes an amount is added for contingency. This means that the standard cost represents what ought to be usually achievable, rather than what has been usually achieved. The proponents of this approach argue that standard costs serve as self-fulfilling predictions: the lower you set the standard cost (within reason), the lower the actual costs will be. The opponents of the minimum cost approach argue that it commits the fallacy of composition (confusing 'sometimes possible' with 'always possible'), ignores statistical fluctuations, can result in unreasonably low costs, and leads to over-optimistic plans.
3. Measure variance against standard cost.
4. Analyse/explain variances.

Cost variances

If there are significant differences between the actual costs incurred in a series of operations, or between the actual costs and the standard costs, this could mean any of three things.

1. Cost overruns – some of the operations are exceptionally expensive. This could mean that some departments or individuals are operating inefficiently.

Identification of waste may result in some corrective action. Another possible explanation is that the standard cost is unreasonably low (either inaccurate or out of date).

2. Cost underruns – some of the operations are exceptionally cheap. This could mean that some departments or individuals have discovered a new way to carry out the operations. Good practice may be worth emulating elsewhere. Or it could be that they are taking unacceptable short cuts or risks. Poor quality may require some corrective action.

3. Group too broad – the operations are not sufficiently similar to make a meaningful comparison. If it is not meaningful to compare all the operations within the cost group, because the cost factors are different, the group needs to be focused by subdivision into clusters with the same cost factors. If this subdivision makes the groups too small or fragmentary, then it may be necessary to regroup at a higher level.

Possible implementation of costing system

1. The first phase implements a single-loop control, which measures actual costs and compares with fixed standard costs. Standard costs and cost groups are captured, but no automated support is offered for calculating them.

2. In the second phase, the processes of calculating standard costs are automated. This should draw on the learning experience of the organization in using the phase 1 system. However, the cost groups are still fixed.

3. In the third phase, the reclustering processes for defining the cost groups are automated. This cannot be done until the organization has reached a certain level of sophistication in measuring and controlling costs. If it is done too early, it will be a theoretical exercise that leaves the business too far behind. It can also distract the organization from learning the basic principles of cost measurement, and the control of overruns and underruns.

Costs: assumptions

Standard costs can be represented as data, or captured as algorithms. In order to represent them as data, we have to impose some restrictions on the kinds of algorithm that can be used, to enable the cost parameters to be 'tabularized'. A reasonable assumption is that all costs can be made up of single cost elements, each with a single 'driver'. In mathematical jargon, this means that costs can be expressed as linear equations. The cost of using a lorry works out at so much per hour, plus so much per mile, plus so much per trip. (This would include an allowance for fuel, wear and tear, tax and insurance, etc.)

$$
\begin{aligned}
\text{Lorry cost} \quad &= (x * \text{hours used}) \\
&+ (y * \text{miles driven}) \\
&+ (z * \text{number of trips})
\end{aligned}
$$

(Overheads and other indirect expenses may thus be calculated as a fixed percentage of direct expenses, or to vary linearly by some other parameter.)

That this is a simplification can be seen if we consider that a full load uphill uses more fuel than a half load downhill. However, non-linear cost equations quickly become unmanageable. Most companies make do with linear cost equations for most, if not all, components of cost.

8.6.5 Account

Accounting can roughly be divided into two functions: financial accounting seeks to record the past and present financial state of the business, and management accounting seeks to enhance the future financial state of the business. Thus financial accounting tends to be concerned with the production of reports, while management accounting tends to be concerned with the making or supporting of decisions (e.g. investment decisions). Often financial accounting creates or assembles information to be used by management accounting. This information is presented as a series of ACCOUNTS, which contain notional amounts of money representing different aspects of the business, in particular income and expenditure, assets and liabilities (broken down by areas and categories). Each CUSTOMER and SUPPLIER will have an ACCOUNT, which allows the mutual liabilities between organizations to be monitored – the complete sets of these accounts are known as the **general ledger, sales ledger** and **purchase ledger** respectively.

These accounts form a financial model of the business. It is a model that originated in late mediæval Italy, known as double-entry book-keeping. Each transaction (such as a movement of materials or money, or a change of ownership or stewardship) is represented as two equal and opposite entries in the accounts – one debit and one credit. (More complex transactions may result in more than two account entries, but the principle remains, that all the entries resulting from a single transaction should sum to zero.)

The trouble with modelling accounts is that you are not modelling reality, but the accountants' model of reality. An information model of a general ledger is therefore a model of a model. There is a choice – to ignore the accountants' models and develop your own from scratch, or to take the accountants' models at face value. The problem with the former option is to reconcile your models with the accountants'. The problem with the latter option is that the accountants' models have been built for different purposes, with deliberate redundancy built in for control (which is the rationale of double-entry book-keeping).

Because general ledger is a model, rather than direct reality, we can only model it by considering its purpose, the requirements it is supposed to fulfil. Typical requirements of an ideal general ledger are as follows:

1. To maintain historical financial accounts, according to the legal requirements and accounting practices within those countries the company trades in.

2. To produce management accounting information (including 'what if' analysis) without impairing the integrity of the financial accounts.
3. To interface with any other accounting systems and ledgers being used by the organization. To be coordinated with non-financial systems.
4. To consolidate groups of companies with different account structures and practices. (Each company may require a stand-alone general ledger, which then interfaces to a corporate level general ledger. Thus the model may need to interface with itself.)
5. To restructure accounts without losing data, and without losing the ability to compare financial performance over time. (Typical organizations change their organization structure frequently; existing GL application packages force the accountants to create parallel or multiple accounts structures to keep up with these changes.)

Let us start by taking the accountants' model at face value. An object is represented as an ACCOUNT, which is a book-keeping device for assembling all financial transactions (individual or aggregated, historical or forecast) about that object. Thus there are a series of TRANSACTIONS (which can be defined as any financially significant events), each resulting in a self-balancing set of debit or credit ENTRYS or POSTINGS to individual ACCOUNTS: see Figure 8.42

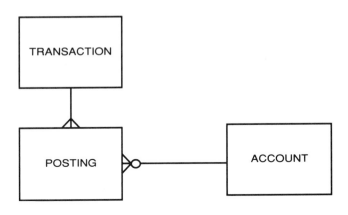

Figure 8.42 Simplified book-keeping

How is the individual occurrence of ACCOUNT defined? Typically, there is a structured account code, which can be broken into three or four parts. Thus expenditure accounts may be identified by a location or cost centre, an expenditure category, and a project or task code. Thus account number S12/4711-WRP contains all costs of category 4711 incurred by project WRP at location S12. This can be depicted by a three-dimensional matrix, as the shaded cell within Figure 8.43 shows.

Of course, this is complicated by the fact that not all combinations of location, expenditure category and project are valid. Perhaps for some expenditure categories, the project is irrelevant. Thus the matrix may not be a regular shape – it may be only one cell thick in places. However, in general, each cell

Figure 8.43 Matrix of accounts

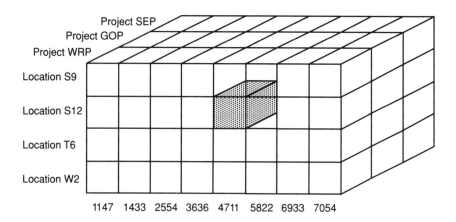

corresponds to an account, to which transactions may be assigned. The existence of an account represents the acceptability of that combination. Thus you might expect to see the following model shown in Figure 8.44.

Figure 8.44 Model of accounts

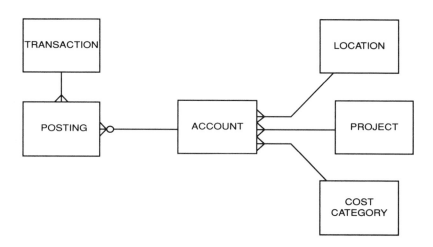

But the postings, and the assignment of the postings to particular accounts, can usually be derived from a set of posting rules. The primary association is between the original accounting event, or TRANSACTION, and the entity types from which the ACCOUNT is defined (Figure 8.45).

Sometimes more than three dimensions will be required; with such representations as Figure 8.41, as the complexity of the situation increases, it becomes increasingly difficult to draw intelligible diagrams. But this is not true of the entity–relationship diagram; its complexity does not explode as the complexity of the situation increases – an additional dimension to the accounts will typically just result in an additional entity type.

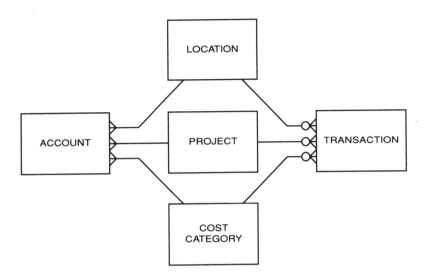

Figure 8.45
Transaction–account
relationship

A hierarchy of accumulation or indirect accounts is typically established by the accountants, in order to aggregate various aspects of the organization's financial performance. Thus we may want to accumulate costs by project regardless of location, or costs by location regardless of project. If there are n dimensions of account, then there are $2^n - 1$ possible ways of accumulating the accounts (since each dimension may be either included or omitted, but at least one dimension must be included). The balances in these accumulation accounts are derivable from the balances in the lower-level accounts, to which direct postings are made. The accumulation occurrence of ACCOUNT can be defined by any arbitrary combination of the categories used to define the posting accounts.

Some internal transactions may be captured in the accounts. For example, a movement of stock, or the secondment of a worker from one warehouse to another, may well result in a debit to the account associated with one warehouse, and a credit to the account associated with the other. Not all internal movements have financial significance, however; thus a movement of stock from one shelf to another within the warehouse would probably have no financial significance and would therefore not be notified to the financial accountants for inclusion in the accounts. (This implies the existence of a set of RULES, determining what kinds of movement are to trigger account entries.)

There is, however, a significant difference between an internal transaction and a real transaction. An internal transaction has no overall effect on the business – it does not change the total amount of cash or physical assets or creditors or debts or other liabilities. A real transaction is one that has a visible effect (however small) on the company balance sheet. Thus it may not be appropriate to model them by the same entity type.

There are also indirect postings to accounts, based on allocation or apportionment rules. These share costs between cost centres, according to set formulas. For example, each department is charged for a proportion of the computer costs, equal to the proportion of the computer time consumed by the department. This is often modelled by including non-financial data (such as computer time) as postings to non-financial accounts. The apportionment formula can then refer to the current contents of a series of accounts, both financial and non-financial. In some cases, the formula may need to refer to the current contents of accumulation accounts. The trouble with this is that it seems to make it necessary to combine accumulation accounts and posting accounts into a single entity type. Whereas the flexibility of accumulation might be better served by keeping the two entity types separate. This is a difficult judgement.

We have now produced a simple model of the accounts of a typical business that mirrors the accountants' own model. But if we review this against the goals of entity modelling, some problems emerge. The two main problems are redundancy and abstraction. The accounts may be redundant in two ways. Perhaps the association of the posting with the account may be redundant, since it follows automatically from the location, category and project with which the original event is associated. And perhaps the posting itself may be redundant, since it can be derived from the attributes of the original event. For example, if the receipt of a SUPPLIER INVOICE results in an ACCOUNT POSTING, then the posting is perhaps nothing more than a copy of the invoice, and contains no new information.

The accounts are an abstraction from the business, since all models are, in some sense, abstractions. FINANCIAL EVENT is a generalization of many other event-based and operational entity types within the model. Perhaps it includes PAYMENT, STOCK MOVEMENT, INVOICE and so on.

8.6.6 Debts and payments

One of the difficulties of book-keeping is matching the payments received from the customers against the debts awaiting settlement. (In accounting jargon, these debts are referred to as receivables. We shall model them with the entity type RECEIVABLE ITEM, which will probably correspond to INVOICE or PREMIUM DUE or CUSTOMER STATEMENT.) If only every RECEIVABLE ITEM were paid separately and in full, then there would be a simple optional one to one relationship between RECEIVABLE ITEM and PAYMENT, and the matching would be a trivial one. (Figure 8.46).

Figure 8.46 Simple item–payment model

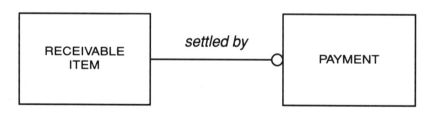

This is unlikely to work, because there will probably be some customers that send a single payment to cover several debts. There may also be part payments (for a variety of reasons, including disputes), and/or prepayments (such as deposits).

This means that the relationship between RECEIVABLE ITEM and PAYMENT will be many to many, and an intersection entity type is required. (Figure 8.47).

A payment may be used to fully or partly settle one or many receivable items. Considerable effort is devoted, in complex accounting systems, to matching the receivable items off against the payments, in order to calculate the settlement items, and to calculate the outstanding balance.

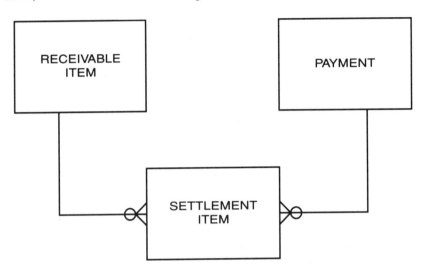

Figure 8.47
Intersection entity type item–payment model

8.6.7 Foreign currency

Many American companies operate exclusively in US dollars. At some stage in the future, European companies may be able to operate exclusively in ecus. But for many companies, at least some transactions may be carried out in some foreign currency. When these transactions are rare (perhaps the occasional overseas purchase or sale), the conversion into the base currency can be kept out of the picture.

One way to model CURRENCY is as an entity type. The trouble with this approach is that every financial attribute must have a value in a specific currency. Thus every entity type that possesses a financial attribute would have a relationship to CURRENCY. Furthermore, if an entity type has more than one financial attribute, it may not always be possible to assume that all the attribute values, even for the same occurrence of the entity type, will be in the same currency. For example, a purchase order could conceivably specify a delivery charge of DM 20, and an insurance charge of US$5. Thus we should need two relationships from PURCHASE ORDER to CURRENCY. The entity–relationship diagram becomes unreadable, because of all the relationships to this rather unimportant entity type.

Foreign currency is therefore one of those areas where it is common to find a model that disobeys the strict principles of pedantic information modelling. The pragmatic (although impure) alternative is to define currency as a **domain,** rather like units of measure. Then, whenever we have a financial attribute, we give it a sister attribute to specify the currency. Thus PURCHASE ORDER, in the example above, would have four attributes: DELIVERY CHARGE AMOUNT, DELIVERY CHARGE CURRENCY, INSURANCE CHARGE AMOUNT and INSURANCE CHARGE CURRENCY. The two currency attributes would take values from a set of predefined codes. There is an international standard ISO list of currency codes, which should be used if possible. Of course, it is often possible to define a **home currency**, so that most financial attributes are in the home currency, thus saving unnecessary duplication of currency attributes.

Meanwhile, there may be a need to maintain currency exchange rates. Usually only the exchange rates between the home currency and each foreign currency are maintained, and conversions from one foreign currency to another are calculated via the home currency. Some banks and organizations performing high volumes of currency transactions may require every pair of exchange rates to be stored, but this is exceptional, and very tedious to maintain.

8.6.8 Assets and liabilities

If costs are assigned to COST CENTRES and revenues are assigned to PROFIT CENTRES, then assets and liabilities may be assigned to RESPONSIBILITY CENTRES. There are two main distinctions that sometimes have to be made, particularly with assets. One is between real assets and operating assets. A REAL ASSET is one that we own, which appears on the balance sheet. However it may or may not be physically present in our organization; perhaps we have leased it out to another company. An OPERATING ASSET is one that is physically present in our organization. However, it may or may not belong to us; perhaps we have leased it in from another company.

Sometimes, accountants are only interested in the REAL ASSETs, whereas the OPERATING ASSETs are only of interest to the parts of the company using them. But there may be complications. Perhaps we have to pay insurance or maintenance on the assets we operate, as well as the assets we own. If the asset is large (such as a building or expensive machine), then there may be a specific ACCOUNT for its maintenance costs. In some cases, an asset may be shared between two organizations. Oil companies sometimes use one another's pipelines, and take temporary responsibility for the oil that belongs to another. In this case, a more complex definition of REAL ASSET would be required.

The other distinction that may be required is that between CAPITAL ASSET, which is a long-term asset, probably acquired in one financial year and disposed of many years later, and WORKING ASSET, which is expected to be acquired and disposed of within the same year. Materials and products, work in progress and unpaid bills, are all usually regarded as working assets. One of the problems with making this distinction, however, is that some working assets are held over from one financial year to another, because no company wants to have an entirely empty warehouse at the financial year-end. Meanwhile, some capital assets may be disposed of within the same year that they were acquired. For example, a vehicle that is wrecked in an accident, or a machine bought to support a production line that is soon afterwards abandoned. If the accountants need to have this type of distinction made within the information model, therefore, they must define clear criteria for the membership of each category of asset. The purpose of this section has been to prompt the appropriate questions.

8.7 Organization

This section considers the modelling of companies and their subdivisions. There is often a need to model other organizations, and there is often a need to model the structure of one's own organization. In some cases, these needs overlap: internal organization units may occasionally play the roles of external organizations, and there may be a need to understand the internal structure of one's customers and other external organizations (including such details as the office locations of different job-holders, responsible for different aspects of the business). So this section considers both external and internal modelling of organizations, including various information needs associated with the personnel function.

8.7.1 Corporation and institution

Many companies and other corporate bodies have a legally defined status. A registered or limited company has certain rights and privileges, from which it derives its status as an entity. The organization for which the information model is being built (the target organization) will usually have business dealings with many such outside organizations. Some of these dealings may be based on formal written contracts, others may be based on informal agreements or standard industry terms.

Other institutions may behave as companies. Your customers may include government departments, trades unions, charities, scout troops. International banks may unwittingly include terrorist and criminal organizations among their customers. What defines the identity of a company? If it changes its name, is it still the same? For some purposes, such as financial ones, you may need to adopt the legal definition. (For example, if a company disappears owing you money, and then reappears trading under a different name, under what conditions can you sue the new company for the old company's debt? And under what conditions can the new company sue you for money that you owed the old company?)

For other purposes, such as market analysis, you may adopt a different definition. (For example, if a new company has the same management as a former competitor, and is trading in the same area, it would be reasonable to predict its competitive behaviour as if it were a continuation of the behaviour of the former company.) ORGANIZATION or ORGANIZATION UNIT can be regarded as a simple object, provided that it is defined by name, and not by the collection of PERSONS that happen to belong to it. But teams can often change their identity if their membership changes significantly. (Pop groups cause particular problems, particularly if they register collective ownership of copyright on songs.)

8.7.2 *Company or person*

Some of the entity types in a typical business information model will represent roles that can be played by either companies or individual people. For example, the entity type CUSTOMER often includes both private consumers, and small or large companies (known in some industries as trade customers). For many purposes, we do not need to distinguish between individual and trade customers. (They may, however, have different credit terms or discount terms.)

When there are significant overlaps between customers and suppliers, it may be appropriate to have an entity type covering both. Sometimes the attempt is made to define a general entity type covering all external individuals and organizations with which the target organization does business. General entity types like this are usually difficult to name, and this proves no exception. Let us look at some attempts, and the problems associated with each attempt.

- CONTRACT PARTNER: this assumes that you have a contract with all the external companies or persons with whom you want to do business. It can, however, be defined to cover those external companies or persons with which you intend/hope to negotiate a contract, but do not have a contract with yet.
- BUSINESS PARTNER: this suggests a high degree of cooperation and liaison, and can be confused with a person that shares the same business with you. It is therefore open to some misunderstanding.
- THIRD PARTY: for some reason, many people think that any outside organization with whom you do business is a third party. This is a misuse of legal jargon, and should be discouraged. A third party is correctly a company or person indirectly involved in a contract. (This will be discussed below.)
- PERSON: this follows the legal jargon, whereby a company is a legal 'person'. It is however confusing for most people, and is therefore not generally recommended, except perhaps where the vast majority of the occurrences of the entity type are persons in the non-legal sense.
- COMPANY OR PERSON: this is a somewhat cumbersome name for the entity type, but is often better than anything else.

The trouble with such a generalized entity type is that it may end up as a catch-all bucket, indiscriminately including everybody and everything. Suppose we define the entity type as anybody from whom payments may be received, or to whom payments may be due: this may include employees, customers, suppliers, banks, pension funds, shareholders, magistrate courts, tax authorities, newspapers and so on. Such an entity type may will be related to every other entity type in the model, and involved in every business process. Such a modelling structure can sometimes be difficult to manage and difficult to implement. Unless there are significant business benefits to be gained from imposing a common structure on all these organizations (such benefits do exist sometimes, but not always), it may be better to model each type of organization separately.

8.7.3 Organization hierarchy

An organization is usually divided into parts, and these parts divided into smaller parts. Thus a company may consist of divisions, and divisions consist of departments, and departments of groups, or whatever. Each division, department or group is managed by one of its employees. Figure 8.48 is one example

Figure 8.48 An organization hierarchy

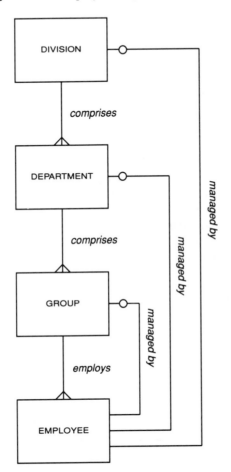

In Figure 8.49, Division 1 has a department with only one group (so the department and the group are identical), and Division 2 only contains one department (so the division and the department are identical). Let us suppose further that Division 3 allocates costs down to group level (thus the cost centre equates to GROUP) while Division 4 allocates costs only down to department level.

This kind of situation leads us apparently inexorably towards an organization hierarchy, modelled as a single entity type ORGANIZATION UNIT, with the reporting relationship represented as an involuted one to many. This bears some similarity with the GEOGRAPHICAL AREA, referred to earlier, since we have the same apparent difficulty relating the EMPLOYEE to the ORGANIZATIONAL UNIT. The

Figure 8.49 A model of divisions

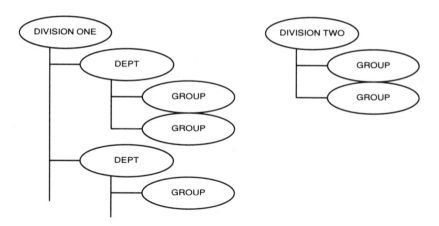

same employee works in a factory, and in a department within the factory, and within a team within the department within the factory. Thus the same occurrence of EMPLOYEE is associated with three different occurrences of ORGANIZATIONAL UNIT. (see Figure 8.50). We resolve this by relating the employee only to the lowest level of ORGANIZATIONAL UNIT. This is in fact easier than geography, since our knowledge of employees and their location within our own organization tends to be rather better than our knowledge of customers and their geographical locations.

Figure 8.50 Organizational unit

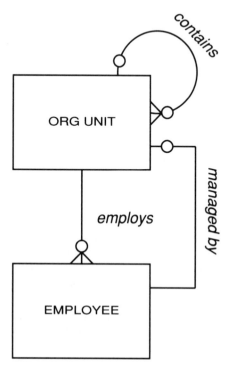

An organization unit tends not to be equivalent to the collection of its specific members. Thus, even if all the members of a department or project team leave and are replaced, it remains the same department or project team. Therefore, an organization unit cannot be identified by its members, but requires a name or some other identification.

Some organizations, however, are interested in all or some of the employees (or job titles) of their customers, either because these individuals (or roles) act as contact points, or because a service is being provided directly to the employees (although paid for by the employer). Modelling the internals of another organization can be more difficult, since the organizational structure may be partially opaque, and varies from one organization to another.

8.7.4 Job

A person has a job. So what is my job? Is it the same as the job my colleague has, who sits at the desk next to mine (who has similar responsibilities, but over a different group of items)? Is it the same as the job I had a year ago (when my job title was the same, but my responsibilities were fewer)? We can define 'job' in a number of ways, as a specific role or responsibility (i.e. mine alone, which I do not share with my colleague) or as a generic role or responsibility (i.e. a job title which I share with my colleagues). A job may be a semi-permanent position (which I hold until promoted, or until I change employment, and which is then filled by my successor) or a fixed-length assignment to a task or project (which I perform until the task or project is completed). The relationship between JOB and EMPLOYEE is often resolved into an intersection entity type called INCUMBENCY. This tends to be required for longer term information needs. If only the current incumbency is required, this may be modelled with a simple relationship between JOB and EMPLOYEE.

8.7.5 Authority

What is an individual allowed to do? A senior manager may be allowed (or indeed expected) to talk to the press, a middle manager may be able to authorize the purchase of capital equipment, while a junior manager may be allowed to hire and fire casual labour. (Note: when we speak of authorizing a PURCHASE ORDER, what we really mean is authorizing the PURCHASE. There is not always a one-to-one relationship between the former and the latter.)

A person has many authorities. Each authority allows him/her to do one specific thing, or to access one specific type(or item) of information. One of the possible authorities is to grant or revoke authority to other people. In some cases, authority may be shared. For example, a manager may share authority for recruitment with the personnel department. Each candidate must be interviewed twice, and both the line manager and the personnel manager must approve the appointment. In many companies, there are several managers who are authorized to sign company cheques. Sometimes there is a rule that one signature is required for cheques up to (say) £5000, while for higher value cheques, two signatures are required. This is another example of shared or joint authority.

Authorization applies to the actions they are allowed to do without higher authority, and also to their access to information. There is a general entity type here, which we may call AUTHORIZATION ITEM, being that for which authorization can be defined – the unit of authorization. Authorization can then be regarded as a relationship between the AUTHORIZATION UNIT and the AUTHORIZATION HOLDER, which may be either an individual person, or a role, or some complex combination of these. But since we have many types of authorization, we probably need an intersection entity type.

Authority may be defined in two ways. Some organizations allow their staff to do nothing until specifically authorized, while others allow everything that is not specifically banned. Thus authorization can be modelled positively (linking those items that are allowed with the people or roles that are allowed them) or negatively (linking those items with the people that are not allowed). These are logically equivalent, but they are not psychologically equivalent. Furthermore, they imply a wholly different set of process controls. For this reason, it is important to model authorization the right way around.

In complex contractual situations, there may be specific authorities and contact names defined within a CONTRACT. This may require modelling the job and authority structures of the CONTRACT PARTNER.

8.7.6 Skills

A person may have many skills. A job (for example, an assignment to a project in a particular role) may require many skills. Thus the matching of people to jobs is, among other things, a matching of skills. Therefore we need to have some way of modelling skills. Skills are both qualitative and quantitative. Thus we can compare the skills of two people in the same area (Edward speaks Arabic better than John does), or compare the skills of the same person in different areas (Edward speaks Arabic better than he speaks French). But often we merely want to know what skills a person has (Anthony speaks Malay but not Urdu), rather than trying to measure the level of skill.

Comparing the level of skill may involve introducing a scale of measurement. A **scale** is a range of values for the appropriate attribute or attributes. A simple scale for skill in a foreign language might be:

- **Native:** equivalent to mother tongue, bilingual.
- **Fluent:** can understand and be understood easily, but imperfectly.
- **Limited:** can understand and be understood with some difficulty.

It would be easy to imagine a more elaborate or sophisticated scale, with more values or dimensions. The complexity of the scale should match the purpose for which the scale is needed. For example, it might be more important to know about a person's ability to converse in his/her technical speciality in a foreign language, or his/her ability to conduct commercial negotiations, than to know about general conversational or cultural fluency.

A skill may be a cluster of abilities, rather than a single indivisible ability. If you can read *and* write in a foreign language, is this one skill or two? Is management a single generic skill, or is project management different to line management?

For each skill or combination of skills, there may be one or more training packages (perhaps formal courses or informal training or a mixture of both) suitable for providing or enhancing the skill. Different packages may be suitable for people with different starting skills or aptitudes. Therefore an information model for the planning of training and career progression within an organization may require an elaborate structure of abilities, actual and potential skill levels, associated with each employee (see Figure 8.51).

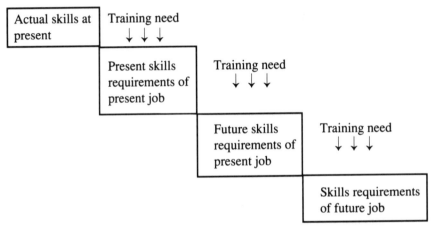

Figure 8.51 A framing model

As well as skills, it may be necessary to model knowledge, or rather knowledgeability. Some companies also attempt to monitor the general aptitudes and capacities of staff, such as judgement or initiative; this can also fit into the model, although it remains an open question whether such traits can be objectively measured.

8.7.7 Job evaluation

One of the functions of a typical personnel department is to classify different jobs within an organization, in order to compare salary differentials. There are several approaches to this evaluation, and the information model will vary according to which approach is adopted. In this section, we offer one approach to this problem, to illustrate how such personnel functions could be modelled. (Figure 8.52.)

We start off with a small number of standard FACTORS into which each job will be analysed. For example, the factors might be (α) skill (β) effort (γ) responsibility (δ) job conditions. Or for managerial jobs, the factors might be

Figure 8.52 Job
evaluation model

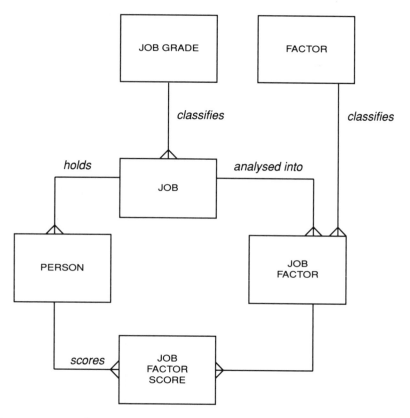

(α) know-how (β) problem-solving; (γ) authority. (In practice, there would be more factors than this, say between ten and fifteen.) Then we can analyse each job against the standard factors. For each JOB and each FACTOR, we determine a score, which indicates the degree of importance that this particular factor has for this particular job, as in Table 8.3. For example, the job of night watchman might score high on responsibility and difficult job conditions, but score low on skill and effort. In the following table, these scores are multiplied by a weight for each factor, and the weighted scores are then totalled. These weights should be understood to mean that responsibility is the factor most highly valued by the employer, while unpleasant or inconvenient job conditions are considered of least importance. Each JOB GRADE is defined as a range of total scores. By weighting and totalling these scores, we determine which jobs belong to which grades. By sheer coincidence, it turns out that the grade A jobs are those with the greatest influence over the weights of the different factors. A scale of pay and benefits can then be defined, with a range of possible salaries for each occurrence of JOB GRADE. These scales are usually adjusted at least once a year. In some organizations, these scales are subject to regular collective bargaining between management and the representatives of the employees.

Table 8.3. Job analysis

Factor	Weight	Watchman	Score	Engineer	Score	Director	Score
Skill	6	1	6	10	60	6	36
Effort	3	1	3	10	30	6	18
Responsibility	10	6	60	3	30	10	100
Job conditions	1	10	10	3	3	1	1
Total			79		123		155
Job grade			E		C		A

In order to determine for each individual employee, how he or she is to be paid, we then need to carry out an individual evaluation of his/her performance and abilities against the job. In some cases, the job itself may be open to negotiation, as well as the salary; thus Indra Patel may be classified as an engineer, but may argue that she deserves the status and reward of a senior engineer. This should be settled by comparing her skills and experience against the job description for senior engineer. In some cases, the evaluation of jobs and job grades requires a much more elaborate structure of point scores and weights than has been demonstrated here. For example, the Hay system is used to determine salaries for all levels of staff including top management, and calls for expert use of a complex series of charts and matrixes. However, the same approach to information modelling should be used, with entity types added only where necessary.

8.7.8 Organizational design

As discussed in the preceding sections, there are four different relationships between a person within an organization, and a task or function. One of the aims of organizational design is to discover people that have responsibility for tasks, without having the necessary expertise or authority. Or perhaps the opposite: there may be people who have knowledge and skills that would be useful to the organization, but which are not currently being used. A valuable tool for analysing an organization is an RAEW matrix, which stands for responsibility, authority, expertise, work.

In the matrix, the rows denote individual people, or perhaps organizational units or departments. Each cell may contain any combination of R, A, E and W. In the example in Table 8.4, we can see several anomalies, including the divided authority for task 3, and the total lack of expertise or responsibility for task 5. Task 2 is the neatest, because all four are in the same place. The organizational redesign process can concentrate on creating and moving the Rs, As, Es and Ws around the matrix (or reclustering the organizational units) until they form a coherent pattern.

Table 8.4 RAEW matrix

R: *responsibility*
A: *authority*
E: *expertise*
W: *work*

Task	1	2	3	4	5	6	7
Person **A**	RA - -		RA - -				
B	R - E -		R- - -		-A - -		
Γ	- - E -		RA - -			-A- -	
Δ		RA EW					
E	- - -W		R- EW	- - EW	- - -W		
Z					- - - W	R - E -	R - EW
H						- - - W	- - - W

The underlying information model for this matrix is shown in Figure 8.53.

Figure 8.53
Information model for
RAEW matrix

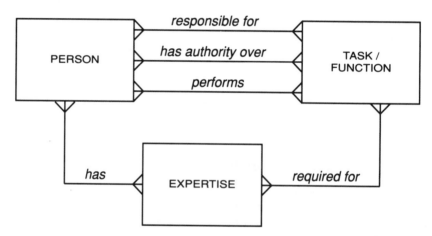

Why have I shown EXPERTISE as a separate entity type, rather than as a single many-to-many relationship between PERSON and FUNCTION, like the other three? I need not have done this, but I have chosen to in order to show that the relationships are still many to many, despite the introduction of an intermediate entity type. (In simple cases, as described in Chapter 2, the introduction of an intermediate entity type resolves a many-to-many relationship into two one-to-many relationships.) Another reason is that the employer is buying the skill of a person. Therefore the employee's expertise can be regarded as his/her marketable commodity. The other three relationships (responsibility, authority and work) are dependent on the current position of the individual within the employing organization, whereas expertise is something that can be picked up by a person and taken along to the next employer.

8.8 Commercial

In this section we consider the modelling of various business agreements, such as intercompany orders and contracts, and the modelling of sales and marketing activities.

8.8.1 Orders

One of the most popular sources of examples for introductory texts and courses in business information modelling is order processing. Thus one of the most common examples of a one-to-many relationship is that between ORDER and ORDER ITEM. Most people are sure that this is a fully mandatory relationship. A customer places an order, and the order consists in turn of order items, each specifying a different product or service, as shown in Figure 8.54. It is expected that purchasing should be a mirror image of this, with SUPPLIER replacing CUSTOMER. This is because the business relationship between the customer and the supplier would surely be modelled in the same way, within both the customer organization and the supplier organization.

Figure 8.54 Popular model of ORDER

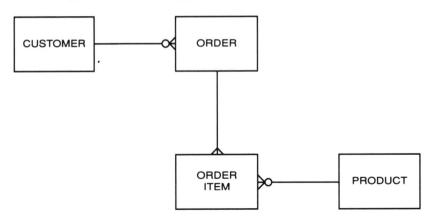

Unfortunately, this example is faulty, for most businesses.[16] This is because it is not a true model of a sale; instead it is a model of the paperwork that results from a sale. It results from a mental image of the order form filled out by the salesman or customer, which usually contains customer and delivery information in the top half, and product and price information as a series of separate lines in the bottom half. Indeed, some information models actually refer to ORDER ITEM as ORDER LINE, to reinforce this mental image, and the association with the paperwork. The definition of ORDER itself often turns out to be circular.

Let us therefore ignore the paperwork, and think about the typical sales process itself. The customer has a series of requirements for different products, perhaps required at different locations, or with different dates when delivery is required. The salesman offers prices for some of these products. The customer may then agree to buy quantities of one or more products, which the salesman then promises to deliver. The simplest and most obvious way of modelling this would be to have one occurrence of ORDER for each product thus ordered. (This is what is meant in the model above by the entity type ORDER ITEM, but there is something wrong with any entity type that requires the word ITEM in its name. This is because every entity is an item.) Then ORDER can be defined as 'that which is ordered'.

These orders are then grouped together into an ORDER AGREEMENT. (This group is what is meant in the model above by the entity type ORDER, although in our terms it is several orders grouped together.) So let us look at the possible motivations for this grouping, which will help us define the entity type properly:

1. It may be easier to negotiate terms of business (date and mode of payment, delivery terms, etc.) once, rather than for each separate ORDER. Discounts may be calculated from the total amounts ordered, rather than separately for each product ordered. Some sales organizations negotiate these terms annually with their customers, rather than reopening the negotiations on every sales visit.

2. The salesman may wish to link the sales of different products, as part of his/her sales tactics. There may be incentives to buy/sell particular combinations of products, or there may be some products that are only available in certain combinations. Equally, such links may be imposed by the customer.

3. There should be an incentive for both customer and supplier to reduce the number of deliveries, since there are fixed costs associated with each delivery. Discounts are sometimes calculated from the total amount included in each delivery, to provide an extra incentive. Thus the ORDER AGREEMENT may be equivalent to AGREED DELIVERY.

4. It is administratively convenient to reduce the number of pieces of paper. Each agreement is given an arbitrary reference number (known as the order number) which allows the orders to be tracked and controlled. Sometimes the customer and the supplier each assign a reference number to the agreement. It is unlikely that they will both assign the same number. It is possible, indeed frequent, that they group the orders differently. Thus what the customer regards as one purchase order agreement may be regarded by the supplier as two or more sales order agreements, or vice versa.

What impact does this have on the model above, which we dismissed as faulty? What we can now see is that the ORDER is of primary interest, while the AGREEMENT may be of secondary interest. Thus there is often a stage during the sales or purchasing process when an ORDER has not yet been grouped into an AGREEMENT. Therefore the relationship between them is partially optional, and thus the relationship between ORDER and CUSTOMER is non-redundant. (Figure 8.55.)

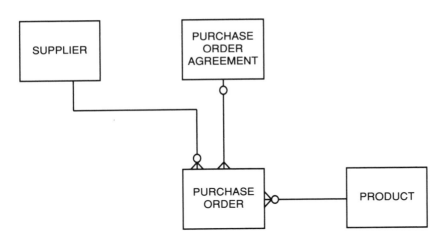

Figure 8.55 Correct model of ORDER

Let us now look at the situation from the perspective of the purchaser. Most businesses have some sales function, and some purchasing function, and some symmetry might be expected between the models of these two functions. (Figure 8.56.)

Figure 8.56 Purchase order model–incomplete

But this misses part of the purchasing function, which typically starts with a requirement for a product (or service) and selects a supplier able to meet the requirement on good terms. Therefore the PURCHASE ORDER exists before it can be associated with a particular SUPPLIER. Furthermore, each possible supplier may use a different reference number for the same product, and offer a different list price. This information may be available before any purchasing requirement exists. Thus there may be an entity type called SUPPLIER PRODUCT, defined as a particular product as supplied by a particular supplier; its attributes include the supplier's reference number, list price, packing quantity, and so on, which may vary between suppliers of the same product. (Figure 8.57.)

Figure 8.57 Complete
purchasing model

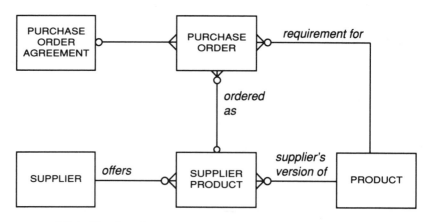

8.8.2 *Contracts*

A contract is a legally binding document, defining the rights and responsibilities of
two or more parties (which may be occurrences of COMPANY OR PERSON). It may contain several clauses, schedules, appendixes and attachments. In some circumstances,
such contracts are negotiated from scratch by two entrepreneurs and their legal
representatives. What is more usual, however, is that each contract is put together
from a standard set of clauses, defining standard terms and conditions of trade. Each
clause in an actual contract, then, may either be standard or modified. (Figure 8.58.)

Figure 8.58 A contract
model

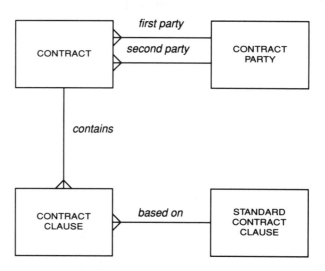

We are usually only interested in contracts in which the target organization is
one of the contracting parties. The target organization may be either buying or
selling some product or service. Some contracts are more complex than this: in
the oil industry, it is common to negotiate exchange contracts, agreeing to
supply one type of hydrocarbon at one location on one date in exchange for
another type of hydrocarbon at another location at another date.

Some contracts involve more than two parties. For example, in the oil industry exchange contracts mentioned above, a third party is usually nominated to verify the quantity and quality of oil delivered by the first or second party to the other. There may be several third-party rôles in a contract, (perhaps one inspector at each location) leading us to a more complex model, as follows in Figure 8.59.

Figure 8.59 More complex contract model

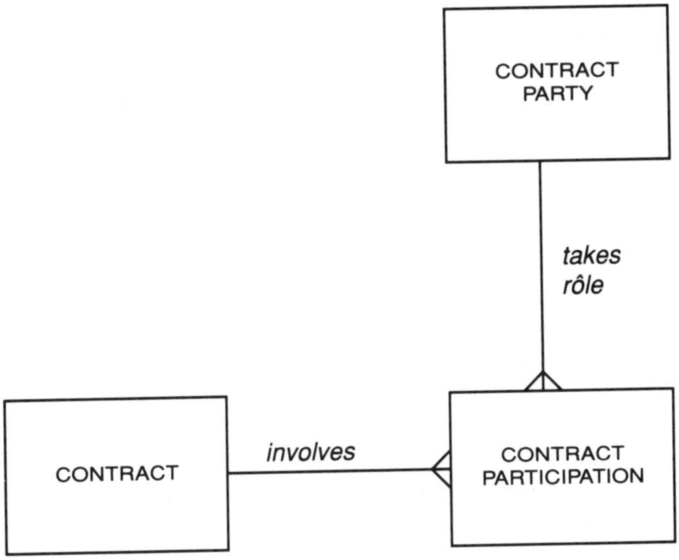

Contract terms and conditions may form a network of rights and counter-rights (if you do this, then we may do that, in which case you may do the other).

8.8.3 Market

A market is a group of customers. Many marketing operations define markets as a combination of geography and some other characteristics. The idea is to define groups of customers that can be handled in a similar way, because they have similar requirements or because they can be expected to respond similarly to given sales tactics. Therefore, what characteristics are chosen depends on whatever is thought relevant to the kinds of product or service being sold, and to the sales tactics being used. Different people may hold different opinions about this, and their opinions tend to change over time, which makes any useful definition of markets fairly unstable.

For those selling to commercial customers, markets may be defined by industry type and size, as well as location. For example, software houses typically divide their operations in three ways: by industry, by computer hardware, and by geographic area. They tend to reorganize regularly, vacillating between these three organization structures. For those selling to domestic consumers, markets may be defined by **demographic** characteristics such as age, sex, social class, ethnic group, **psychographic** characteristics, such as striving for individuality or acceptance.

We often speak of a GROUP as if it were a consistent and uniform entity. This is especially true of nations and nationality, where we commonly speak of the attributes of Chinese people in general, as if they were all alike. Such demographic generalizations are often necessary injustices. It is important to keep the attributes of the GROUP separate from the attributes of the MEMBER.

Where populations are constructed by statistical analysis, there may be problems in counting. For example, a demographer may estimate that there are so many children of a certain ethnic minority and/or class background living in a certain place, but be unable to name them as individuals. Thus we may have a collective entity type of POPULATION, without being able to define a relationship between it and PERSON.

Markets may be defined from three perspectives: pre-sale, sale and post-sale. The **pre-sale** perspective has to do with the sales tactics, how much sales resources do we want to devote to selling to this or that market, what kind of campaigns or promotions are appropriate, what advertising media to use and so on. The **sales** perspective has to do with what products or services the customer actually gets sold. This is particularly important in the financial sector, where the terms and conditions offered to a particular customer depend on the market. (Thus, for example, wealthy customers are offered a differently coloured credit card from the rest of us.) The **post-sale** perspective has to do with the actual provision of service to the customer. Superficially, these three perspectives appear to be the same. But if we look closely, we often find that the three concepts of market are used for incompatible purposes, especially where what is being marketed is intangible services rather than fast-moving consumer goods.

This can be seen more clearly with an example. Suppose that a financial service package is designed for sale in the UK to a group of professional customers, e.g. doctors. Then the market for the service is UK doctors. Suppose further that it is intended to promote this service initially in a particular geographical area, e.g. Greater Manchester. Then the market for the initial sales campaign is doctors in Greater Manchester. Now consider the following test cases:

1. A doctor in South Wales requests the service, having learnt of it from his sister in Manchester. He belongs to the market for the service, but not the market for the campaign. We decide to let him have the service, because there is no reason not to.
2. A doctor in New South Wales requests the service, having learnt of it from her brother in Manchester. She does not belong to the market for the service or for the campaign; we cannot let her have the service because of the differences between financial systems in UK and Australia.
3. A doctor who has signed up for the service then moves from Manchester to South Wales. We continue to provide him with the service.

4. A doctor who has signed up for the service then moves from Manchester to New South Wales. We cannot continue to provide her with the service.

5. A doctor who has signed up for the service is then elected to Parliament and ceases to practise as a doctor. However, he wishes to continue receiving the service.

6. An accountant or lawyer in Manchester receives a mailshot by mistake, since her address has been incorrectly included on a list of Greater Manchester doctors. She perceives that the service would be of value to any professional, not just doctors, and requests the service. We decide to let her have a similar service, but with significant variations, due to the differences between the professions. (For example, indemnity insurance will be at a different level, with different conditions.)

Thinking through these and similar test cases (together with the users whose concept of MARKET is being modelled) helps clarify exactly what is meant by MARKET.

From these examples, we can see that there are three ways each customer can be classified, corresponding to the three market perspectives outlined above:

- The **target group** for a particular campaign, which defines which potential customers will be contacted.
- The **eligibility group**, which defines what terms and conditions (if any) are allowed to a particular customer, depending upon the characteristics of the customer at the time of sale.
- The **service group**, which defines the service provided to the customer, depending not only on the terms and conditions of the agreement with the customer, but also on his/her current characteristics.

If the entity type MARKET is used to refer ambiguously to these three groupings, then the membership of each market is likely to be confusing. In particular, the target groups are likely to be much more overlapping, and much more changeable, than the eligibility groups and the service groups. There may even be a marketing strategy, to provide greater flexibility in targeting and eligibility, while consolidating service groups in order to achieve consistency of service and economies of scale. In such a situation, therefore, MARKET is a two-faced (or, more accurately, three-faced) entity type, and it is necessary to pull the different concepts apart into separate entity types.

8.8.4 Requirement

In a previous section, we considered INTENTION. We often refer to the intentions of our customers as REQUIREMENTS. Consider an estate agent (as they are called in the UK) or realtor (as they are called in North America), trying to match house-hunters with the available houses. The houses have definite characteristics: so many bedrooms, so many square metres, type of heating, state of repair, location, and so on. Thus there is a many-to-many relationship between HOUSE and CHARACTERISTIC. We may resolve this many-to-many relationship in the usual way by introducing an intermediate entity type called HOUSE CHARACTERISTIC. (Thus an occurrence of CHARACTERISTIC might be 'gas-fired central heating', and an occurrence of HOUSE CHARACTERISTIC might be the details of the gas-fired central heating for a particular house.)

The house-hunters, on the other hand, have perhaps only a vague set of preferences and trade offs. 'Either three bedrooms or two large bedrooms.' 'Would pay up to £X for a house in perfect repair, but could only go up to £Y for a house that needed attention.' 'Prefer easy access to shops, but would consider somewhere further out if there was good parking.' Each house-hunter, therefore, has a set of *intentions,* of what kind of house to look for, and what price to offer. This usually represents a hopeful ideal, however, rather than an inflexible demand. The estate agent, therefore, is faced with a complex set of requirements, which it may be impossible to completely fulfil, at an acceptable price. The agent then tests the reaction of the house-hunter to various alternatives, each of which falls short of the house-hunter's ideal requirements in a different way. By observing the reaction, the agent can then judge which of the requirements is fixed, and which may be open to compromise.

What happens if the house-hunter finds a house that completely fulfils the initial requirements. 'Oh, well if there are so many three-bedroom houses on the market for so little, perhaps I can afford a four-bedroom house without going over my budget.' Thus the response may be to increase the requirements. But usually, the requirements are already difficult to satisfy. Even the very rich house hunters want more than they can get, and have to accept compromises. This relationship is illustrated in Figure 8.60.

Figure 8.60 Houses and house-hunters

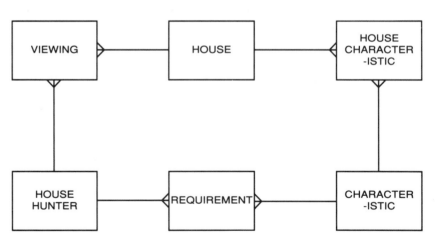

8.8.5 Benefits

Marketing can be defined as the systematic matching of product features to purchaser needs, or vice versa, to generate benefits. Some writers and sales trainers insist on two levels of matching. An ADVANTAGE is the result of matching a product feature with an unstated need, or with the needs of hypothetical purchasers. A BENEFIT is the result of matching a product feature with the explicit needs of actual purchasers. The point of this distinction is to prevent the salesman rabbiting on about some supposed benefit of the product that is in fact of no interest at all to the sales victim. A benefit is what the customer really wants, not what the salesman thinks he ought to want. (Figure 8.61).

Figure 8.61 Needs and benefits

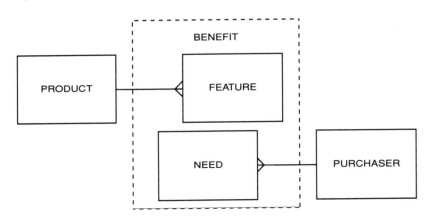

Thus we can divide NEED into two subtypes: STATED NEED and INFERRED/ GUESSED NEED. The former relates to named occurrences of PURCHASER (or POTENTIAL PURCHASER), whereas the latter may relate to demographic classes or other groups of possible purchasers.

8.9 Intelligence and knowledge

Earlier in this chapter, we discussed the modelling of information as a substance. In this section, our concern will not be with what information is 'made of', but with its pattern. Form rather than content.[17] It would be impossible in this book to give a complete account of the modelling of knowledge that would satisfy the proponents of artificial intelligence. However, many of the objects that are manipulated by so-called expert systems are discussed in this book.

What else must we do, before we can use the information model as a basis for designing a knowledge-based system instead of just a database system? First, let us note that most expert systems are stand-alone, personal decision-support systems, not interfaced (let alone integrated) with corporate data systems. Thus huge opportunities are missed.

8.9.1 Facts and explanations

One of the things that makes facts interesting is that they can be explained in many ways. There are many jokes that rely on giving unexpected, but perfectly valid answers to 'why' questions. 'Why did the chicken cross the road?' 'Why do firemen wear red braces?' This complexity of explanation has serious business consequences. Suppose a firm wants to analyse the behaviour of a major competitor. The first step is to obtain facts. The next step is to try to interpret the facts. Each fact may have multiple explanations. An explanation may explain several different facts. Both facts and explanations have sources. 'Why have they bought a warehouse in Belgium?' 'Why have they cancelled their stand at the trade fair in New Orleans?' 'Why are they suddenly recruiting so many research biologists?' If we want to manage these facts and their explanations systematically, we need to understand their structure, by representing them in an information model.

If we assume that a company has a consistent business strategy, then we can expect a certain level of consistency in its observed behaviour, and can eliminate incompatible explanations. (Observed behaviour may include public announcements, which it is not always appropriate to take at face value.) Many organizations, however, have inconsistent or evolving strategies, which makes it considerably more difficult (but not impossible) to analyse their behaviour.

We may also be interested in the business strategies of our customers and/or suppliers; these companies are more likely than competitors to reveal their business strategies to us, but here too, we must be careful not to be too credulous. After all, a popular business strategy (known as vertical integration) leads a company to compete with its former customers and/or suppliers, thus a customer or supplier may secretly intend to develop a product or service that competes with ours, or may suspect us of intending to do likewise.

Each FACT has a SOURCE, and one or more EXPLANATIONS. Each explanation may be compatible with some other explanations, and incompatible with yet others. Explanations may include a REASON (or CAUSE) and a CONDITION. Similar to explanations would be EXCUSE or JUSTIFICATION. There are also some interesting relationships to be modelled between PROBLEM, FAULT and SYMPTOM. As Bill Kent points out, it is not always easy to determine whether two perceived problems in a computer system are two symptoms of the same underlying program bug, or can be counted as two separate bugs.[18] This can have important contractual implications, whenever there is a service agreement (between the software developer and the software user) specifying the length of time taken to fix each fault.

8.9.2 Patterns

If you want to explain the (business) environment, you have to be able to perceive and recognize patterns of behaviour, including those of your competitors and customers. These patterns are then used to determine an appropriate response. Human beings are much better at matching and manipulating patterns than computers are. However, in order to record and communicate patterns, it may be necessary to name and describe patterns. We use patterns to recognize entities.

To identify a bald eagle we look for a large hawk with a white head and tail and a flat-winged glide. To tell a mule deer from a whitetail deer we look for large ears, a white, ropelike, black-tipped tail, and for equally branching antlers if it is a male. ... In similar ways we look for patterns in electrocardiograms and seismograms to ascertain the cardiac condition of a person or the geological structure of a valley.[19]

A pattern is an array of characteristic features.

There are conflicting forces in the definition of a pattern: for convenience it must be abstract and simple, for effectiveness it must be specific and precise; there is therefore a creative tension in the level of detail. A designer consciously manipulates and creates patterns, using a pattern language. 'We impose rather than discover a pattern when we use a template to mount a ski binding or a pattern to cut the material for a dress.'[20] Christopher Alexander has developed a method of architecture based on the systematic combination of patterns.[21]

8.9.3 Rules, constraints and policies

During this chapter, we have discussed many aspects of organizational structure. An organization sees the world in a certain way, and behaves in a certain way; in the end this is what characterizes the organization and differentiates it from its competitors. This can be expressed as a series of rules – perception rules, interpretation rules and action rules.

Specific rules will appear in the information model. For example, there may be a rule stating that a credit limit must be set for each customer; this may well be expressed as a mandatory attribute CREDIT LIMIT of the entity type CUSTOMER. For another example, there may be a rule stating which versions of which products may be sold in which countries; this may well be expressed as a relationship between PRODUCT VERSION and COUNTRY. Representing a rule in this way allows the content of the rule to change (i.e. a specific product version may be released in additional countries, or withdrawn from others), but assumes that the structure of the rule remains fixed. In fact, it is possible to see the information model itself as nothing more than a collection of rules, within which the organization structures its knowledge and its actions.

Other kinds of rules may determine what processes may be carried out at any given time. Thus there may be a rule stating that payment must be received from a customer, and cleared by the bank, before goods can be delivered. This kind of rule may be easier to express by means of a process model such as a **process dependency diagram**, showing which sequences of operations are acceptable to the organization. Process models are for this reason included in many methodologies, but are not described further in this book.

A problem may arise, however, in large organizations, where some users, especially in central staff functions, may see their role as the maintenance of rules. Thus the personnel department may spend much of its time negotiating rules and guidelines for line management, and monitoring the application of these rules, rather than performing direct personnel operations. The planning department lays down general business rules and operating policies, while the accounts department maintains a fat volume of accounting rules, dictating how costs are to be allocated and distributed between accounts.

The typical daunting prospect for the analyst is a loose-leaf file of paper, documenting these rules. Updates are circulated from time to time, so that the original ring-binder is now overflowing, in danger of bursting apart when opened. The users describe the contents indiscriminately as rules, but at first glance they may just appear to be a random collection of codes and numbers. Another difficulty is that all rules are strictly provisional, in that they are subject to the decisions of the organization's leaders. Any rule may be overridden in a special case, or entirely overthrown. Even legal constraints can be altered by new legislation or precedent.

As a result of this, you may be tempted to introduce a generalized entity type called RULE or POLICY or OPERATIONAL CONSTRAINT or something like that. This solution is usually a cop out. It reveals no insight into the organization, and indicates that neither the structure nor the content of the rules have been analysed. So the aim of this section is to lead you away from this over-generalized solution, to unpack RULE into its parts.

There are two possible approaches. The bottom-up approach is to examine every rule (or a representative selection of rules) to determine the structure of each. The top-down approach is to go back to what the rules are doing for the organization, Most rules can be expressed as tables. A simple table can often be translated directly into an entity type, with each row becoming an entity occurrence, and each column becoming an attribute. The example in Table 8.5 suggests an entity type called CUSTOMER CATEGORY, with maximum discount as an attribute.

Table 8.5 Customer category

Customer category	Maximum discount
Major industrial	33%
Minor industrial	25%
Government	33%
Foreign	15%
Private	15%

More complex tables require more entity types to represent them. If the information contained in each cell of a two-dimensional matrix is Boolean, in other words it can only take one of two values, yes/no or true/false, then the information may be represented as a many-to-many relationship between two entity types: one for the rows and one for the columns. Otherwise, an intersection entity type is required, whose attributes are the cell values.

The example in Table 8.6 suggests three entity types: CUSTOMER CATEGORY and PRODUCT CATEGORY with maximum discount as an attribute of a third intersection entity type: CUSTOMER PRODUCT SUPPLY (which represents the conditions for the supply of a product of a given category to a customer of a given category).

Table 8.6 Customer – product relationship

Product Category	Standard make	Special make	Parts and spares	Service
Customer category	Maximum discount			
Major industrial	33%	25%	33%	25%
Minor industrial	25%	15%	25%	15%
Government	33%	33%	33%	33%
Foreign	15%	10%	30%	10%
Private	15%	5%	15%	5%

Tables with repeating items, or with cross-references to other tables, may require several entity types. Complex rules can often be represented as a decision table, showing how a series of possible actions depends on a series of values. Thus, in Table 8.7 the action **P** is to be carried out whenever **A** is true, **B** is home and **C** is zero, and also whenever **A** is not true and **B** is home.

Table 8.7 Decision table

Condition A	Yes	Yes	Yes	Yes	No	No
Condition B	Home	Home	Home	Abroad	Abroad	Abroad
Condition C	Zero	Positive	Negative	-	-	-
Action P	X				X	
Action Q				X		X
Action R			X			
Action S		X				

An abstract information model of this structure would look like Figure 8.62.

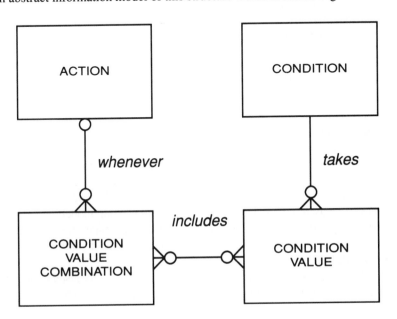

Figure 8.62 Model of a decision table

Or if we can restrict the conditions to Boolean two-valued yes/no, the CONDITION VALUE becomes redundant, and it could look like Figure 8.63. But this is still too generalized to make much sense to the business. What you need to do now is break the rules down into groups, relating particular groups of actions to particular groups of conditions.

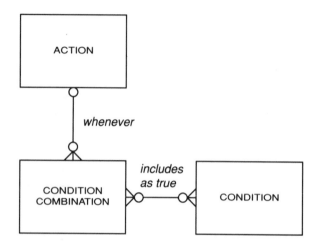

Figure 8.63 Condition values

We have stated that many rules can be overridden with the correct authority. Even large companies sometimes sail close to the wind in adherence to legal restrictions (whether deliberately or otherwise). Furthermore, rules about the conduct of business may be breached by employees or customers. (The fact that this may result in the employee being dismissed, or the customer being sued, does not alter the possibility of its happening.) Because rules are broken, it is dangerous to define any action or behaviour in terms of the rule that it follows – because it may not follow any rule.

8.10 Summary

In this chapter, we have progressed from simple entities (such as physical objects and people) to more difficult ones, asking what kinds of entity can exist, both generally and in a business environment. These questions of existence are what philosophers call ontology.

Previous chapters have demonstrated that information modelling can be applied to a wide variety of situations. This chapter backs this argument up, by demonstrating the huge range of things that can be modelled. But the examples in this chapter only represent a tiny fringe of the information modelling carpet. I hope the reader will be encouraged to seek and analyse many more examples, from all aspects of his/her working and non-working life, in order to further develop the skills of information modelling.

Throughout this book, I have drawn on many varied sources for inspiration about information modelling. I have made this visible in order to show to the reader how he or she may, if desired, continue to learn about information modelling while reading novels, while watching films, while studying entirely different subjects.

The main characteristic of a good modeller is an alert and nimble mind. As you consider the examples in the book, you will find yourself observing similar patterns and structures occurring all over the place. You may continue to learn for the rest of your life.

Notes

1. Cited in W. V. O. Quine, *From a Logical point of View* 2nd edn, Harvard University Press, Cambridge, MA, 1961, p. 77.
2. The other components of Fordism were mechanization, decomposition of labour (also known as Taylorism), and assembly-line production.
3. Herbert Simon, 'The architecture of complexity' *Proceedings of the American Philosophical Society*, vol. 106, December 1962, pp. 467–82, reprinted in H. Simon, *The Sciences of the Artificial*, 2nd edn, MIT Press, Cambridge, MA, 1981.
4. I use this somewhat ugly word to make it clear I mean the process, rather than the end-product, of assembly.
5. John Stuart Mill, *A System of Logic*, Longmans, London, 1930.
6. Quine, *op. cit.*, p. 2.
7. Peter Littlechild, writing in the *Guardian*, 20 October 1988.
8. This corresponds loosely to the old programming concepts of CALL BY NAME and CALL BY REFERENCE.
9. Remember that any noun or noun phrase should be considered as a potential entity type.
10. I am indebted to Ernie Akemann for this example.
11. G. Bateson, 'Form substance and difference', *General Semantics Bulletin*, No 37, 1970.
12. P. F. Strawson, *Individuals*, Lowe and Brydone, London, 1959, p. 46.
13. You are the first party, your insurers are the second party, and everyone else is a third party. And, as Chico Marx once pointed out, there ain't no sanity clause.
14. Jon Elster, *Logic and Society*, John Wiley, Chichester, 1978, p. 84.
15. See Sir Geoffrey Vickers, *The Art of Judgement: A study of policy-making*, Chapman and Hall, London, 1965.
16. This was pointed out to me by Deepak Singhal.
17. Bateson attributes this distinction to Pythagoras. G. Bateson, 'Form substance and difference', *General Semantics Bulletin*, No. 37, 1970.
18. W. Kent, *Data and Reality*, North Holland Elsevier, Amsterdam, 1978, p. 8.
19. Albert Borgmann, *Technology and the Character of Contemporary Life*, University of Chicago Press, Chicaco, IL. 1984, p. 73.
20. *Ibid.*, p. 73.
21. Christopher Alexander, *A Timeless Way of Building*, Oxford University Press, New York, 1979.

Index 1: Concepts and topics

Index 2: Entity types and other objects